CW01095823

I.B.TAURIS SHORT HISTORIES

I.B.Tauris Short Histories is an authoritative and elegantly written new series which puts a fresh perspective on the way history is taught and understood in the twenty-first century. Designed to have strong appeal to university students and their teachers, as well as to general readers and history enthusiasts, *I.B.Tauris Short Histories* comprises a novel attempt to bring informed interpretation, as well as factual reportage, to historical debate. Addressing key subjects and topics in the fields of history, the history of ideas, religion, classical studies, politics, philosophy and Middle East studies, the series seeks intentionally to move beyond the bland, neutral 'introduction' that so often serves as the primary undergraduate teaching tool. While always providing students and generalists with the core facts that they need to get to grips with the essentials of any particular subject, *I.B.Tauris Short Histories* goes further. It offers new insights into how a topic has been understood in the past, and what different social and cultural factors might have been at work. It brings original perspectives to bear on the manner of its current interpretation. It raises questions and – in its extensive bibliographies – points to further study, even as it suggests answers. Addressing a variety of subjects in a greater degree of depth than is often found in comparable series, yet at the same time in concise and compact handbook form, *I.B.Tauris Short Histories* aims to be 'introductions with an edge.' In combining questioning and searching analysis with informed history writing, it brings history up-to-date for an increasingly complex and globalized digital age.

www.short-histories.com

'*A Short History of Transatlantic Slavery* provides a magisterial overview of the transatlantic slave trade and slavery from the mid-fifteenth to the late nineteenth century. Synthesizing a vast field of scholarship, including the latest important works, Kenneth Morgan here addresses the organisation of the slave trade, plantation slavery, resistance, abolition and emancipation, and the legacy of slavery. The author spans Europe, Africa, North, Central and South America, and includes essential information about slave demography and culture, the legal underpinnings of slavery, plantation economies and the great push to destroy inhuman bondage. Specialists and non-specialists alike will welcome this readable and succinct handbook, which should appear on the reading lists of many university courses.'

– Stephen D. Behrendt, Associate Professor in History, Victoria University of Wellington, co-author of The Diary of Antera Duke: An Eighteenth-Century African Slave Trader

'This is an impressive book by one of Europe's leading historians of slavery and the transatlantic slave trade. Kenneth Morgan provides a comprehensive and very readable assessment of the European and African origins of slavery, of slaveholders and the enslaved, of the transportation of Africans to the Americas and of their experiences of enslavement and emancipation. Building on the latest scholarly work, Morgan has fashioned a penetrating assessment of how the institution of slavery was adapted over space and time, and in the process became ever more difficult to eliminate. Readers of this book will learn a great deal about and better understand not just historical slavery but also the myriad ways in which it ended. Both experts and those who are new to the subject will benefit from Morgan's able synthesis of a vast amount of scholarship, and his confident survey of the history of slavery across four hundred years and four continents. *A Short History of Transatlantic Slavery* is an excellent introduction to this fascinating subject.'

– Simon P. Newman, Sir Denis Brogan Professor of American History, University of Glasgow, author of A New World of Labor: The Development of Plantation Slavery in the British Atlantic

A Short History of . . .

the American Civil War	Paul Anderson (Clemson University)
the American Revolutionary War	Stephen Conway (University College London)
Ancient China	Edward L Shaughnessy (University of Chicago)
Ancient Greece	P J Rhodes, FBA (Durham University)
Ancient Rome	Andrew Wallace-Hadrill (University of Cambridge)
the Anglo-Saxons	Henrietta Leyser (University of Oxford)
the Byzantine Empire	Dionysios Stathakopoulos (King's College London)
the Celts	Alex Woolf (University of St Andrews)
Christian Spirituality	Edward Howells (Heythrop College, University of London)
the Crimean War	Trudi Tate (University of Cambridge)
English Renaissance Drama	Helen Hackett (University College London)
the English Revolution and the Civil Wars	David J Appleby (University of Nottingham)
the Etruscans	Corinna Riva (University College London)
the Hundred Years War	Michael Prestwich (Durham University)
Irish Independence	J J Lee (New York University)
the Italian Renaissance	Virginia Cox (New York University)
the Korean War	Allan R Millett (University of New Orleans)
Medieval Christianity	G R Evans (University of Cambridge)
Medieval English Mysticism	Vincent Gillespie (University of Oxford)
the Minoans	John Bennet (University of Sheffield)
the Mongols	George Lane (SOAS, University of London)
the Mughal Empire	Michael H Fisher (Oberlin College)
Muslim Spain	Alex J Novikoff (Rhodes College, Memphis)
New Kingdom Egypt	Robert Morkot (University of Exeter)
the New Testament	Halvor Moxnes (University of Oslo)
Nineteenth-Century Philosophy	Joel Rasmussen (University of Oxford)
the Normans	Leonie Hicks (Canterbury Christ Church University)

the Ottoman Empire	Baki Tezcan (University of California, Davis)
the Phoenicians	Mark Woolmer (Durham University)
the Reformation	Helen Parish (University of Reading)
the Renaissance in Northern Europe	Malcolm Vale (University of Oxford)
Revolutionary Cuba	Antoni Kapcia (University of Nottingham)
the Risorgimento	Nick Carter (Australian Catholic University, Sydney)
the Russian Revolution	Geoffrey Swain (University of Glasgow)
the Spanish Civil War	Julián Casanova (University of Zaragoza)
the Spanish Empire	Felipe Fernández-Armesto (University of Notre Dame) and José Juan López-Portillo (University of Oxford)
Transatlantic Slavery	Kenneth Morgan (Brunel University London)
Venice and the Venetian Empire	Maria Fusaro (University of Exeter)
the Vikings	Clare Downham (University of Liverpool)
the Wars of the Roses	David Grummitt (University of Kent)
the Weimar Republic	Colin Storer (University of Nottingham)

Chiwetel Ejiofor in *12 Years a Slave* (dir. Steve McQueen, 2013).

A SHORT HISTORY OF TRANSATLANTIC SLAVERY

Kenneth Morgan

I.B. TAURIS

LONDON · NEW YORK

Published in 2016 by
I.B.Tauris & Co. Ltd
London • New York
www.ibtauris.com

Copyright © 2016 Kenneth Morgan

The right of Kenneth Morgan to be identified as the author of this work has been
asserted by the author in accordance with the Copyright, Designs and Patents Act
1988.

All rights reserved. Except for brief quotations in a review, this book, or any part
thereof, may not be reproduced, stored in or introduced into a retrieval system, or
transmitted, in any form or by any means, electronic, mechanical, photocopying,
recording or otherwise, without the prior written permission of the publisher.

Every attempt has been made to gain permission for the use of the images in this
book. Any omissions will be rectified in future editions.

References to websites were correct at the time of writing.

ISBN: 978 1 78076 386 6 (HB)
ISBN: 978 1 78076 387 3 (PB)
eISBN: 978 0 85772 855 5

A full CIP record for this book is available from the British Library
A full CIP record is available from the Library of Congress

Library of Congress Catalog Card Number: available

Typeset by Fakenham Prepress Solutions, Fakenham, Norfolk NR21 8NN
Printed and bound in Great Britain by T.J. International, Padstow, Cornwall

Contents

List of Maps, Tables and Illustrations

FRONTISPIECE

Chiwetel Ejiofor in *12 Years a Slave* (dir. Steve McQueen, 2013).
Credit: Regency Enterprises/The Kobal Collection

MAP

TABLES

FIGURES

Preface

To attempt a wide-ranging synthesis of slavery, the slave trade and abolition in the transatlantic world across four centuries is a daunting task within 75,000 words, which is the remit of this book. One wants to do justice to the vitality and significance of modern scholarship in this field but it is necessary to do so succinctly, without space to follow through all strands of the subject that ought to be explained fully. But it is also a necessary challenge, because an up-to-date synthesis of the main contours of transatlantic slavery is essential for students as a guide to more detailed scholarship. In writing this volume, I have tried to do justice to the main findings of historians on transatlantic slavery in thematic chapters, beginning with the emergence of the slave trade in the Atlantic world and ending with the aftermath of slavery and abolitionism. Recent research is highlighted in the book, but I have also drawn upon older studies that have stood the test of time.

No one could hope to read all of the significant studies on transatlantic slavery to write a volume such as this, but I have aimed to offer wide coverage. Hopefully, depth is not sacrificed in the quest for breadth. My thanks go to all the fine scholars upon whose published works I have drawn. In 2012 a fellowship at the Robert H. Smith International Center for Jefferson Studies at the University of Virginia, Monticello, gave me the opportunity to present a seminar on themes considered in Chapter 5. My thanks go to the Center's director, Andrew Jackson O'Shaughnessy, and his staff for their friendly scholarly cooperation during my stay in Charlottesville. In 2013 an earlier version of Chapter 1 was presented at the 45th annual Settimani di Studi of the Istituto Internazionale di Storia Economica 'F. Datini', and subsequently published in Simonetta Cavaciocchi (ed.), *Serfdom and Slavery in the European Economy 11th-18th Centuries* (Firenze University Press, 2014). Parts of Chapter 6 draw upon material I presented in Kenneth Morgan (ed.), *Slavery in America: A Reader and Guide* (University of Edinburgh Press/University of Georgia Press, 2005) and Kenneth Morgan, *Slavery in the British Empire: From Africa to America* (Oxford University Press, 2007).

Thanks are due to Jerome S. Handler, Michael Tuite, the University of Virginia Library and the Virginia Foundation for the Humanities for permission to reproduce images of slavery from material gathered on their website (http://slaveryimages.org/).

Timeline

1501	On 3 September the Spanish Crown signed documents authorizing the introduction of African slaves to their colonies in the Americas.
1510	On 22 January King Ferdinand of Spain authorized a shipment of 50 slaves to Santo Domingo, which began the slave trade to the Americas.
1518	Emperor Charles V of Spain established the *asiento* system and thereby legalized the slave trade to Spanish American colonies.
1522	On 28 December the first major uprising by slaves in the Americas broke out in Hispaniola (now the Dominican Republic).
1562	John Hawkins carried 300 slaves from West Africa to Hispaniola, displaying the potential profits of this trade.
1618	The Company of Royal Adventurers of London established Fort James at Bathurst, Gambia.
1619	The first cargo of Africans landed in North America in the English settlement at Jamestown, Virginia.
1621	The Dutch West India Company was formed, a corporation that would become a significant operator in the transatlantic slave trade.
1655	On 10 May England conquered the Spanish colony of Jamaica.
1670	The first slaves arrived in South Carolina.
1672	The English Parliament granted a charter to the Royal African Company, granting it a monopoly in conducting the English slave trade between Africa and the Americas.

1673   The Compagnie du Sénégal, a leading French slave trading enterprise, was formed.

1676   In Virginia slaves and indentured servants combined in Bacon's Rebellion.

1685   The French government enacted the *Code Noir* in all of its colonial settlements. This code required religious instruction for slaves and outlawed slave work on Sundays and holidays.

1693   Gold was discovered in Brazil's Minas Gerais region, requiring the importation of large numbers of slaves to conduct mining operations.

1698   The Royal African Company lost its monopoly status for conducting the English slave trade between Africa and the Americas.

1713   The London-based South Sea Company received the *asiento*, a contract that permitted it to carry 4,800 slaves annually to the Spanish colonies for thirty years.

1739   On 9 September the Stono slave revolt broke out in South Carolina.

1748   The French political philosopher Baron de Montesquieu published *L'esprit des lois*, an important condemnation of slavery.

1752   The British Parliament chartered the Company of Merchants trading to Africa, the successor to the Royal African Company.

1760   On 7 April Tacky's slave revolt broke out in Jamaica.

1763   Britain settled Grenada and St Vincent and introduced slaves into both colonies.

1763   On 23 February a large slave revolt began in Berbice, a Dutch colony. It was not suppressed until 1764.

1772   In a landmark legal case, Knowles v. Somersett, Lord Chief Justice Mansfield abolished slavery in England.

1778   Virginia banned slave importation.

1780   Pennsylvania's legislature passed a measure for gradual abolition of slavery within the state's borders.

1786   The Clapham Sect, a group of British abolitionists, established the Committee for the Relief of the Black Poor.

1787   British abolitionists established the Society for Effecting the Abolition of the Slave Trade.

1787	The US Constitution was signed on 17 September. It counted three out of every five slaves for the purposes of taxation and representation. The document also stated that Congress could not prohibit the African slave trade until 1808.
1787	Sierra Leone was founded by Britain as a colony for emancipated slaves.
1791	On 22 August a major slave revolt broke out in the French colony of Saint-Domingue.
1791	The revolutionary French National Assembly abolished slavery in all French colonial possessions.
1792	The Danish Crown issued an order stating that all imports of African slaves into Danish colonies would end in 1803.
1794	On 22 March the US Congress prohibited the slave trade to all foreign ports and banned the outfitting of any foreign vessels in US ports for the purpose of slave trading.
1799	On 29 March the New York legislature enacted a bill for the gradual emancipation of slaves in the state.
1800	On 30 August the Virginia authorities discovered and suppressed the slave revolt led by Gabriel Prosser.
1802	On 12 May Napoleon restored slavery to all French colonial territories where it had been outlawed by the French National Assembly in 1791.
1803	Denmark banned the slave trade.
1804	New Jersey enacted a gradual emancipation of slaves.
1804	Victorious blacks declared Haiti (formerly Saint-Domingue) as the first independent black republic in the Western Hemisphere.
1807	On 25 March 1807 Britain abolished her slave trade, with the act taking effect on 1 March 1808.
1808	On 2 March 1807 the US Congress banned slave imports, with the law becoming effective on 1 January 1808.
1810	Venezuela ended the slave trade.
1812	A series of slave revolts known collectively as the Aponte Rebellion erupted throughout Cuba.
1814	On 15 January the Netherlands government ended Dutch involvement in the slave trade.
1815	The French government of Louis VIII enacted a measure to end the slave trade, but it was weakly enforced.

1815	At the Congress of Vienna eight victorious powers declared their opposition to slavery.
1817	The British government provided £400,000 in compensation for Spain's promise to end the slave trade north of the Equator.
1817	On 19 December an Anglo-Portuguese treaty agreed that Portugal would abolish the slave trade north of the Equator.
1818	On 4 May Britain and the Netherlands signed a bilateral treaty to end the slave trade.
1819	The British Parliament authorized the creation of Courts of Mixed Commission to be established in Sierra Leone to decide the fate of slave ships seized off West Africa.
1819	The French government banned its slave trade.
1820	On 30 May Spain abolished the slave trade south of the Equator.
1822	On 2 July Denmark Vesey was hanged as the alleged ringleader of a slave conspiracy in Charleston, South Carolina.
1823	British abolitionists founded the Anti-Slavery Society.
1823	Between 18 and 20 August a slave revolt occurred in Demerara.
1823	The British government announced a detailed programme of slave amelioration.
1824	The British Parliament declared that participation in the African slave trade was an act of piracy.
1825	Programmes of gradual abolition of slavery became effective in Bolivia, Paraguay, Peru, Chile and Argentina.
1829	Slave emancipation was enacted in Mexico.
1830	The governments of Great Britain, Portugal and Brazil signed a treaty in which Brazil agreed to end the African slave trade south of the Equator; but this legislation was not enforced for many years.
1831	France passed a law that sanctioned the seizure of French slave ships and the imprisonment of their owners.
1831	During August the Nat Turner slave revolt occurred in Southampton County, Virginia.
1831	Bolivia abolished slavery.

1831/2   Between 25 December 1831 and 4 January 1832 a large slave revolt, known as the Baptist War, occurred in Jamaica.

1833   On 1 August Britain passed an Emancipation Act, which ended slavery in most British possessions.

1834   On 1 August Britain inaugurated a system of Apprenticeship for former slaves.

1835   Slave revolts occurred in the Cuban cities of Jaruço, Havana and Matanzas.

1835   On 25 January the great Malê Muslim slave revolt erupted in Bahia, Brazil.

1838   On 1 August the British government abolished Apprenticeship.

1839   Britain enacted the Palmerston Act, which permitted British vessels to search Portuguese ships suspected of taking slaves to the Americas.

1839   In July the Spanish slave ship *Amistad* was seized off the Cuban coast when the Africans on board revolted and killed the captain.

1840   Between 12 and 23 June the World Anti-Slavery Convention was held in London.

1845   Britain enacted the Aberdeen Act, which permitted British ships to search Brazilian ships suspected of carrying slaves to the Americas.

1846   The Swedish king granted slave emancipation in Swedish colonies.

1847   The Danish king, Christian VIII, issued a law of free birth for the children of slaves born in the Danish West Indies.

1848   On 27 April the French government abolished slavery in French colonies.

1848   On 2 July slaves were freed in the Danish West Indies.

1850   In September the Brazilian government enacted the Queirós Law, which ended the slave trade to Brazil.

1852   Ecuador passed a law to free all slaves in the country.

1852   All remaining slaves in Colombia were liberated.

1852   Harriet Beecher Stowe published a bestselling antislavery novel, *Uncle Tom's Cabin*.

1854   Argentina completed a programme of the gradual abolition of slavery.

1854   Venezuela completed a programme of gradual freedom for slaves.

1861   On 12 April the Confederate bombardment of Fort Sumter, South Carolina began the American Civil War.

1862   Paraguay completed a programme of gradual abolition of slavery.

1862   An Anglo-American slave trade treaty brought British vessels to Cuban waters in search of illegal slave imports.

1863   The Netherlands abolished the slave trade for Dutch citizens and freed slaves in Dutch colonies.

1863   On 1 January the Emancipation Proclamation became effective in the United States, declaring all slaves free except those in states that were no longer in rebellion.

1865   On 9 April the American Civil War ended with the surrender of the Confederacy.

1865   On 18 December the 13th Amendment, which abolished slavery, became part of the US Constitution.

1867   The last recorded shipload of African slaves arrived in Cuba.

1867   Spain passed a law to stop the Cuban slave trade.

1870   On 23 June Spain enacted the Moret Law, which began the process of emancipating slaves in Cuba.

1871   On 28 September the Brazilian government passed the Rio Branco Law, which began the process of slave emancipation in Brazil.

1873   Slavery was abolished in Puerto Rico.

1880   Spain enacted the Law of Patronato, which began a process of gradual emancipation in Spanish colonies.

1880   On 7 September the Brazilian Anti-Slavery Society was established.

1885   The Brazilian government passed the Sexagenarian Law, which freed all slaves in Brazil who were 65 or older.

1886   Spain abolished slavery in all its colonies, including Cuba.

1886   The Brazilian government pledged to enact a gradual abolition of slavery.

1888   On 13 May slavery officially ended in Brazil.

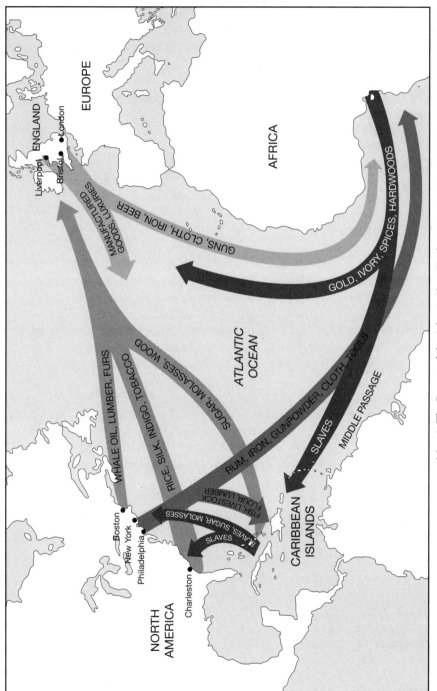

Map 1: The Routes of the Atlantic Slave Trade

Introduction

Slavery was an extreme form of dependency for centuries that coexisted with other forms of institutionalized dependency and servitude such as debt peonage, convict labour, serfdom and indentured labour.[1] The coercive and permanent nature of slavery, however, has been singled out as a particularly inhuman form of bondage. Existing in a state of complete unfreedom, forced to work according to the demands of owners, and perpetuating their condition through their children being born into slavery, the enslaved have endured bondage until set free, usually by statutory enactment of abolition. From the ancient world to the rise of transatlantic slavery, many societies in Europe, Africa and the Middle East contained slaves. Human bondage was therefore a common phenomenon. Some slaves lived in societies where the majority of people were non-slaves. This was the case in Greece and Rome in ancient times. Other slaves were part of societies dominated by slavery. This was the norm during the eighteenth and nineteenth centuries throughout the Caribbean, Brazil and the southern colonies in North America that became the US South. Hundreds of thousands of slaves fell into both categories.[2]

It might be supposed that campaigns and protests over the past two centuries have led to an end to slavery. But far from having disappeared as a result of growing pressure for human rights in the modern world, slavery and bondage still exist in Asia, Africa and Europe. Contemporary exploitation of conditions akin to slavery involves selling people like objects, forcing them to work for little or no pay and holding them at the mercy of employers. Slave-based businesses in the contemporary world include prostitution

1

in Thailand, water-selling in Mauretania, charcoal production in Brazil, general agriculture in India, and brickmaking in Pakistan.[3] According to the International Labour Organisation (ILO), around 21 million men, women and children today are in a form of slavery. Anti-Slavery International, a charitable non-governmental organization, expends great efforts to secure freedom for such people.[4]

A Short History of Transatlantic Slavery explores the significance of slavery over time and in space within the Atlantic world, drawing parallels between slavery and other forms of unfree labour and explaining the difficulties involved in ending slavery. The coverage of the book is broad. Six detailed chapters cover the main features of the transatlantic slave trade, slavery and emancipation over the course of four-and-a-half centuries. Combining the slave trade, slavery and emancipation within a book of this length is a challenging task, but this survey will show how slavery depended on replenishing enslaved workers through continuation of the slave trade, and how abolishing the slave trade and emancipating slaves were complex processes that gathered momentum over many years. The book contends that slavery and emancipation in the Atlantic world can only be understood by covering the links in the chain that created slavery, from initial capture of Africans, through the voyages of the enslaved across the Atlantic, to the experiences of slaves in the Americas, and to their achievement of freedom.

The geographical focus of *A Short History of Transatlantic Slavery* is on the mainland Americas and the Caribbean but with plenty of contextual reference to the European background of slave traders and planters and to the African origins of slaves. The role of masters in controlling slaves and organizing their living and work routines is an essential part of slavery. The behaviour and reactions of slaves to their condition of bondage is an equally important component of slavery. This book will yoke together these two perspectives on the evolution of slavery in different societies, taking account of the unbalanced power relations that characterized the interaction between owners on the one hand and slaves on the other.

This book examines the varieties of transatlantic slavery over time, including the use of domestic slaves in households and racial slavery based upon staple plantation production in the Americas. The gender and age dimension to the use of slaves is important, with some slave societies drawing upon adult male slaves in particular (dominant throughout the transatlantic slave trade) or turning to a greater use of child slavery (the international slave trade in the nineteenth century). The differences between gang work on plantations and task work, the gradation of skills among the slave labour force, and the different climatic and geographical conditions of slavery are further aspects of the variety of slavery that will be explored.

A Short History of Transatlantic Slavery explains the persistence of a system of human bondage that evolved over time into different forms as a permeable labour institution that was difficult to eradicate. Slavery constantly reinvented itself as different societies adapted to various uses for slaves. This adaptability meant that it was very difficult to end slavery and the slave trade altogether, because a demand always existed for supplies of new captives. The advantages to owners and employers arising from the necessity of a large, unfree workforce in relation to alternative supplies of labour, such as various forms of temporary servitude and free waged work, is an important theme that will help to explain slavery's persistence.

The transatlantic slave trade comprised the largest form of enforced inter-continental migration in world history. Over 10 million slaves were shipped from coastal regions of West Africa to the Americas between 1501 and 1867. Chapters 1 and 2 are devoted to the scale and organization of transatlantic slaving. The major national carriers of slaves across the Atlantic were the English, the French, the Dutch, the Spanish, the Portuguese, the Americans and the Brazilians. Their quantitative contribution to the scale of the slave trade can be gauged by statistical estimates gathered together in a major database, discussed in Chapter 1. These data are deployed to determine the major regions for the supply of slaves in West Africa and the main regions of slave disembarkation in the Americas. Fluctuations over time in levels of national engagement with the slave trade are assessed. Chapter 1 also discusses the continuation of the transatlantic slave trade after initial points of slave disembarkation through an intra-Caribbean slave trade and through internal slave trades in the United States and Brazil.

Chapter 2 examines the organization of the slave trade. Chartered trading companies conducted slave-trading enterprises in the seventeenth and early eighteenth centuries, but over time they were largely superseded by private merchants acting in partnerships for slave trading voyages. The slave trade in the North Atlantic was largely organized on a triangular basis. The first leg of the triangle consisted of voyages from a home port to West Africa, with commodities for sale or barter to middlemen for slaves. The second leg comprised the Atlantic crossing, known as the Middle Passage. The third leg was the voyage home after slaves had been sold in the Americas. The slave trade in the South Atlantic, by contrast, followed a bilateral pattern between West Africa, largely south of the Equator, and South America. The human and economic aspects of the slave trade are discussed, with emphasis on the complexity of the arrangements necessary for successful conduct of a slaving voyage. The level of slave trade profits and the economic impact of transatlantic slaving on the nations participating in the trade are also summarized in Chapter 2.

Chapter 3 focuses on the work and life of slaves on plantations. These large agricultural holdings were the site where African slaves and their descendants produced staple crops for export to European markets. Sugar was the predominant plantation commodity throughout the Caribbean, Brazil and Louisiana; coffee was also grown in the West Indies and Brazil. Rice plantations were found in South Carolina and Georgia. Tobacco plantations dominated Virginia and Maryland. Throughout the nineteenth-century American South, from the Carolinas to Alabama and Mississippi, cotton became the main staple crop. The history of plantation slavery in the Americas is very much connected to the particular type of staple crop produced. Chapter 3 examines connections between slave life and work in these different American regions, in relation to crop production.

Planters aimed to produce a self-sustaining slave population through natural increase, but, with the exception of the US South, this proved difficult to achieve. Chapter 3 outlines the demography of slavery, with particular attention to problems of fertility, mortality and nutrition. Sugar, it will be seen, was the plantation crop most associated with heavy levels of mortality. The intermixture between new supplies of African slaves and the emergence of a Creole (i.e. American-born) workforce on the plantations is discussed, with consideration of its crucial significance for the slave culture created in the Americas. The different work patterns of plantations are analysed – gang labour, task work, skill levels in the workforce

– along with the gender division that was an important part of labour. Chapter 3 also discusses the main features of slave beliefs and customs and how these were transformed in the Americas. Despite the hardships and deprivations of living as slaves, African-Americans forged a vibrant, multifaceted culture based on a blending of African regional customs and the experience of life in the Americas.

Slaves lived and worked under conditions of unfreedom and forced labour and therefore it is not surprising that resistance, in a variety of forms, was an important aspect of their consciousness and actions. Chapter 4 explores the varying types of slave resistance and how these were dealt with by owners. Day-to-day resistance, in the form of verbal insolence and work stoppages, was common. This is discussed in relation to how these practices shaped the ability of slaves to bargain and negotiate with masters within the power relations of slavery that were stacked against them. Running away was another common form of slave resistance. The chapter will select examples of geographical locations where slave runaways were prominent to discuss their common patterns. Slave rebellions were the major overt form of slave resistance in the Americas. There were many short-lived revolts, but relatively few were successful. This will be explained. The most important slave rebellion in the Western Hemisphere was the Saint-Domingue/Haitian revolt of 1791–1804, the first time in history that a massive slave revolt (involving more than 100,000 people) was successful. The reasons for this success and its implications are analysed.

Before *c.* 1750 slavery was accepted as an institution by most educated commentators; it was seen as a normal part of human societies. Occasional critics of slavery had publicized their views in the seventeenth century, but no antislavery movement had emerged. Matters changed considerably after the mid-eighteenth century for a variety of reasons, including changing philosophical views about slavery associated with Enlightenment thinking, the rise of Christian notions of benevolence in relation to slavery, legal decisions about the enslaved, the arguments of Adam Smith over the superiority of free labour to slavery, and the mobilization of antislavery campaigns. Chapter 5 analyses the shift in attitudes towards an antislavery stance, and then concentrates on the mobilization of abolitionist groups in the campaigns to end the slave trade throughout the Atlantic world. The chapter discusses the reasons for varied endings to the slave trade. It also explains the international attempts by abolitionists to combine their efforts to attack the continuation of the slave trade through diplomatic pressure, naval patrols and international treaties. My discussion emphasizes the diverse reasons why different national slave trades were abolished.

Chapter 6 concentrates on the movements for slave emancipation throughout the Americas. Gaining freedom for slaves usually occurred about thirty years after national slave trades were prohibited. The mixture of proslavery support, government inertia and the predominance of gradual emancipation schemes in the process of working towards slave freedom will be explained. Whether the process of emancipation was mainly a top-down affair achieved by governments or whether it was achieved through abolitionist pressure will also be discussed. The chapter shows that there was no set pattern from one nation to another, and that many impediments existed before legislative freedom for slaves was possible. In one notable case, that of the United States, slave emancipation was bound up with complex national political debates and the fighting of a bloody civil war. In other cases, nations enacted slave emancipation laws in peaceful circumstances. It was common, as Chapter 6 will show, for individual polities to opt for what was effectively a gradual transition to full freedom for former slaves through Apprenticeship or similar schemes.

Slavery has had an enduring impact on the making of the modern world. Over four centuries it was a central part of a massive international diaspora of people taken against their will to many parts of the Atlantic world. The epilogue considers long-term effects of transatlantic slavery, which was a crucial matrix for the formation of African-American culture. The racial prejudice associated with black slavery has had an enduring impact on modern life. The epilogue concludes with a discussion of the philosophical and legal aspects of the movement for reparations for the descendants of slaves and a section dealing with the memorialization of slavery through anniversaries, ceremonies, museum exhibitions and monuments.

1

THE FLOWS OF THE SLAVE TRADE

The scale of the transatlantic slave trade can only be estimated rather than calculated precisely. Over the past century numerous scholars have attempted to determine the extent of the trade, but their estimates have varied widely. Greater precision on this matter is more readily available today, however, than at any previous time. The collective research endeavour that has produced the online Transatlantic Slave Trade Database offers historians the most detailed opportunity ever available to analyse the flows of slaving in the Atlantic world. Dealing with the most important form of forced migration between continents in modern history, the database includes information on 33,367 voyages that embarked 10,148,288 slaves in Africa and on 33,048 voyages that disembarked 8,752,924 slaves, mainly in the Americas, between the early sixteenth and the mid-nineteenth century.[1] This covers about 80 per cent of all transatlantic slave trade voyages.[2] The compilers of the database calculated the overall volume of the slave trade from information on individual voyages and from inferences made from missing data to create estimates of the total transatlantic slaving traffic.[3]

The revised database provides historians with a firm basis for quantitative enquiries into the extent and characteristics of transatlantic slaving across time and space. The numbers matter because they provide the best estimates available of the contours of the slave trade, allowing the historian to pinpoint the importance of some national flags in transporting Africans against their will to the Americas and the peripheral nature of other flags. The database also provides statistics on fluctuations in the scale of the slave trade in different epochs and during wartime and peacetime. Only by contextualizing the flows of slaves according to these recently compiled data can the extent and persistence of transatlantic slaving be analysed in depth.[4] This chapter uses the estimates in the revised database to discuss the distribution of the slave shipments according to national flags, the African region of departure, and the American region of arrival over the entire course of transatlantic slaving.

NATIONAL FLAGS AND THE SLAVE TRADE

The national flags that dominated the slave trade were the major Western European trading powers that competed with one another for overseas trade and empire in the early modern period: Spain, Portugal, France, the Netherlands and England. These nations had the financial resources and the commercial motivation to conduct long oceanic voyages. The slave trade formed just one line of commerce followed by vessels from these nations, and was closely connected to direct commodity trades between European ports, Asia and the Americas. The Africans supplied via the slave trade and the goods taken in direct commerce with American destinations were linked to the emergence and growth of a plantation sector that produced staple crops on agricultural estates for exportation back to the Old World. The major plantation staple commodities were sugar (pre-eminently), tobacco, rice, cotton and coffee. All these crops needed to grow in warm climates; they required a large labour force to carry out multifarious tasks including planting, harvesting and transporting the crop to ships.[5] Staple crops grown on plantations catered for a strong growing market for tropical groceries among European consumers. Smoking tobacco, taking snuff, sweetening tea and coffee with sugar, and using sugar and rice in cooking, all advanced considerably as consumer products because of slave-grown commodities. Cotton, which only became a significant export crop after 1800, was the one major product among these staple commodities that was connected to clothing rather than to food and drink.[6]

In five cases – Portugal, Spain, France, the Netherlands, England

– the ships involved in the slave trade conducted triangular voyages beginning in their home country, sailing out to Africa, buying slaves there, transporting them across the Atlantic for sale in the Americas, and then returning westwards to their original port of departure.[7] In the case of the Brazilian slave trade, ships usually sailed on a bilateral basis between Brazilian ports and the west coast of Africa.[8] Merchants in North America also organized slaving voyages, beginning while the thirteen colonies were part of the British Empire before 1776 and continuing after the formation of the United States. This, too, was a triangular trade, with ships sailing from North American ports to exchange goods in West Africa for slaves, who were taken to mainly West Indian destinations, and then a final leg of the voyage back to their North American provenance region. Denmark was the main smaller flag to participate in the triangular slave trade; other minor slave-trading polities included Sweden and Brandenburg/Prussia.[9]

THE FLOWS OF THE SLAVE TRADE

The flows of the slave trade were very modest in the sixteenth century: only 2.2 per cent of the embarked captives during the entire slave-trade era were placed on vessels before 1600 (Table 1). Transatlantic slaving voyages increased significantly from the second half of the seventeenth century onwards. They maintained high levels of slave shipment, amounting to 1–2 million embarked African captives in each quarter-century between 1701 and 1850: that was the peak period in which transatlantic slaving flourished. Table 1 shows the main contribution of national flags to the slave trade. The Spanish and the Portuguese (via the Luso-Brazilian trade) had the longest involvement with transatlantic slaving. Conquest and settlement by the Iberian powers in Central and South America and the Caribbean in the sixteenth century paved the way for the deployment of slave labour. The Spanish did not develop a plantation sector until the second half of the eighteenth century, while the Portuguese supplied slaves mainly for the Brazilian sugar industry.[10] The Iberian powers continued to send slaves to their American territories until the end of the Brazilian and Cuban slave trades in 1851 and 1867.

Table 1 shows that the Iberian powers were responsible for

Table 1: Slave embarkations by flag, 1501–1866[11]

	Spain/Uruguay	Portugal/Brazil	Great Britain	Netherlands	USA	France	Denmark/Baltic	Totals
1501–1525	6,363	7,000	0	0	0	0	0	13,363
1526–1550	25,375	25,387	0	0	0	0	0	50,763
1551–1575	28,167	31,089	1,685	0	0	66	0	61,007
1576–1600	60,056	90,715	237	1,365	0	0	0	152,373
1601–1625	83,496	267,519	0	1,829	0	0	0	352,843
1626–1650	44,313	201,609	33,695	31,729	824	1,827	1,053	315,050
1651–1675	12,601	244,793	122,367	100,526	0	7,125	653	488,064
1676–1700	5,860	297,272	272,200	85,847	3,327	29,484	25,685	719,674
1701–1725	0	474,447	410,597	73,816	3,277	120,939	5,833	1,088,909
1726–1750	0	536,696	554,042	83,095	34,004	259,095	4,793	1,471,725
1751–1775	4,239	528,693	832,047	132,330	84,580	325,918	17,508	1,925,314
1776–1800	6,415	673,167	748,612	40,773	67,443	433,061	39,199	2,008,670
1801–1825	168,087	1,160,601	283,959	2,669	109,545	135,815	16,316	1,876,992
1826–1850	400,728	1,299,969	0	357	1,850	68,074	0	1,770,979
1851–1866	215,824	9,309	0	0	476	0	0	225,609
Totals	1,061,524	5,848,265	3,259,440	554,336	305,326	1,381,404	111,041	12,521,336

Source: http://www.slavevoyages.org/tast/assessment/estimates.faces

55.2 per cent of the embarked slaves taken across the Atlantic between 1501 and 1866.[12] The leading Iberian ports in the trade were Lisbon, Bahia, Recife and Rio de Janeiro.[13] The volume of the Portugal/Brazil trade was especially large in the nineteenth century: four out of every ten Africans taken by that national flag to the Americas were sent between 1801 and 1866. Table 1 shows that Portugal/Brazil embarked many more slaves than Spain/Uruguay. A caveat needs to be registered, however, about this. Until 1789 Spain pursued a policy of *asiento* agreements whereby other countries were licensed to carry slaves to Spanish America. The Spanish and Portuguese crowns were unified for sixty years after 1580. Portugal held the first official *asiento* from 1595 until the Portuguese revolt against Spain in 1640. Thereafter *asiento* holders included the Netherlands, France and Britain. Whereas it was once thought that Spain largely relied on these trading partners to take slaves to Spanish America, recent research has found that ships sailing under the Spanish flag also conveyed large numbers of captives to Spain's colonies.[14]

England, the Netherlands and France played a minimal role in the flows of the slave trade in the sixteenth century. Each of these nations sent out voyages of exploration to the Americas before 1600, but none of them had yet settled significant colonies across the Atlantic. The establishment of colonies by these powers during the seventeenth century led to the emergence of a significant slave trade for each of these flags. England colonized much of the east coast of North America in the seventeenth century and acquired a number of Caribbean islands. France and the Netherlands also settled colonies in the West Indies during the seventeenth century, with the Dutch gaining an important foothold in territories (Demerara, Essequibo, Berbice and especially Suriname) on the 'wild coast' (as they termed it) of the northern end of South America. England carried the largest volume of slaves of these three powers. This reflected the fact that Britain acquired much more territorial acreage in the Americas than her northern European rivals, allowing scope for a larger plantation sector: by *c.* 1775 the British Empire in the Americas covered more than twice the square miles of the Dutch and French Atlantic empires combined; and the French and Dutch colonies in North America and the Caribbean had only a quarter of the British population in the same regions.[15]

The British slave trade grew in the last four decades of the seventeenth century and reached its peak during the eighteenth century: between 1660 and 1807, when Britain abolished its slave trade, vessels sailing from English ports to North America and the Caribbean embarked more than three million slaves (Table 1). Britain was the leading slave-carrying nation in the eighteenth century.[16] London was the main English slaving port from the mid-seventeenth century until around 1720, when the English branch of the trade lay mainly under the auspices of the London-based Royal African Company.[17] But after the British slave trade was opened to non-chartered companies in 1698, Bristol's private merchants challenged London's position in the trade to assume dominance among British slave-trading ports in the 1720s and 1730s.[18] Liverpool overtook Bristol and London to become the leading port in the British slave trade between 1740 and 1807. During that period, Liverpool became the busiest port in the world for dispatching slaving voyages. Its merchants effectively drew together the human capital needed to conduct the slave trade successfully.[19]

British North American colonial shipping contributed to slave trade flows during the eighteenth century, notably from Rhode Island. Newport became the main North American port connected with transatlantic slaving, assuming greater importance than the much larger port of New York. Newport's merchants had good commercial connections in the Caribbean but had the added advantage of having a cluster of rum distilleries in Rhode Island – using molasses from the West Indies as their main ingredient – to supply alcohol to West African traders in return for slaves.[20] After the American Revolution, a slave trade from the United States embarked nearly 177,000 slaves in the half-century after American independence (Table 1). Most of these were delivered via Charleston, South Carolina to southern US markets before the abolition of the African slave trade to the United States in 1808. Thereafter American vessels supplied slaves to colonies of other powers in South America and the Caribbean; in some cases, this meant deploying American vessels in illegal slaving ventures.[21]

The French slave trade always had a smaller volume than the British slave trade in each quarter-century covered by Table 1, but French merchants still embarked 1.38 million slaves during the entire period of transatlantic slaving – an 11 per cent share in the trade. As with Britain, the eighteenth century was the peak period for the French slave trade. In 1794 France abolished slavery in all its possessions, but Napoleon, when ruler of France, restored slavery in territories growing sugar cane in 1802. The French slave trade was outlawed in 1815 but continued until 1831, with the French flag sometimes being used illegally thereafter. French transatlantic slaving declined significantly in each quarter-century after 1800, but still carried 17,000 slaves annually in 1820–5, a figure matching the numbers of the 1770s (Table 1).[22]

Nantes dominated the French slave trade, accounting for more slaving expeditions than the combined share of its rivals – Le Havre, La Rochelle, Bordeaux, St Malo and Honfleur. Nantes, situated near the mouth of the Loire River about thirty miles from the French Atlantic coast, was well placed geographically to participate in transatlantic slaving ventures. Nantais merchants accounted for 42 per cent of the Africans dispatched on French vessels in the eighteenth century.[23] On the eve of the French Revolution, the Nantes economy relied on the slave trade. Between one-third and one-half of all tropical produce entering Nantes at that time comprised payments for slaves acquired from Nantais merchants.[24] Between 1813 and 1841 Nantes embarked 102,000 slaves, concentrating on the Bight of Biafra as an embarkation centre and Cuba as a destination for slave sales.[25]

The Netherlands had a lesser role in the slave trade than either Britain or France, but was still ranked fifth among the national flags taking slaves to Atlantic markets. The Dutch slave trade began in the second quarter of the seventeenth century, when merchants in Amsterdam undertook most of its organization. The peak period for Dutch slave trading lay in the first three-quarters of the eighteenth century, when the trade became concentrated at Middelburg and Vlissingen (i.e. Flushing) in Zeeland. Until 1738 the private Dutch West India Company (WIC) monopolized transatlantic slaving, but the Middelburg Commercial Company then became a vigorous competitor in the trade. The Dutch slave trade reached its peak around 1770 but declined towards the end of the American War of Independence. Britain's navy captured Dutch ships in the fourth Anglo-Dutch War of 1780–4. The plantation economy in Suriname, the largest Dutch slave colony, was then heavily in debt and not importing many slaves. Dutch participation in the French revolutionary wars from 1795 brought its slave trade to a halt.

The Netherlands decreed the end of its slave trade in 1814, but authentic Dutch slave voyages ceased before 1800.[26] Dutch investors also acquired slaves through Sweden, Brandenburg and Kurland, but these ventures were more concerned with trading expeditions along the West African coast than embarking slaves for an Atlantic crossing.[27]

The only other flag significantly involved in transatlantic slaving was Denmark, which accounted for more than 100,000 embarked slaves over time (Table 1). The ships in the trade were mainly owned in Copenhagen. The Danish slave trade was generally small in scope, but it rose significantly in the last quarters of the seventeenth and eighteenth centuries: those two periods account for over half of the Africans loaded during the entire Danish slave trade. In common with other minor carriers, the increase in Danish slaving activity in those periods reflected the timing of the increased volume of overall transatlantic slaving. Brandenburg vessels and Dutch interlopers joined Danish ships in supplying slaves to the Danish West Indies.[28] Denmark's small colonies in the Caribbean – St Croix, St Thomas and St John – lacked extensive demand for supplies of enslaved Africans. However, Denmark participated strongly in an inter-Caribbean slave trade that handled almost as many captives as those brought directly from Africa.[29]

AFRICAN REGIONS OF DEPARTURE

African regions of departure for the transatlantic trade were largely located along *c.* 3,000 miles of coastline, stretching from the Senegal River in the north to Benguela in the southwest. These areas in sequence from north-west to south-east were Senegambia, Sierra Leone, the Windward Coast, the Gold Coast, the Bight of Benin, the Bight of Biafra and West Central Africa. The regions named are those adopted in the revised edition of the transatlantic slave trade database.[30] Supplies of slaves were unobtainable from regions above the Senegal River, owing to the Sahara desert and the territories controlled by Moroccans. Slaves were similarly unavailable from arid territories to the south of Luanda. In any case, Europeans did not need to penetrate so far in a southwesterly direction to gather the captives needed to sustain the slave trade. There were minor exceptions. Thus for brief periods in the late seventeenth and early eighteenth centuries, slaves were taken from Madagascar to the West Indies, Massachusetts and New York.[31]

After 1800 a further African region came to the fore as a slave provenance area for transatlantic destinations: this comprised southeast Africa and some Indian Ocean islands. This occurred because of the increased demand for slaves from the Americas and because Britain and other powers put diplomatic and naval pressure on several West African regions to curtail their shipment of slaves across the Atlantic. No other significant areas of supply were tapped for the slave trade during its entire existence. Various British plans for unlocking Africa's agricultural potential were mooted during the second half of the eighteenth century.[32] But there were no schemes for Europeans to establish plantations in Africa rather than in the New World. The prevalence of diseases such as malaria, lack of European knowledge of West Africa beyond its coastal areas, and the firm control of African rulers and notables over European penetration of the African continent all militated against setting up a plantation sector in West Africa. Nevertheless, the Portuguese had firm control of Luanda and Benguela and many of the slaving networks connected to those ports.[33]

Table 2 shows that some regions were heavier suppliers of slaves than others, and that there was no consistent trend towards ship captains having to penetrate ever further south because slave supplies had been exhausted in more northerly areas. Considerable fluctuations occurred over time in the volume of slaves embarked from different West African regions. But clearly there were complex reasons why European and American slave traders tapped slaves from different regions. For instance, it would have made sense – in terms of distance and costs – for slave supplies from Senegambia to reach mainly Caribbean destinations and in greater numbers than Africans emanating from more southerly West African regions, but that was not the case in most periods. African cultural, economic and demographic conditions were more important than considerations of the shortest distance from the West African region of slave provenance to their place of American disembarkation. [34]

Table 2 shows the trends in slave supplies from the eight African areas. West Central Africa stands out as the main regional contributor. Between 1514 and 1865 it accounted for more than 5.7

Table 2: Slave embarkations by African regions, 1501–1866

	Senegambia and offshore Atlantic	Sierra Leone	Windward Coast	Gold Coast	Bight of Benin	Bight of Biafra	West Central Africa and St. Helena	Southeast Africa and Indian Ocean islands	Totals
1501–1525	12,726	0	0	0	0	0	637	0	13,363
1526–1550	44,458	0	0	0	0	2,080	4,225	0	50,763
1551–1575	48,319	1,168	0	0	0	3,383	8,137	0	61,007
1576–1600	41,778	237	2,482	0	0	2,996	104,879	0	152,373
1601–1625	23,862	0	0	68	3,528	2,921	322,119	345	352,843
1626–1650	30,360	1,372	0	2,429	6,080	33,540	241,269	0	315,050
1651–1675	27,741	906	351	30,806	52,768	80,780	278,079	16,633	488,064
1676–1700	54,141	4,565	999	75,377	207,436	69,080	293,340	14,737	719,674
1701–1725	55,944	6,585	8,878	229,239	378,101	66,833	331,183	12,146	1,088,909
1726–1750	87,028	16,637	37,672	231,418	356,760	182,066	556,981	3,162	1,471,725
1751–1775	135,294	84,069	169,094	268,228	288,587	319,709	654,984	5,348	1,925,314
1776–1800	84,920	94,694	73,938	285,643	261,137	336,008	822,056	50,274	2,008,670
1801–1825	91,225	89,326	37,322	80,895	201,054	264,834	929,999	182,338	1,876,992
1826–1850	17,717	84,416	6,131	5,219	209,742	230,328	989,908	227,518	1,770,979
1851–1866	0	4,795	0	0	33,867	2	156,779	30,167	225,609
Totals	755,513	388,771	336,868	1,209,321	1,999,060	1,594,560	5,694,574	542,668	12,521,336

Source:http://www.slavevoyages.org/tast/assessment/estimates.faces

million (45.5 per cent) of the Africans transported to the Americas. West Central Africa first emerged as a significant supplier of slaves in the last quarter of the sixteenth century. It expanded its slave supplies rapidly in the first quarter of the seventeenth century, when it easily assumed the most prominent position among all provenance regions for the transatlantic slave trade. West Central Africa was a particularly important contributor to slave supplies in the peak years of transatlantic slaving activity between 1726 and 1850. The main ports handling slave departures from this region were Cabinda, Luanda, Benguela and Malembo.[35] Between 1701 and 1867 Luanda shipped 1,632,000 (or 37 per cent) of slaves embarked from Angola, while Benguela shipped 671,100 (15 per cent).[36]

After 1575 West Central Africa was always the largest single slave-supplying region in each quarter-century apart from 1701–25 (Table 2). The Kingdom of Kongo was a major supplier of slaves before 1700, with additional captives coming from the Vili to the north of the Congo River and some Mbundu states to the south and east. During the eighteenth century several remote inland states, including the provinces of Luanda and Kazembe, became the main suppliers of slaves to the coast. This resulted from a shifting slaving frontier that was more noticeable in West Central Africa than in any other provenance region for slaves.[37] The Portuguese had a stronghold in Angola while the Dutch concentrated on trade north of the Congo River at Cabinda and Loango and north of Luanda at the mouth of the Bengo River. English and French slave ships also called frequently at various ports in West Central Africa.[38] The English and French challenged the Luso-Brazilians for slave supplies from ports north of Luanda in the late eighteenth century, notably at Cabinda, but the French slave trade with Angola collapsed suddenly after the Saint-Domingue slave revolt (1791) and English competition with Portuguese-speaking traders ended with the abolition of the British slave trade.[39]

The second most important slave provenance area for the transatlantic slave trade over time was the Bight of Benin, which contemporaries referred to as the Slave Coast. French, British and Portuguese traders were the main purchasers of slaves in this region.[40] The Bight of Benin embarked on transatlantic slaving later than West Central Africa, only beginning to traffic for slaves modestly in the first half of the seventeenth century. Matters changed considerably thereafter. The slave trade from the Bight of Benin had a swift upward increase in volume in the half-century after 1675; but it then declined gradually in all but one quarter-century period up to 1850 as other African regions, such as the Bight of Biafra and West Central Africa, expanded their slave exports. Yet even in the second quarter of the nineteenth century, the Bight of Benin was the third out of eight African regions for slave embarkations to the Americas (Table 2).[41]

Allada, situated behind coastal lagoons, dominated the export slave trade from the Bight of Benin in the seventeenth century. Thereafter the two main contributors to slave supplies in that region were the Yoruba Kingdom of Oyo and Dahomey. The reorganization of the slave trade at the Bight of Benin in the eighteenth century involved the rise to significance of Ouidah as a major slave trading port. Both the Oyo and the Dahomeans used this port extensively.[42] Almost half of the estimated slave departures from the Bight of Benin between 1650 and 1865 emanated from Ouidah. Porto Novo took over as the leading slave trading port from this African region in the last quarter of the eighteenth century, but it faded away after 1800 when Lagos became a significant slave embarkation centre in the Bight of Benin. Nearly 90 per cent of the slaves leaving the Bight of Benin after 1800 were Yoruba in origin.[43]

Third in order of the volume of the slave trade from African regions was the Bight of Biafra. This area comprised the innermost bay of the Gulf of Guinea. Today it includes much of Nigeria. Slaves were acquired at a modest level from the Bight of Biafra before the mid-seventeenth century. Export totals began to increase after 1650 but it was not until the eighteenth century that the slave trade from the Bight of Biafra grew significantly in volume. The peak period of growth was in the century after 1750 when the Bight of Biafra embarked nearly three-quarters of the captives it took during the entire era of transatlantic slaving. Between 1751 and 1825, the Bight of Biafra was only exceeded as a region of slave supply by West Central Africa.[44]

The rise of the Biafran slave trade was closely connected to the rise of the Aro in supplying slaves in the Niger Delta and Cross River hinterlands.[45] Probably more than 90 per cent of slaves leaving the Bight of Biafra were Igbo. They were recruited at inland fairs and taken via creeks and lagoons on boats to three ports on the coast of the Niger Delta: Bonny, Old Calabar and New Calabar (also known as Elem Kalabari). Before 1807 the Bight of Biafra was heavily dominated by British traders, notably from Liverpool; it became the major supply area for vessels taking slaves to British American markets in the eighteenth century. After the British abolition of the slave trade, other powers engaged in transatlantic slaving at the Bight of Biafra: these were principally the Luso-Brazilians, the Spanish and the French.[46]

The fourth slave provenance area in West Africa was the Gold Coast, which accounted for 9.7 per cent of the overall slave trade to the Americas (Table 2). The Gold Coast supplied enslaved Africans on a very modest scale in the second quarter of the seventeenth century. Thereafter its slave trading activity grew, though for most years before 1700 traders were more interested in collecting gold from the region rather than human captives.[47] The exhaustion of gold supplies from the late seventeenth century, however, reoriented much external trade at the Gold Coast towards the dispatch of slaves.[48] During the eighteenth century, warfare between the Akan and their rivals, the Asante, supplied an increased number of captives from the Gold Coast. This prolonged struggle for mastery led to successful Asante armies establishing a strong centralized state that captured Akans and supplied them to Muslim traders in the northern areas of the Gold Coast and in large numbers to ships for transatlantic destinations.[49]

During the seventeenth and early eighteenth centuries, slave trading activity along the Gold Coast centred on forts and castles belonging mainly to Portuguese, English and Dutch slave traders. These structures usually had guns on their parapets pointing out to the ocean as a means of protection against rivals; they had compounds to hold slaves; and they included sufficient space for storerooms and quarters for armed personnel and local African employees. Rivalry among European powers meant that forts were sometimes captured and held by other nations. These forts declined in significance over time as a result of fierce competition from private traders, and they were a pale shadow of their former strength by 1800. Two forts – Anomabu and Cape Coast Castle – accounted for more than four out of every ten slave departures from this region. At the forts slave ship captains interacted with European officials, local headmen (known as *caboceers*), inland suppliers of slaves,

Kenneth Morgan

Fig. 1: Cape Coast Castle, Ghana, 1990s

agents who handled gold and slave sales, and members of African elites.[50] The abolition of the British and American slave trades, along with British naval enforcement against slave trading, had a major impact in reducing the flow of slaves from the Gold Coast from 1808 onwards, as Table 2 shows.[51]

The last three slave provenance areas in West Africa were the Upper Guinea regions of Senegambia, Sierra Leone and the Windward Coast. Collectively, they shipped more Africans across the Atlantic than the Gold Coast during the entire course of the slave trade, but individually they were the least three important areas of slave supply in West Africa. The Senegambian slave trade lasted longer than the equivalent traffic at the two other regions. In only one quarter-century (1751–75) did the Windward Coast dispatch more slaves for the transatlantic slave trade than Senegambia. Gambia/James Fort and Senegal/St Louis together accounted for more than a third of slave departures from Upper Guinea over time.[52]

The supply of slaves in Upper Guinea was strongly influenced by the Muslim holy wars conducted in the interior of the region that consolidated Futa Jallon as an Islamic state.[53] Liverpool merchants dominated the slave trade with Upper Guinea in the second half of the eighteenth century through establishing strong cultural and economic networks with traders along the coast, on Bunce Island in the Sierra Leone River, and on small offshore depots such as the Banana Islands and the Iles de Los.[54] Upper Guinea was the one exception to the pattern of high levels of slave departures following an initial upsurge of slave trading. This suggests that other West African regions offered better opportunities for slave ships and their captains over the course of transatlantic slaving activity.[55]

Southeast Africa played only a marginal role in the transatlantic slave trade before the later eighteenth century. But it was a region that witnessed a rapidly expanding level of slaving activity to meet the increased demand for plantation labour in the Atlantic world in the first half of the nineteenth century. Thus Table 2 shows that more than 400,000 Africans were shipped from that region to Atlantic markets between 1801 and 1850. Many slaves from southeast Africa in that half-century emanated from Mozambique, the Mascarene Islands and the Zambesi valley.[56] This branch of the slave trade flourished as the European powers blockaded West African sources of slave supply in an effort to expand abolitionist pressure on slave trading; but more important in the supply of slaves from southeast Africa was rising demand for Africans in Río de la Plata and Brazil. The growth of slave supplies from the Indian Ocean to transatlantic destinations underscores the propensity of slaving to adapt to other supply areas after diplomatic pressure and naval patrols curtailed the slave trade from West Africa. There was a ready market for Africans in many parts of the Americas where slave emancipation took a long time to come to fruition during the nineteenth century.[57]

AMERICAN DESTINATIONS

After disembarkation and sale in the Americas, most slaves became workers on plantations growing staple crops. The plantation sector absorbed probably around 90 per cent of the Africans trafficked to the Americas over time; the remaining slaves were destined for work in households, on livestock properties and in urban occupations.[58] The continuing problem of substantial mortality – caused by inadequate diet, overwork and many fatal diseases – combined with the expansion of plantations into new areas led to the continuance of the slave trade for such a long time. Of course, those parts of the Americas where natural growth among slave populations increased markedly (such as the Chesapeake and South Carolina after 1700, or Barbados after *c.* 1750) had a lower demand for African captives than those places where slave mortality remained high (such as Jamaica, Cuba and Brazil). It was a truism that slave disembarkation areas dominated by sugar cultivation had the highest rates of slave mortality.[59]

Disembarkation regions for slaves in the Americas outnumbered embarkation areas for captives in Africa. Nevertheless, Table 3 shows that most slaves were delivered to two major broad regions: Brazil and the Caribbean. This reflected the fact that sugar was the main staple crop produced in those territories. Over the entire era of the slave trade Table 3 shows that Brazil accounted for 45.4 per cent of the enslaved Africans disembarkations, whereas the Caribbean's share was 37.3 per cent. As a supplement to the figures in Table 3, recent estimates of the slave trade to Spanish America suggest that 1.5 million slaves arrived directly from Africa in Spanish America between 1520 and 1867 and an additional 566,000 slaves disembarked in Spanish America from New World colonies such as Brazil and Jamaica.[60]

Brazil was a minor disembarkation point for slaves in the sixteenth century. But the spread of sugar plantations there in the seventeenth century, organized by the Portuguese and the Dutch, boosted the demand for fresh supplies of slaves after colonists had acquired the necessary capital and credit to purchase Africans.[61] From the first quarter of the seventeenth century, slave imports to Brazil grew without fail in each quarter-century up to 1850, by which time a coffee boom was also stimulating the demand for enslaved Africans. In the two centuries after 1650 – except for 1751–75 – this was the largest single broad disembarkation region for slaves (Table 3). The backbone of the Brazilian trade lay in the extensive shipment of slaves from the Bight of Benin and Angola to Pernambuco, Bahia and southeast Brazil.[62] From 1600 onwards almost all of the organization of this branch of the slave trade was based in Pernambuco, Bahia and Rio de Janeiro rather than in Lisbon. This reflected the fact that

Table 3: Broad disembarkation regions for slaves, 1501–1866

	Europe	Mainland North America	British Caribbean	French Caribbean	Dutch Americas	Danish West Indies	Spanish Americas	Brazil	Africa	Totals
1501–1525	452	0	0	0	0	0	8,923	0	0	9,375
1526–1550	0	0	0	0	0	0	35,534	0	0	35,534
1551–1575	0	0	0	0	0	0	40,671	2,461	0	43,132
1576–1600	188	0	0	0	0	0	84,242	26,814	0	111,244
1601–1625	85	0	567	0	0	0	117,709	156,468	0	274,829
1626–1650	0	100	26,639	545	0	0	61,482	163,938	172	252,876
1651–1675	1,281	3,970	86,770	16,746	52,190	0	32,292	204,575	2,457	400,282
1676–1700	1,615	11,077	196,501	21,394	71,967	18,146	14,021	259,475	493	594,689
1701–1725	158	39,303	280,470	82,147	53,413	8,059	37,856	423,161	0	924,567
1726–1750	3,968	106,671	357,150	212,325	73,051	4,515	17,435	468,690	516	1,244,321
1751–1775	1,090	118,822	580,824	309,733	118,145	18,271	21,030	476,010	428	1,644,353
1776–1800	23	30,687	594,879	390,929	50,606	37,763	69,212	621,156	1,373	1,796,627
1801–1825	0	77,613	183,701	63,517	25,355	17,223	254,777	1,012,762	32,224	1,667,172
1826–1850	0	91	10,751	22,880	0	5,021	333,781	1,041,964	99,908	1,514,396
1851–1866	0	413	0	0	0	0	163,947	6,899	17,998	189,257
Totals	8,860	388,747	2,318,252	1,120,216	444,728	108,998	1,292,912	4,864,374	155,569	10,702,656

Source: http://www.slavevoyages.org/tast/assessment/estimates.faces

ships sailed bilaterally between West Africa and Brazil rather than operating a triangular trade from Lisbon.[63]

The discovery of gold in the Brazilian province of Minas Gerais between 1693 and 1695 boosted the traffic in slaves to northeastern Brazil. Pernambuco had extensive plantations in its hinterland, and served as an entrepôt for other areas of Brazil that used slaves, including mining areas and coastal areas of Amazonia. Pernambuco's slave trade peaked in the late 1810s and early 1820s in response to increased plantation output and the opportunities for increased slave trading afforded by the abolition of the British and American slave trades.[64] After 1760 the rapid growth of cotton production in the Amazonian region boosted the number of slave vessels attracted to Pará and Maranhão.[65]

Bahia, a large region of extensive sugar production, was another important Brazilian reception area for slaves. Overall some 1.3 million slaves were imported to Bahia during the Atlantic slave-trade era, the majority of them after 1650. By that time Africans had replaced Amerindians as the major source of labour on Bahian sugar estates. Merchants supplied slaves to these plantations and to the mines of Minas Gerais. The emergence of a large-scale coffee industry in São Paulo, Rio de Janeiro and Minas Gerais in the first half of the nineteenth century was a further stimulus to the Brazilian slave trade. Though Britain tried to restrict the Brazilian slave trade after the Napoleonic Wars, the import of slaves to Bahia continued through to 1850. Bahia was overall the largest receiving port in the transatlantic slave trade apart from Rio de Janeiro.[66]

Between 1790 and 1830 Rio de Janeiro supplied slaves to the Minas Gerais mines and to Río de la Plata, Rio Grande do Sul, Santa Catarina, São Paulo and Espírito Santo for herding, craftwork and domestic labour. Its share of the Brazilian slave trade increased significantly in the last century of its operation: between 1750 and 1800 half of the slaves entering Brazil came via Rio, but between 1810 and 1830 between 70 and 90 per cent of them came through this port.[67] A clandestine trade in slaves operated in the 1830s whereby vessels claiming Portuguese nationality and a destination in Montevideo, Uruguay landed African captives surreptitiously along the Brazilian coast.[68]

Table 3 shows that the English slave trade to the Caribbean began modestly in the second quarter of the seventeenth century. This was the period when several islands in the Lesser Antilles were settled by English adventurers and largely turned over to sugar cultivation; they included Barbados, St Kitts, Antigua and Nevis. Slave imports to the English West Indies rose swiftly in the second half of the seventeenth century. In that period, estates established in the eastern Caribbean expanded their output and Jamaica, in the western Caribbean, was captured from the Spanish (in 1655) and soon planted with sugar cane. The peak period of the British slave trade to the Caribbean came in the eighteenth century – almost four out of every five slaves disembarked from British ships in that region arrived during that century (Table 3). Kingston, the leading port of Jamaica, dominated the slave deliveries among specific disembarkation points in the British West Indies.[69] In addition to increased plantation output from existing colonies, Britain acquired productive new slave frontiers in two batches during the eighteenth century: the Windward Islands 'ceded' by France to Britain after the end of the Seven Years' War (Grenada, Saint Vincent, Dominica and Tobago) and Trinidad, Demerara, Essequibo and Berbice, captured from Spain and the Netherlands in the Napoleonic Wars.[70]

Table 3 shows that the Spanish Americas were the third main broad disembarkation region for African captives in the slave-trade era, lagging substantially behind supplies of slaves to the British Caribbean but exceeding those delivered to the French West Indies.[71] Spanish America was the only area to receive slaves for the entire period from 1501 to 1866. European rulers in Spanish America in the sixteenth century found Native American populations were neither numerous nor accessible enough to undertake all the work demanded by settlers and they rapidly turned towards African slaves for the production of agricultural, mining and fishery exports but more importantly for providing food, clothing, shelter and other services to towns and for producing goods (sugar, tobacco, hides, cacao, flour) for other Spanish colonial markets. The Jesuits made extensive use of slaves in coastal Ecuador, Peru and Córdoba (modern Argentina) to work farms, cane lands, vineyards and livestock ranches.[72]

The Spanish American slave trade reached its greatest height in the nineteenth century when over 750,000 enslaved Africans were disembarked at Spanish American markets, notably in Cuba.[73] That was the era when Spanish vessels were largely Cuban-based. The boom in sugar, coffee and tobacco production in Cuba in the 1820s and 1830s stimulated the demand for fresh slave supplies.[74] Spanish silver mines in today's Bolivia and Peru and cattle ranches in the Río de la Plata region were also supplied with slaves.[75] Cartagena was a major entrepôt for the reception of slaves, who were dispatched to Colombia, Peru and other colonies in New Spain. Cartagena, which had an excellent natural harbour, enabled transatlantic slave traders to concentrate their slave deliveries at one port on the northern mainland of South America rather than sailing on to Portobello on the Panama coast, which was considered unhealthy.[76]

The French slave trade delivered slaves to three main Caribbean markets: Saint-Domingue (renamed Haiti in 1804) and two Windward Islands, Martinique and Guadeloupe.[77] The early French slave trade before 1715 – a modest affair – was dominated by Martinique, followed by Saint-Domingue and Guadeloupe.[78] Disembarkations in the French slave trade were heavily concentrated in the period 1725–1800: those years accounted for more than four in five of the African captives delivered to the French Caribbean in the Atlantic slave-trade era. In that period, the sugar and coffee plantations of Saint-Domingue boomed as the main markets in Francophone America for new supplies of slaves. This reflected Saint-Domingue's position as the premier producer of sugar cane in the world until its plantation system was devastated by slave rebellion in the 1790s.[79] Saint-Domingue had the advantage over other French Caribbean destinations in having a large local market for slaves and the prospects of rapid sales and reloading of ships. Its demise during the 1790s had calamitous effects on the French plantation economy. The slave trade to Saint-Domingue never recovered.[80]

The delivery of slaves to Dutch and Danish colonies in the Americas was collectively fewer than half of the slaves disembarked in the French Caribbean and fewer than a quarter of the enslaved Africans reaching the British Caribbean (Table 3). The Dutch imported more than 50,000 slaves into Suriname, Demerara, Essequibo and Berbice in each quarter-century between 1650 and 1800. This trade escalated between 1750 and 1775, when plantation investment in Suriname was at its height, to reach a level of nearly 120,000 slave deliveries. Much smaller numbers of slaves ended up at St Eustatius and Curaçao, which were mainly entrepôts for the reshipment of slaves and goods to intra-American destinations. Paramibo, the capital of

Suriname, was the major port receiving slaves from Dutch vessels.[81] But economic troubles in the Dutch colonies, notably indebtedness on Suriname plantations, and the collapse of the Dutch slave trade in the early 1780s reduced the number of slave disembarkations and they never recovered.[82]

The small Danish slave trade served three Danish islands just to the east of Puerto Rico: St Croix, St John and St Thomas. More than half of the slaves disembarked in Danish Caribbean islands during the slave trade era arrived between 1750 and 1800 (Table 3). The main destination was St Croix, which had a sizeable population of British investors, with St John and St Thomas lagging behind. Denmark had a small plantation sector: only about 17,000 people lived in the Danish Caribbean by 1770. In addition, Danish plantations were encumbered with debts by that stage, which did not encourage extensive importation of Africans.[83]

The other significant area for slave deliveries shown in Table 3 consisted of mainland North America – the thirteen British colonies before the American Revolution and largely the same territories as states of the USA. This trade was substantially larger before 1776 than afterwards except that on an annual basis more slaves entered the USA between 1803 and 1807 than in any other years of the slave trade era. The North American slave trade was mainly linked to the tobacco areas of Virginia and Maryland and the swampy rice-growing lowcountry areas of South Carolina and Georgia. By the mid-eighteenth century the large influx of enslaved Africans to South Carolina had created a black majority in that colony.[84]

Modest numbers of slaves were imported into Pennsylvania and New York, but this trade diminished over time because those colonies had no plantations in need of a large unfree labour force. The overall level of slave disembarkations was much lower in North America than in the British Caribbean. This reflected more even sex ratios and better demographic growth on mainland North America than in the West Indies, resulting also from less arduous work regimes, possibly a better diet for the enslaved, and the absence of a plantation crop that matched sugar (prior to cotton).[85] The US Congress banned slave imports into the United States in 1807 and most states in the union had already legislated against the slave trade before that date; but slaves were still delivered to the

Lower South, especially to Charleston, right up to the time of the congressional ban.[86]

FINAL PASSAGES

Disembarkation at a principal port in North and South America and the West Indies, followed by sales to planters, was the norm for most Africans who survived the Middle Passage. But it was not the end of voyaging for them all. Many thousands of slaves, though not the majority, were then reshipped to other destinations. These final passages of slaves on their voyages from Africa to the New World are not included in the revised transatlantic slave trade database. One recipient of slaves via these final passages was Venezuela. Around 101,000 captives were disembarked there via an intra-American slave trade from other colonies. At various times between 1526 and 1811 captives were unloaded in Santo Domingo, Caracas, Curaçao, Puerto Rico, Trinidad and the Danish Caribbean before being taken to Venezuela.[87] Slaves who ended up in Ecuador and Peru during the seventeenth century had often been imported at Cartagena before being dispatched to Panama and sold to coastal traders plying Pacific coastal routes.[88]

Around 15 per cent of slaves arriving in Anglophone America were dispersed from their original place of disembarkation to other destinations in North America and the Caribbean before the abolition of the British and US slave trades. This amounted to around 72,000 captives altogether. Barbados and Jamaica were the main suppliers. Secondary ports that barely participated in the direct transatlantic shipment of slaves benefited from the intercolonial movement of slaves as merchants transferred Africans from glutted ports in search of high slave sale prices elsewhere.[89] Before 1700 Virginia and South Carolina relied considerably on slaves imported from the Caribbean but thereafter most slaves entering those colonies came directly from Africa. South Carolina, in fact, took more than 21,000 slaves from the West Indies between 1670 and 1808. The Mississippi Valley was another significant recipient of slaves originally disembarked in the Caribbean, accounting for nearly 12,000 slaves. Louisiana colonists travelled to West Indian islands to purchase these captives during the Spanish period of control in the Mississippi Valley, because

Spain (under the 1494 Treaty of Tordesillas) did not trade with West Africa. Slaves initially imported to the Caribbean were also reshipped to other British mainland colonies such as Pennsylvania, Maryland and Georgia.[90]

An inter-island slave trade in the British Caribbean operated between 1807 and 1825. This transferred about 22,000 slaves from long-settled colonies such as Barbados and St Kitts to territories acquired more recently by Britain with a demand for new slave supplies, such as Trinidad, Demerara and St Vincent. This traffic, which was legal owing to a loophole in the British slave trade abolition act, reflected a rational response to economic imperatives: slave prices were higher in colonies suffering from a shortage of labour than in those where sufficient slaves were in place to carry out plantation tasks. Abolitionist pressure eventually led to the end of this trade in the early 1820s, mainly through implementation of the Slave Trade Laws Consolidation Act in 1824. From 1 January 1825 no colonial official had the right to license the intercolonial movement of slaves within the British Caribbean.[91]

INTERNAL SLAVE TRADES

Internal slave trades flourished during the nineteenth century in two of the largest nations with extensive plantations: the United States and Brazil. In the case of the former, the domestic slave trade arose from the ending of transatlantic slave imports in 1808 and the subsequent need for additional slaves to meet the expansion of the plantations into new southwestern states between the western frontiers of Virginia and the Carolinas and the Mississippi River Delta. In the case of the latter, an internal slave trade served a shifting regional plantation economy. In both Brazil and the United States these internal slave trades moved slaves from areas where they were oversupplied to regions that had a continuing demand for additional labourers to cultivate staple crops.[92]

In the United States between 1790 and 1860 more than 1 million slaves were transported from the Upper South to the Lower South. Two-thirds of these slaves moved as a result of sale. Every Southern village and town experienced these transactions. This trade solidified the South's commitment to chattel slavery because planters could increase the prices of slaves for sale from the Upper South to the Lower South and thereby produce a source of surplus capital. The Cotton Kingdom in the US South was created partly by these transfers, which enabled slaves to be moved from areas where excess slave labour existed to regions in need of new slave supplies. New Orleans, Louisiana became the major centre for the sale of slaves via the domestic trade by the 1840s. Natchez, Mississippi was the second largest slave mart in the internal slave trade. Hundreds of traders in New Orleans operated auctions where over 100,000 enslaved men, women and children were packaged and priced for sale.[93]

The internal slave trade in Brazil operated on a smaller scale than the domestic slave trade in the United States. It was largely active after the end of the transatlantic slave trade to Brazil in the early 1850s. Probably around 5–6,000 slaves per year were transferred in the internal Brazilian slave trade in the 1850s and 1860s, rising to an annual figure of 10,000 in the 1870s. The main direction for these internal slave movements were from small and medium-sized farms in the northeast (not from sugar plantations) to the booming coffee economy areas of Rio de Janeiro province and São Paulo. Few slaves moved with their owners; rather, the trade consisted of sales of enslaved men and women taken via a coastwise trade.[94] Only with the formal ending of slavery in different polities did this domestic transfer and sale of enslaved people come to an end.

2

THE SLAVING BUSINESS

The transatlantic slave trade was a highly complex form of international commerce that connected three continents. There was a North Atlantic trading system in the slave trade and also a South Atlantic system, both determined by ocean winds and currents. In the North Atlantic, ships sailed north of the Equator in a clockwise direction and took advantage of westerlies from North America and the Caribbean and northeast trade winds off the coast of West Africa and directed towards the Americas. In the South Atlantic, which operated south of the Equator, vessels were blown in an anticlockwise direction by westerlies across the ocean from South America towards Africa and then picked up southeast trade winds to sail back across the ocean. Thus two slave trading systems operated in the Atlantic, a northern one in which voyages originated in Europe and North America and a southern one in which voyages began in Brazil and Río de la Plata.[1] The one main exception to this division was that slave vessels emanating from northeastern Brazilian ports followed North Atlantic winds and currents when gathering slaves in Africa from north of the Equator but took advantage of South Atlantic winds and currents when embarking slaves in Africa south of the Equator.[2]

Most ships in the North Atlantic slave trade followed a triangular route between Europe, Africa and the Americas. Generations of historians have therefore referred to transatlantic slaving by its geometrical shape, as a triangular trade.[3] The first leg of the triangle was usually an outward voyage from a home port such as Bristol, Liverpool, London, Nantes, Amsterdam or Newport, Rhode Island to the West African coast. Ships sailed laden with manufactured goods that could be exchanged for slaves in Africa. Sometimes they stopped en route at the Canary Islands or Cape Verde to replenish water and provisions, but often they sailed directly to Africa. The second leg comprised the infamous Middle Passage. This was the name given to the Atlantic crossing from Africa, after slaves had embarked on board ship, to the disembarkation point for slaves in the Americas. The third and final leg comprised the voyage home after the slaves had been sold. Vessels normally returned to their original port of departure. In the South Atlantic system, however, many vessels sailed bilaterally between Brazil and West Central Africa. The return voyage from Africa to South America still constituted a 'middle passage' in practice even though it did not form part of a triangular route.

CHARTERED TRADING COMPANIES

The organization of the slave trade in the sixteenth and seventeenth centuries was often conducted by large chartered merchant companies. The main such company in the Netherlands was the Dutch West India Company (known as the WIC, 1621–1791). France had several chartered slave trade organizations, including the Compagnie des Îles de l'Amérique (1635–51), the Compagnie de l'Occident (1664–67), the Compagnie des Indes Occidentales (1664–73), the Compagnie de Guinée (1685–1720) and the Compagnie du Sénégal (1673–1763). The chief English companies were the English Guinea Company (1618–60), the Company of Royal Adventurers Trading to Africa (1660–72) and the Royal African Company (whose monopoly period was 1672–98). The South Sea Company, founded in London in 1711, was a public–private partnership that arranged contracts with the Royal African Company over the supply of slaves.[4] There was also a Brandenburg African Company (1682–1718/21), a fairly small branch of the 'Guinea' traffic.[5]

These chartered trading organizations had headquarters in leading cities of their respective countries; they attracted monied

Fig. 2: Ramparts and guns at Cape Coast Castle, Ghana, 1986

investors on a joint-stock basis to pool resources for the risks of long-distance oceanic commerce such as the slave trade. Though investors were sometimes private, state support was the mainstay of these companies. Each company had an elaborate management structure. The Royal African Company, for instance, was managed by a Governor, Sub-Governor, Deputy Governor and twenty-four assistants. It held two General Courts each year, one for the election of officers and the other for hearing statements about the company's stock. The Court of Assistants, chosen annually by shareholders, dealt with most of the company's business.[6] The Dutch West India Company was controlled by two chambers in Amsterdam and Zeeland, Holland, which comprised lawyers, bankers and merchants among its personnel and investors, and by a director-general in Africa supported by a council, superintendent, a small group of high-ranking officers, and factors as head of outposts.[7]

Chartered companies maintained forts and trading castles on the West African coast, principally in Senegambia and along the Gold Coast. These large-scale structures had originally been built in many cases to protect the European access to gold from Africa, but they were later adapted for the slave trade. They had stores and dungeons for holding slaves before they were placed on board ship for the Middle Passage. The trading castles were controlled by a figurehead, often designated a governor, who was responsible to the headquarters of the company. They were staffed by employees dispatched from Europe and by local *gromettos* or black servants. Castle slaves in the forts built and maintained these trading castles; they provided domestic services to the fort inhabitants; and they served as interpreters and liaisons between Europeans and Africans in and near the forts. These large establishments comprised living quarters, barracks and guns pointing outwards to sea to withstand enemy assaults.[8]

The Royal African Company – to take a representative example – usually maintained between fifteen and twenty fortified establishments on the Gold Coast and Senegambia, housing 200–300 civilian and military personnel. These people had a high risk of mortality: between 1684 and 1732, one in three of the Royal African Company's complement died in the first four months in Africa and more than three men in five died in the first year.[9] The company's Agent-General resided at Cape Coast Castle on the Gold Coast. He marshalled the services of sailors and native crew in small craft and canoes, and received the accounts of the company's factors at factories and dependent lodges such as Anomabu and Accra.[10]

Great rivalry over the forts existed among different nations. With the potential riches to be gained from the sale of gold and slaves, forts were often attacked and taken over by rival powers.

Fig. 3: Dixcove Fort, Gold Coast, 1727

Cape Coast Castle was originally controlled by the Swedes and the Danes before it was captured by the English and became the headquarters of the Royal African Company on the Gold Coast in the 1660s. Elmina, the major fort to the west of Cape Coast Castle and the largest one in West Africa, was operated by the Portuguese from 1482 until it became the headquarters of Dutch slaving in Africa in 1637. St Louis, near the mouth of the Senegal River, changed hands several times between the French and the English in the seventeenth and eighteenth centuries. Large forts flourished for decades, sometimes for centuries; but many smaller establishments lasted only for a handful of years before falling into decay and then being abandoned. Important forts were still trading in slaves by the early nineteenth century – Cape Coast Castle until 1807, Elmina until 1814 and Anomabu until 1839.[11]

Despite elaborate structures, many chartered trading companies experienced organizational and financial problems. The Royal African Company had been established with an initial capital of £110,000 and a wealthy and influential Board of Directors. This initial capital proved insufficient, however, for its needs. The forts, factories and lodges in West Africa drained its finances and large sums of money were owed to the company from the sales of slaves on credit in the Caribbean. By 1712 such were the financial burdens of the company that it was technically bankrupt. The operational difficulties of the Royal African Company lay in its relative inflexibility. The company relied on chartered ships sent out at set intervals. A syndicate of shareholders invested in these voyages.[12] It was not just the English chartered organizations that experienced difficulties in operating the slave trade; French companies in the trade suffered from insufficient capital and resources, lack of skilled agents in Africa, and internal quarrels among their leaders.[13]

The Iberian nations largely avoided the use of companies to conduct their slave trade. In the case of Spain, the supply of slaves from West Africa to Spanish America, including New Spain (Mexico), New Granada (Colombia) and Cuba, was often handled under an *asiento* (contract or licence) agreement whereby other European nations undertook slave shipments. Contracts issued for individual voyages bought from the Spanish Crown were the norm before 1595; thereafter *asiento* rights granted for a period of years became more common.[14] Such licences were frequently awarded to

Portuguese traders until the separation of the Spanish and Portuguese crowns in 1640.[15] There were no *asientos* granted between 1641 and 1663; the Dutch and the French then held the *asiento* in the decades before the end of the War of Spanish Succession.[16]

After the Treaty of Utrecht (1713) Britain received the *asiento*. The Royal African Company technically oversaw the arrangement but in practice farmed out this branch of the slave trade to the South Sea Company. Britain retained her *asiento* rights until the end of the War of Austrian Succession in 1748.[17] It was not until 1789 that Spain relinquished the use of the *asiento* and pursued policies of free trade that enabled Spanish subjects to buy slaves in any foreign country and sell them in a Spanish colony free of duty. This came about because Spain had finally realized the importance of the slave trade for commercial expansion and the development of her colonies.[18] But not all of the slaves arriving in Spain's American colonies came under *asiento* arrangements. Between 1641 and 1789, for example, most slaves entering the Spanish Americas were purchased by Spanish merchants from ports in the Americas controlled by other European powers. The ports in this intra-American slave trade included Curaçao, Cartagena and Kingston, Jamaica.[19]

PRIVATE MERCHANTS

Despite the activities of large trading companies, most slaves were acquired and shipped by private merchant partnerships operating from European and American ports. Private traders took shares in slave vessels when and where they chose; they dispatched vessels to Africa at different intervals to take account of changing supply and demand situations; they were not required to send an annual ship to the same places on the African coast year after year. Private merchants in the British slave trade also benefited from a shift in political interests in London after 1698 from those who favoured a monopolized trade conducted by a chartered company to those whose political lobbying promoted unregulated trade. Private traders lacked the sheer amount of capital of the large chartered organizations, but their flexibility in operating the slave trade, notably the scope for conducting commerce in West Africa beyond parts of the coast dominated by forts, was a crucial factor in establishing their role in transatlantic slaving.[20]

The transatlantic slave trade was one of the riskiest of eighteenth-century commercial activities. For success in the trade, care was needed on each leg of the voyage. To cope with the capital needs of hiring ships, fitting them out and paying for cargoes, merchants engaged in slave trading took shares in voyages on an ad hoc basis. In other words, a group of investors combined for a particular voyage to Africa and the Americas; they came together specifically for that venture. They might involve themselves in further slave voyages, but before each venture the arrangements were worked out again from scratch. The leading shareholder was known as the ship's husband. He took care of the final accounting for the voyage. In France, the investment in slave ships was divided between *armateurs* (shipowners) and *négociants* (merchants). The possibility of holding relatively small shares in ships meant some investors could be men of modest capital such as shopkeepers, mariners, ship captains, or other retailers, but most investors were merchants.[21] Over time in the British slave trade (and also in the slaving business of other powers) a number of captains upgraded their status to that of merchant. Sometimes captains of slave vessels graduated to become major investors in such ventures.[22] Merchants in the slave trade were generally clustered at notable ports. This reflected the way in which such centres could draw upon their hinterlands for suitable exports to sell in West Africa, and could tap a pool of maritime traders and workers to conduct the trade regularly.[23]

THE SLAVE TRADE IN WEST AFRICA

Loading vessels with trade goods in demand in West Africa was vital for the conduct of the slave trade. Captains needed to take the right assortment of commodities by product category, price and quality to meet consumer demand on different parts of the African coast.[24] Any notion that such demand was simple, unchanging and geared towards cheaper goods is wide of the mark. Africans were discriminating purchasers of trade goods. They were discerning about colour, texture and prices; their tastes changed over time; and most goods they bought were not cheap gewgaws. Ship captains needed a finely tuned knowledge of the consumer goods of different Africans. They built up a repertoire of catering for these needs by establishing contact with specific regions of the African coast and with particular traders there. The diary of Antera Duke, a slave dealer and Efik chief from Old Calabar, contains many details of transactions between captains and African traders that illustrate this point.[25]

Textiles dominated the trade goods shipped to Africa to purchase slaves. East Indian cottons and some silks were important among textile exports. The bright colours, designs and finishing of these wares were superior to anything that the textile industry in Africa could produce.[26] From the 1740s onwards in the British slave trade, English-produced woollens and linens, many of them manufactured in Lancashire, took an increasingly prominent part in the outward cargoes carried from British ports to Africa.[27] These textiles were used for garments such as shirts and dresses. Woollens were also in demand in Africa; they were suited to cool evening temperatures, and could be used as wraps or shawls. Textiles were generally sold on parts of the West African coast that had little or no textile industry.[28]

Many other goods apart from textiles were exported to Africa. Copper and brass ware, iron products, gunpowder, gunflints, lead shot, muskets, pistols, glass beads and alcoholic beverages all found their way into the holds of slave-trading vessels. Guns were readily sold in West Africa by slave traders because indigenous societies lacked the techniques to make such weapons themselves.[29] Metals in demand in West Africa were ones where internal supplies could not meet consumer needs or where locally produced metals were regularly more expensive and poorer in quality than imported products.[30] The availability of a particular commodity also helped fuel the wheels of trade. At Luanda, Brazilian alcohol, in the form of cheap sugar cane brandy, was a prime commodity used to barter for slaves.[31] Rhode Island slave traders specialized in selling a fiery variety of rum from New England distilleries to acquire African captives.[32]

The location of trade in West Africa was decided before ships embarked on their voyages. Captains carried letters of instruction from their owners stating where they should trade, with whom, and on what terms. Merchants tried, as far as possible, to cultivate trade with certain parts of the African coast, by captains experienced in the rigours of slave trading.[33] Crew who had sailed before on a 'Guinea' voyage were also much prized. They were not usually paid wages until they had delivered slaves for sale. This helped to prevent crew members absconding from a difficult trade before they had carried out the main part of their task. But there was always a high turnover of crew on slaving voyages owing to mortality levels, desertion and the impact of the press gang in wartime.[34] Sometimes captains were instructed to pick up slaves at more than one place in West Africa; and sometimes they were requested to trade at one place for gold, redwood, camwood and ivory, and then to proceed elsewhere to get their slaves. In most instances, however, slaves were gathered at one trading point in West Africa.[35]

Along the Gold Coast, the slave trade continued to be organized largely through the European forts well into the eighteenth century. At Cape Coast Castle the slave trade was facilitated by the use of company slaves. These were the property of Britain's Company of Merchants Trading to Africa. Company slaves were paid a subsistence wage and played an important part in maintaining the castle.[36] They were supplemented by white workers sent out to Cape Coast Castle, who often suffered from ill health caused by infectious diseases, poor diet and climatic alterations. Skilled workers among this group were used to train the company slaves to carry out essential tasks. Professional officers, soldiers and apothecaries were also present at Cape Coast Castle. In order to maintain the trading fort and barter successfully for gold and slaves, these white personnel worked alongside mulattoes and the company slaves, thereby operating within a cooperative mixture of races that was largely unknown to Britons at home or in the Americas.[37]

The fort-trade organization of slaving comprised one way of organizing the slave trade in West Africa, but African authorities would not allow traders to establish forts or factories on most stretches of the coast. Ship captains therefore had to devise different ways of gathering slaves. They mainly resorted to ship-trade organization that had several variants. Near the Sierra Leone River and associated areas, slaving was conducted on small offshore islands, such as Bunce Island, the Banana Islands and the Iles de Los. At Bonny, slave trading was organized on board ship, with African merchants dealing directly with ships' captains and crew.[38] On the Loango coast Dutch ships established temporary lodges on the beach, sometimes gathering slaves at more than one location.[39] In most parts of West Africa, slave ship captains had to moor offshore or anchor near the openings of river estuaries; there were no ports with docks, such as existed in Europe.

Much of the success of a slave-trading voyage depended upon the skill, behaviour and business acumen of captains, who had delegated authority from their merchant employers. Their dealings on the African coast were by no means easy. They had to take account of local supply conditions; they needed to be aware of local political impediments to trade; and they hoped to avoid rainy seasons when diseases spread rapidly and the supply of slaves from the interior was impeded. Palavers, in which gifts were exchanged during elaborate ceremonies, were often conducted near the coast with African notables; these involved detailed negotiations over slave purchases. At Anomabu a Palaver House served as a court of justice in which elders presided over decisions concerning credit, debt and pawnship (on which see below).[40]

Captains had to establish and maintain good relations with African middlemen, who supplied slaves from the interior of the continent to vessels, and they needed the acquiescence of local rulers. Thus the success of captains' dealings in West Africa depended on business skill, cultural interaction with suppliers, and knowledge of climatic and seasonal conditions. In the early Portuguese slave trade, captains often dealt with *lançados* on the Upper Guinea coast. These were Portuguese traders resident on the coast, where they lived under the protection of African chiefs. In Angola the Portuguese captains bargained for slaves through intermediaries known as *pombeiros*, or itinerant traders.[41] On certain parts of the coast, such as Old Calabar, some African traders could read and write English.[42] Long-standing friendships and connections between English captains and these African traders considerably aided the British dominance of the slave trade in the Bight of Biafra. In the Upper Guinea region, the success of Liverpool traders in the second half of the eighteenth century was closely connected to the iterative trade they established with Eurafricans along the coast and on offshore islands.[43]

Captains bartered their goods with local middlemen, dealing in local units of account. These units might be copper or iron rods, manillas or cowries. Manillas were horseshoe-shaped bracelets made from brass and copper, used as a form of currency, notably in the

Niger delta. Cowries were shells gathered from the Maldives in the Indian Ocean, shipped to Amsterdam or London, and then sent out on slave vessels to the Bight of Benin, where they had widespread use. Africans in pre-colonial times did not use numeric currency; rather they calculated the number of goods they received in these units of account.[44] The currency used in certain areas of West Africa, notably by the Akan peoples along the Gold Coast, consisted of an 'ounce' of gold dust. This amounted to the nominal value set on goods that cost around 40 shillings in Europe but sold along the African coast for £4. The use of gold as money involved boxes and bags to hold the gold dust, spoons to transfer the gold dust to weighing scales, and weights and brushes.[45]

Some middlemen with whom captains dealt on the African coast were mulattoes, others were indigenous Africans. There were also European traders resident there. To ensure slaves were delivered for the goods supplied, captains relied on trust and prior commercial connections. They might need to observe 'dashes' with local rulers as a gesture of goodwill; this meant the offer of gifts as a token of friendly exchange. In Old Calabar and Bonny, where the English concentrated much of their eighteenth-century slave trade, credit was associated with transactions that exchanged goods for slaves in the form of pawns or pledges. A pawn was a relative of an African trader who was placed temporarily in the custody of ship captains; the pawn was released once the slaves had been delivered to the ship. This was a form of debt bondage in which people were held as collateral to guarantee trust. It was used widely, but not everywhere, in West Africa during the slave trade era, and was suitable for trade transactions in an environment where most business was not recorded on paper or with institutional mechanisms but carried out in a face-to-face manner.[46]

Captains and their crew usually stayed on shipboard in Africa; they did not venture into the interior, nor did they stray far from their vessels while they lay anchored. They erected temporary houses on their ships covered with mats to conduct business. On occasions crew members were sent on canoes upriver to gather slaves but this was usually carried out by African middlemen and their helpers. In Bonny in the late eighteenth century, large canoes dispatched to gather slaves could hold around 120 people.[47] But there were also overland routes to inland slave marts, often conducted via caravans of slaves escorted by armed guards such as those organized in Angola by local authorities between Loango Bay, Malemba and Cabinda on the coast and Malebo Pool and other interior places.[48] Captives often arrived at the coast in poor health after a long march from inland areas. A chief of several of the forts on the Gold Coast, for example, reported in 1789 that slaves brought to the coast over long distances arrived 'in general poor in flesh; great eruptions over all their skin; very scrophulous, and frequently have bad ulcers.'[49]

The reasons why white men did not penetrate the interior of Africa are not hard to find. Europeans had little knowledge of the geography of Africa beyond fifty or a hundred miles from the coast. By the time of the American Revolution, Africa was one of the major blank spaces on maps produced in Europe.[50] It was not until Mungo Park's expedition of 1795/6 to the Niger River that serious attempts to explore beyond coastal areas occurred. Until then, the geography of Africa was often based on mythical places, people or polities. Many Africans had formidable fighting skills that could withstand attempts at entering their territories. Tropical diseases, such as malaria, were a further significant barrier to European penetration of sub-Saharan Africa.[51] Nor did Europeans have the linguistic skills to converse with many African ethnic groups. But it was not just European reluctance that determined that the white personnel on slaving voyages remained on or near the coast, for a crucial aspect of the transatlantic slave trade was that African polities and rulers had the power to determine who penetrated inland – and for social and political purposes it suited them to keep the Europeans at bay on the shore.[52]

Unlike other parts of Africa, the Portuguese in West Central Africa were involved in seizing African slaves through expeditions into the hinterland of ports such as Luanda and Benguela. Portugal had established the colony of Luanda in 1576 and Benguela in 1617. This gave Portuguese administrators and traders a foothold in Africa from which they could organize raids to acquire slaves.[53] In the seventeenth century, the Portuguese at both ports liaised with African merchants (*guenzes*) who visited inland fairs where they traded with *pombeiros* who had travelled from the coast with European and African merchandise. The merchant communities at Luanda and Benguela relied on the Portuguese authorities for protection and to raid neighbouring populations when slaves were needed.[54] During the eighteenth century, they deployed black troops (*guerras pretas*) to expand warfare and enslavement in that region. Between 1730 and 1750 the rulers of Kakonda, Kabunda and Kablunda became vassals of the Portuguese; they supplied captives from inland conflicts to Portuguese slave traders. Some of these slaves were acquired through warfare and others through tribute or as repayment for debts. By the 1780s traders in Benguela operated through three or four large firms that maintained close ties with merchants in Rio de Janeiro. The financial connections between Brazilian merchants and foreign merchants and colonial authorities in Benguela provided the credit necessary to facilitate the gathering of slaves by itinerant traders connecting the coast to hinterland markets.[55]

Slaves were supplied to the ships by various methods. Some were gathered close to coastal areas but others were marched hundreds of miles to the coast. Contemporary estimates of the late eighteenth century suggest that on the Gold Coast only between one-quarter and one-third of the captives were inhabitants of the coast; the rest were purchased at inland markets.[56] In the eighteenth century the average march of slaves to the coast was about sixty-three miles in the Bight of Biafra, around 125 miles on the Upper Guinea coast and in the Bight of Benin, about 190 miles for the Gold Coast and Senegambia, and around 380 miles in Loango and Angola.[57] Between 1824 and 1841 most slaves exported from Rio Pongo, Upper Guinea, travelled over 100 miles between enslavement and embarkation points; but in southern Sierra Leone the distance was often less than fifty miles.[58] Between 1822 and 1837 most captives leaving the Cameroons for the Americas originated within 200 miles of the coast.[59] Slaves were marched in coffles in a line. The men were chained by their ankles to prevent them from escaping. Sometimes shackles could chain several people together. Yokes could also be used for this purpose. Spiked collars, neck rings, handcuffs and leg irons were used as devices for restraining and punishing slaves.[60]

Black Africans were just as culpable in the supply of slaves as white Europeans were in shipping them to the Americas. Sophisticated supply mechanisms existed whereby Africans became willing accomplices in supplying other Africans to English ship captains. Slavery was an institution with a long history in African societies. For many centuries there had been various slave trades in existence on the African continent. There was a long-standing supply

Fig. 4: Mandingo slave traders and coffle, Senegal, 1780s

of slaves to Islamic countries and to the Indian Ocean as well as indigenous slavery within Africa.[61]

Africans intended for the transatlantic slave trade were largely captured in war or through kidnapping or raids; they might also be taken in lieu of debts. Slave raiding in the hinterland of the Senegal River involved *grande pillage* (where a local king sent several hundred soldiers to attack a village) and lesser pillage and kidnapping. Seizing individuals – a practice known as 'panyarring' – was common in some parts of West Africa, notably among the Fante, and this could be a source for the supply of slaves to the coast.[62] Indigenous merchants at places such as Bonny and Old Calabar (in the Bight of Biafra) and Ambriz, Cabinda and Malemba (in West Central Africa) acted as middlemen in procuring slaves for export markets.[63] The determining factors for the sale of slaves into African slavery or into the Indian Ocean, Mediterranean or Atlantic trades were relative supply elasticities and the tactics of middlemen. Certain areas, such as the Bight of Biafra, had well-known inland slave fairs at which Africans were acquired before their destination was decided.[64]

The demographic balance of slave cargoes assembled for transatlantic slaving followed a particular pattern. Slave traders preferred to take a ratio of two adult men for each adult woman.

This was partly because they considered (rightly) that young adult men in good physical condition would be the easiest to sell in the New World for field labour on plantations.[65] But it was also the case that African societies were often more willing to release men into the slave trade than women. Within Africa, women were valued for their work and reproductive role and there was therefore a reluctance to sell them in large numbers into the transatlantic slave trade. Prime young females were kept as wives in African areas where polygamy

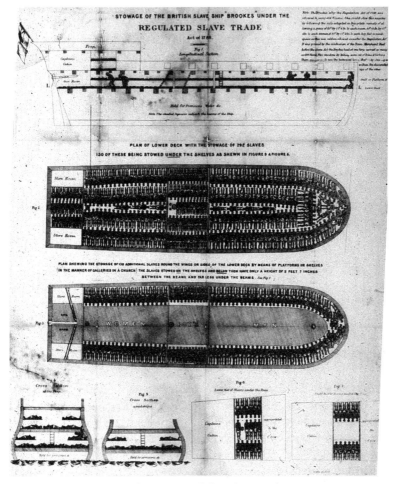

Fig. 5: Plan of the Liverpool slave ship *Brookes*, 1789

was practised.[66] Adolescent boys and girls featured regularly among the captives from the late eighteenth century onwards. Children became an ever larger component of slaving cargoes during the nineteenth century. Whereas they had once been regarded as a liability and only taken on board to complete cargoes of slaves, the increasing availability of children in some coastal West African markets and the insatiable demand of sugar and coffee plantations for newly imported labourers, coupled with declining shipping costs, led to their being taken in larger numbers.[67]

In coastal Africa it was imperative to load slaves on shipboard as efficiently as possible: the longer the stay on the coast, the greater the susceptibility of slaves and crew to disease. Provisions such as yams and rice were loaded to feed the slaves during the Atlantic crossing and fresh water taken on board.[68] Slaves were chained together beneath deck, side by side, rather in the manner depicted in the famous print of the Liverpool slave ship the *Brookes* that was widely published and circulated at the beginning of the British abolitionist campaign against the slave trade.[69] Captives were allowed up on deck for air and exercise for one or two hours a day, but were otherwise kept confined. Misdemeanours by slaves on board ship were often punished by flogging. Sadistic captains in the slave trade gave an even blacker reputation to the trade than it had perforce acquired of its own accord. Barracoons were frequently erected on slave vessels for confining troublesome captives.[70] A poem entitled 'The Sorrow of Yoruba' (1790) summarized the pain involved in treating the enslaved on board ship: 'At the savage Captain's beck, / Now like brutes they make us prance: / Smack the Cat about the Deck, / And in scorn they bid us dance.'[71]

THE MIDDLE PASSAGE

For enslaved Africans, the experience of the Middle Passage was one of misery and confusion. They had never sailed across the ocean before; many experienced terror; and they had no idea of what lay in store for them at the voyage's end.[72] Father Lorenzo da Lucca, for example, travelling on a slaving vessel from Angola to Bahia in 1708, described slaves lying side by side in filth in a chaotic atmosphere that had 'one shouting on one side, one on the other.

Others crying, some lamenting, others laughing.'[73] Another priest described a voyage from Luanda to Bahia in 1666/7 as 'a pitiful sight to behold ... The men were standing in the hold, fastened one to another with stakes, for fear they should rise and kill the whites. The women were between the decks, and those that were with child in the great cabin, the children in the steerage pressed together like herrings in a barrel, which caused an intolerable heat and stench.'[74] Olaudah Equiano, who left one of the earliest published autobiographies by a former slave, concurred. He recalled how, on first boarding a slave vessel in West Africa, he 'received a salutation in my nostrils as I had never experienced in my life ... with the loathsomeness of the stench.'[75]

The Middle Passage lasted for four, five or six weeks, and was associated with mortality and with slave resistance. In the first half of the eighteenth century, 16.3 per cent of the slaves taken on board English slaving vessels died en route to the Americas; after 1750, the mortality loss fell to 10 per cent and less.[76] This was a higher loss of life on oceanic voyages than in other long-distance trades such as the shipment of convicts to Australia. In the British slave trade the provision of doctors on all slaving voyages after the passing of Dolben's Act (1788), for instance, does not appear to have improved mortality rates.[77] Many slaves succumbed to serious diseases while impounded in coastal West Africa awaiting shipment. For the Portuguese slave trade to Brazil, it has been argued that drought, disease and famine in Angola were major reasons for slave mortality on the Atlantic crossing.[78] Pre-embarkation losses among captives were also high in the French slave trade.[79] Though some slaves died from respiratory problems such as inflammation of the lungs, mortality on the Middle Passage occurred largely through diseases caught in Africa. The prime cause of death comprised gastroenterital complaints, caused by dirty, unhygienic conditions and contaminated food and water. Dysentery and severe diarrhoea were the chief symptoms of gastroenteritis. Deaths also occurred through dropsy, scarlet and yellow fever, malignant fever, tuberculosis, and a host of other diseases.[80]

The cycle of mortality depended on how long slaves had been stowed on the African coast to await shipment. The longer slaves were kept in compounds, the greater the chance of disease breaking out. The incidence of disease followed the normal pattern of an epidemic,

Fig. 6: Africans in the hold of a slave ship, 1827

with deaths rising during the first third of the Middle Passage to reach a peak before falling and levelling off later in the voyage. Apart from diseases, some slaves committed suicide in despair at their captivity, usually throwing themselves overboard into the ocean. Towards the end of the voyage, dehydration sometimes occurred as water supplies became depleted and gastro-intestinal problems worsened.[81] In one notorious incident, that of the Liverpool slave ship *Zong* (1781), unhealthy slaves were deliberately thrown overboard to a death by drowning as the vessel neared Jamaica so that the insurance on their loss could be collected by the owners. This resulted in a famous court case that the owners lost.[82]

Crew mortality was also higher on slave-trading voyages than on other oceanic crossings. In fact, crew were subject to mortality levels as soon as they reached the West African coast, as a famous sea shanty chorus emphasized: 'Beware and take care the Bight of Benin, / There's one comes out for forty goes in.'[83] Crew deaths peaked during rainy periods on the West African coast when the yellow fever virus and malarial parasites accumulated in mosquitoes drawn to stagnant pools of water. The Gambia River was one area particularly affected by this disease environment. Non-immune crew members of slaving vessels could die there at epidemic rates.[84]

Not all slaves accepted their situation with passivity; some staged risings on shipboard to attempt to overthrow their captors. Most of these rebellions (which are further discussed in Chapter 4) occurred fairly soon after ships sailed from Africa; and though most were put down, they nevertheless added to the misery, despair and riskiness of slaving voyages. The process of enslavement in Africa and the prevalence of uprisings on slave ships underscore the violence that characterized the traffic in black human beings. Physical coercion, brutality, injuries and abuse, including sexual exploitation of women, were everyday occurrences for Africans drawn into the vortex of the transatlantic slave trade.[85]

Captains exercised strong discipline on board slave ships against both slaves and crew. Contemporary evidence reveals many instances of bullying by captains, with a repertoire of different tactics used. Captains sometimes singled out vulnerable people for intimidation, such as black sailors, a ship's boy or a cook. They used the cat-o'-nine-tails, a long rope with knots, to punish insubordinate slaves and crew members. They sometimes reduced provisions for the crew and slaves on lengthy voyages and exploited the crew by selling clothing, brandy and tobacco at inflated prices. Captains maintained firm control over everyone on board ship in order to consolidate their power.[86]

Ports of disembarkation for slave ships were largely decided by merchants before ships set sail from their home ports. Merchants capitalized on commercial connections with particular regions. They were often well informed about levels of demand for slaves and slave prices in the New World. Letters of instruction to captains advised them of alternative destinations where they could sell their slaves. Most ships disembarked Africans at one pre-arranged port or harbour in the Americas, but if markets for slave sales were slack at particular ports the ships would then sail to another destination. There were also disembarkation areas which frequently re-exported slaves to other destinations. Most Africans imported into Dominica, Barbados, Grenada and Saint Vincent between 1784 and 1806, for example, were re-exported. As mentioned in Chapter 1, transfers of slaves from the Caribbean to Spanish American colonies were extensive over time.[87]

Specific 'Guinea' factors in colonial ports were recommended for the handling of slave sales. Merchants and captains sought to build

Fig. 7: Advertisement for slave sale, Charleston, South Carolina, 26 April 1760

up relationships of trust with such agents so that transaction costs could be minimized by dealing with the same personnel for successive voyages.[88] Letters of instruction to ship captains named the factors in various colonial ports with whom they were expected to trade. Sometimes these included family relatives of slave merchants acting in conjunction with their principals at home. But they also included independent merchants acting on commission who realized the sale of slaves was one of the most reliable ways of undertaking business for good profits in the plantation colonies.[89]

SLAVE DISEMBARKATION IN THE AMERICAS

Slave vessels entering mainland American and West Indian harbours observed quarantine laws and paid import duties on the slaves they imported. Sales were advertised in local newspapers and a day and time publicized for the start of the sale. Some slave sales were held

Group of Negros, as imported to be sold for Slaves.

Fig. 8: Newly arrived slaves, Surinam, 1770s

on shipboard, others were conducted on shore. Selling slaves as though they were commodities was disturbing even to some white planters. When John Pinney first left Dorset to sail to his plantations in Nevis, he felt uneasy at the prospect of purchasing slaves. 'I can assure you,' he wrote home to a friend, 'I was shock'd at the first appearance of human flesh exposed to sale. But surely God ordained 'em for the use and benefit of us: otherwise his Divine Will would have been made manifest by some particular sign or token.'[90] Not all white men involved in buying or selling slaves would have justified their activities by the same reasoning as Pinney, but they set aside sensitivities about the morality of their actions in order to focus on business gains.

The beginning of a slave sale was sometimes marked by a scramble, as the surgeon Alexander Falconbridge vividly described in the early 1790s with regard to the West Indies:

> On the day appointed, the negroes were landed, and placed together in a large yard, belonging to the merchants to whom the ship was consigned. As soon as the hour agreed upon arrived, the doors of the yard were suddenly thrown open, and in rushed a considerable number of purchasers, with all the ferocity of brutes. Some instantly seized such of the Negroes as they could lay hold of with their hands. Others, being prepared with several handkerchiefs tied together, encircled with these as many as they were able. While others, by means of a rope, effected the same purpose. It is scarcely possible to describe the confusion of which this mode of selling is productive ... The poor astonished negroes were so much terrified by these proceedings, that several of them, through fear, climbed over the walls of the court yard, and ran wild about the town; but were soon hunted down and retaken.[91]

Other sales were conducted in a more orderly way. They often involved captains marching their slaves through a town or port where they were intended to be sold and placing them in rows for examination and purchase. The sales ended with cash auctions to dispose of slaves lingering on hand.[92]

Prospective purchasers were mainly local merchants and planters who bought slaves singly, in pairs, or in lots. Credit was commonly offered for slave sales except in circumstances where planters were in funds and cash could be demanded. Typically, credit was arranged for the marketing of the healthiest and strongest slaves, which were sold first. Credit sales continued as smaller, less desirable slaves were sold. Often these transactions were effected with bonds (preferably) or promissory notes to give reasonable assurance that debts would be paid on time. Finally, 'refuse' slaves – the elderly, the invalid, the sick – were sold in a 'vendue' cash auction as sellers found offering credit too risky for slaves with particularly high expected mortality or for those too weak to be of use in the plantation economy. The aim was to sell all slaves, whatever their age or physical condition. The process involved the commodification of people, selling off the remaining slaves at the end of a sale rather like a shop owner marking down the price of damaged fruit in order to sell his produce.[93]

Buyers of slaves often expressed preferences for particular African ethnic groups. Thus, for instance, slaves from Old Calabar were invariably in poor repute in colonies such as South Carolina, Antigua and Jamaica: they were considered unreliable workers and physically less tough than other Africans. Conversely, in Jamaica and some Leeward islands there was a marked preference for slaves from the Gold Coast and the Bight of Benin. In Virginia, several planters expressed a preference for slaves from Senegambia. These were thought to be in good physical condition and hard workers. In the French Caribbean, planters preferred slaves from West Central Africa over those from Sierra Leone, the Windward Coast and the Bight of Biafra. The selection of slaves from particular African regions could only operate, however, when incoming cargoes arrived from different West African ports, providing purchasers with plenty of choice.[94]

Many attributes accorded to slaves from particular regions of West Africa were based on stereotypes. Europeans commonly used ethnographic labels that grossly oversimplified African identity groups.[95] Moreover, the fact that planters and other buyers desired slaves from those areas did not mean necessarily that they received them. The slaves on offer for sale at disembarkation points in the Americas were the product of supply conditions; and buyers purchased slaves more on the basis of those available to buy rather than waiting for ships to bring in Africans of the preferred ethnicity and then cherry-picking them. Thus a heterogeneous package of slaves – by age, gender, price, ethnicity – was the norm for slave arrivals in the Americas. Needless to say, families were often split up during sales, if this had not already happened during the process of procuring slaves in Africa. Slave sales were the final step of the disorienting passage of people experiencing separation, confinement and coercion before they were fashioned, via a seasoning process, into plantation slaves. Seasoning, which involved saltwater slaves adjusting to the work and health demands they encountered on plantations, could take between one and two years.[96]

It was common for the number of crew to be reduced in the Americas: once the control over slaves was no longer required, fewer crew were needed for the homeward-bound voyage. Crew were usually therefore paid the reminder of their wages at American ports. Some decided to jump ship there in any case because they had had their fill of serving on a 'Guinea' vessel. There are also instances of slave ship captains intimidating crew in the hope that they would desert ship on reaching their transatlantic destination before their wages were paid.[97]

Payment for slaves sometimes took the form of crops or cash, but a safer and preferred form of remittance was to send home the proceeds in bills of exchange at specified intervals. These were rather like modern cheques, the major exception being that they did not necessarily have to be cashed via banks; they could, and often were, passed on and signed by the parties specified on the bills for funds to be released by a nominated payer. Such a cashless payment system was common in all long-distance trade over the centuries when the slave trade flourished. To ensure bills were honoured, slave merchants at European ports increasingly used merchant houses and financiers who would accept bills at sight and guarantee to pay them. Such merchants were always men of substantial business experience with an excellent reputation for honouring payments. Arrangements for dealing with the factors' bills to be cashed were usually undertaken through coordination between merchants, ship captains and colonial factors before a slaving voyage began.[98]

Substantial amounts of capital were invested in slave-trading voyages. British slave merchants, for example, sank large amounts of capital into the trade. Bristol merchants invested £50,000–60,000 annually in the slave trade c. 1710–11, over £150,000 per annum in the 1730s, and £280,100 on average in the period 1788–92. The annual sums invested in Liverpool's slave trade were c. £200,000 in 1750 and probably more than £1 million in 1800.[99] These large sums were raised to service a potentially lucrative trade: the total value of slaves sent to Jamaica during the eighteenth century, for instance, was about £25 million.[100]

What profits were made in the slave trade? And what happened to those profits? For the French slave trade, it has been shown that, after risk, maturity and duration are taken into account, there was often a higher return to investors from intercontinental trade than from alternatives.[101] It was once argued that the profits of the British slave trade amounted to 30 per cent on capital invested by the 1780s.[102] But this profit figure has long been discarded and convincingly downgraded. Between 1770 and 1792 profits per venture in the Bristol slave trade came to 7.6 per cent. Evidence taken largely from Liverpool shows that, in the second half of the eighteenth century, a rate of return of between 8 and 10 per cent on annual investment in slave-trading voyages was the norm.[103] Any business generating such returns regularly today would consider this a satisfactory return on invested capital. The return on British government 3 per cent consols during the eighteenth century, a relatively risk-free form of investment, was usually around the 3.5 per cent mark. Slave trading profits were therefore worth the efforts of merchants despite the riskiness and long-drawn-out nature of the voyages.[104]

The contribution of slave-trading profits to the economic development of European nations participating in the trade has been a controversial topic ever since Eric Williams argued in *Capitalism and Slavery* (1944) that the gains were substantial and linked to the origins of industrialization in Britain. He argued that profits from the slave trade 'provided one of the main streams of accumulation of capital in England which financed the Industrial Revolution', and that 'the triangular trade made an enormous contribution to Britain's industrial development. The profits from this trade fertilized the entire productive system of the country.'[105] These generalizations have proven highly contentious. Some historians follow their broad thrust in arguing that the slave trade, and by extension overseas demand, made a critical contribution to the origins of British industrialization in the late eighteenth century. Others are more sceptical of the scale of the impact of the slave trade on British economic growth, and emphasize that it did not make much difference 'at the margins.' These latter historians usually offer supply-side explanations of Britain's transition to an industrialized economy.[106]

Nevertheless, the demand created by the slavery–sugar nexus

was a stimulus to British economic performance. It has been argued that Caribbean-based demand may have accounted for about 35 per cent of the growth of total British exports between 1748 and 1776, and for about 12 per cent of the increase in British industrial output in the quarter-century before the American Revolution.[107] It would be incorrect to claim that the wealth flowing home from the slave trade was a major stimulus for industrialization in Britain.[108] But it would not be unfair to claim that the slave–sugar trading complex strengthened the British economy and played a significant, though not decisive, part in its evolution.[109]

Britain was the one Western European power where the slave trade and Atlantic commerce generally had a significant link to industrialization in the eighteenth century. In the case of the Netherlands, Spain, Portugal and France, such a connection is difficult to make mainly because of their later industrialization. But even in the case of Britain, the contribution of income earned through trade beyond Europe was modest compared with the income derived from internal sources such as the agricultural sector. The slave trade was probably more important for its major participants for the stimulus it gave to expansion into the colonies than for the contribution of the economic gains from slavery and the slave trade to levels of national economic growth.[110]

Though attempts to connect the profits of the slave trade to national industrialization or national economic growth have led, mainly on the basis of evidence relating to Britain, to arguments that question the scale of the impact, new research on the Netherlands suggests that future investigation of the gross margins of the slave trade upon national economies is a fruitful line of enquiry. Consideration of such gross margins would include estimates of activities that factored into the operation of slave voyages, including ship construction, sailors' wages, insurances, commissions and equipment. A recent study has suggested that, in the Dutch case, the gross margins achieved in the Dutch transatlantic slave trade were quite large, amounting to somewhere between 63 and 79 million guilders in the seventeenth and eighteenth centuries.[111]

3

PLANTATION SLAVERY

Slaves in the Americas lived and worked in a variety of locations. Domestic slaves, living in small numbers in households, were common throughout the Americas in both rural and urban settings. Africans purchased by urban businessmen and householders were found in cities such as New York, Philadelphia, Kingston, Port-au-Prince and São Paulo; they often worked as manual labourers or petty retailers or as maritime workers in ports. In rural environments slaves were used for livestock supervision on pens or engaged in a variety of non-plantation agricultural activities.[1] The diaspora of slaves from Africa to the Iberian colonies in the Caribbean and mainland South America contributed significantly to non-plantation economic activities. Blacks in Hispaniola, Cuba, Central America, Colombia, Venezuela and Brazil were deployed in production of cacao, hides, maize, wine and pearls, in gold mining, on dairy and livestock farms, in textile mills and ironworks, as muleteers, street vendors and stevedores, and in tasks that provided food, clothing, shelter and other services to urban environments such as Mexico City, Lima, Cartagena, Havana, Rio de Janeiro and Buenos Aires.[2]

Though slaves were found in highly varied settings, most Africans taken to the Americas lived and worked on plantations, which were large agricultural estates, with sufficient acreage for the cultivation of staple crops that could be marketed to European consumers. Sugar was the most dominant staple crop found on plantations. It was the backbone of estates operated by slave labour throughout the Caribbean and Brazil, and was also cultivated successfully in Louisiana. Other prominent staple crops grown on plantations were tobacco in Virginia and Maryland, rice in the lowcountry areas of South Carolina and Georgia, coffee in Brazil and some Caribbean islands, and cotton throughout the southern states of the USA from the Carolinas across in a westward direction towards the Mississippi River Valley and Texas. A smattering of plantations in the Americas also grew ginger and cacao.[3] The tropical produce produced by slaves on plantations was closely tied to marketing such commodities in Europe, where it was intertwined with increasing demand for new consumer foodstuffs and beverages. It was during the early modern period, when slave plantations first flourished, that Europeans acquired a sweet tooth and the nicotine habit.[4]

The mature plantation complex had several interconnecting characteristics. First, the work force was dominated by slave labour. Plantation owners found, after experimentation with enslaved Native Americans and white indentured servants, that the continuous unfreedom associated with slavery was necessary to operate plantations productively. Second, the slave plantation population was frequently not self-sustaining: heavy mortality rates necessitated a supply of newly enslaved workers via the transatlantic slave trade. Third, plantations were large-scale agricultural enterprises requiring anything from fifty to several hundred workers. Owners supplied the capital and equipment and employed agents to organize and supervise the slaves. Fourth, plantations involved owners in some form of legal jurisdiction over their slave charges: owners determined working hours and conditions, dealt with disputes, and meted out punishments. Fifth, plantations were created to supply distant markets (mainly in Europe) with staple products that met growing consumer demand for tropical goods, with plantation owners securing profits on their investment. Sixth, until the nineteenth century political control over the plantation complex lay in the metropolitan centres of Britain, the Netherlands, France, Portugal and Spain.[5]

Whatever the location and type of work in the Americas, the circumstances under which slaves lived were circumscribed by their status as heritable chattel property. Orlando Patterson argued that slaves lived in a setting of metaphorical 'social death', whereby they were powerless against the total control exercised by masters.

The capture of slaves in Africa and their sale in the Americas were important components of social death because they replaced the previous identities of Africans with a new status, that of being a slave. This process was then deepened by slaves being renamed, branded and dressed differently according to their new position and to their rejection from free society and their total unfreedom. In this situation, all social bonds were rendered redundant unless validated by masters.[6] Patterson's notion of social death needs, however, to be approached critically: to depict slaves as totally estranged from their circumstances plays down the scope within slave systems for the enslaved to exercise agency and to struggle against alienation. Slave agency operated within strict boundaries about what it could achieve positively, but it would be incorrect to interpret slave work and life as though Africans and Creoles merely reacted passively to the parameters set by their masters.[7]

All transatlantic slave societies had a mixture of African-born and Creole slaves (i.e. those born in the Americas). Africans predominated in American destinations that relied heavily on the transatlantic slave trade to maintain population levels, which was particularly the case in the Caribbean, but over time Creole slaves became an increasingly significant portion of the slave population. This was particularly the case in slave societies that experienced positive demographic growth, such as the United States, and in various American settings after slave imports were prohibited by different polities. All slaves in the Americas, whatever their place of birth, were increasingly bound up in a process of creolization – in other words, a process by which their roots, customs and working lives in Africa were transformed by moving to the New World. The pace and nature of creolization was highly complex and varied in different slave societies, involving the retention of some aspects of the African background of slaves and the acquisition of a new culture that might be termed Afro-Creole or African-American. The degree to which African ethnicities were retained or refashioned, in a new environment, into creolized cultures is widely debated by historians.[8]

WHY AFRICANS BECAME SLAVES

Large-scale adoption of African slave labour on American plantations was partly the result of the operation of various branches of the international slave trade financed and organized by European, North American and Brazilian merchants. But it was not just the regular supply of enslaved Africans that was responsible for the widespread use of Africans as slaves, which brought in its wake a racial transformation of the population of the Americas. Social and cultural reasons for enslaving Africans also assumed significance. European attitudes towards Africans in the early modern period partly reflected a widespread ethnocentrism and xenophobia towards 'others.' Some Englishmen, for example, regarded Jews with suspicion and frequently viewed Irish Catholics or Scottish Highlanders with hostility or downright hatred. Yet none of these groups was enslaved. The enslavement of Africans was therefore something more than just ethnocentrism: it consisted of racial prejudice. Blackness, in terms of skin colour, had negative connotations for many Europeans in the early modern era (though these associations were probably less marked in Portugal and Spain, where there had been a longer history of regular contact with Africans, than in North America).[9]

Blackness suggested connections with the Devil. Africans were also associated with Noah's curse in the Bible on the sons of Ham, even though the relevant passage, in the Book of Genesis, Chapter 9, vv. 18-27, makes no reference to blacks at all.[10] Africans were known to be heathens, something that made them seem barbaric to many Christians in Western Europe. They were feared for their supposed lust and savagery. Africans were singled out for their sheer difference from Europeans – in their physiognomy, gestures, languages, dress and behaviour. Together, an amalgam of negative attitudes emerged in the sixteenth and seventeenth centuries that constituted racial prejudice towards Africans.[11] That these sociocultural characteristics of Africans were important in singling them out for slavery reflected the fact that the enslavement of white people was not contemplated in the European colonial empires.[12]

Such attitudes were underpinned by the widespread tolerance of slavery by Europeans in the sixteenth and seventeenth centuries. European trading nations knew that slavery had existed in human societies since ancient times; that various passages in Scripture condoned the existence of slave societies; and that the educated classes widely accepted the practice of slavery. Though some dissenting voices were troubled about the moral implications of enslaving other people, notable European jurists such as Hugo Grotius did not question the existence of slavery.[13] John Locke, the philosopher of liberty, stressed the nature of contractual obligations between rulers and ruled, and the natural right of the ruled to withdraw their consent when governed in an unjust manner. But slaves were explicitly excluded from this contract theory. The reasons why Locke and other advocates of natural rights theories condoned enslavement appears to have lain in their acceptance of slavery as a flourishing African institution.[14] Slaves were a major form of wealth in Africa and a large Islamic slave trade had flourished there for centuries before European merchants participated in the traffic. Thus European intellectuals could have a clear conscience about slave trading, because many Africans had already bartered away their liberty before they came into the hands of ship captains on the West African coast.[15]

Negative perceptions of black Africans coupled with a virtually non-existent antislavery posture created the cultural outlook whereby European traders and New World settlers were morally untroubled in enslaving black human beings. Additional factors explain why Europeans resorted to Africans as the large-scale labour force for plantations. One was that European states engaged in slave trading all had strong centralized administrations and substantial military capacity. They frequently waged war against each other in the early modern period, but state centralization and military threats curtailed individual European powers from capturing and selling each other's subjects. Political factors perhaps were as important as cultural attitudes in explaining why European captives were not the solution to the large-scale labour demands of plantation America.[16]

A second important reason why planters resorted to Africans for their workforce lay in the fact that only workers in a state of continuous unfreedom could be compelled to undertake the rigours of such work to provide a regular labour force for the plantations. Plantations required permanent unfreedom, with heritable continuation of labour, to be productive – or so Europeans thought. Throughout the sixteenth and seventeenth centuries Europeans viewed slavery as an institution that only applied to non-Europeans.[17] Africans were regarded as outsiders in European societies; they were therefore eligible for enslavement. It is noteworthy that enslaved Africans in the Americas originated from outside the groups responsible for their enslavement.[18]

In most American areas where plantation slavery became established, Africans were not the initial first choice of labourers. Commonly, settlers either coerced Native Americans to work on staple crop cultivation or made use of European contract labourers such as indentured servants or *engagés*. Attempts to persuade or compel Native Americans to carry out plantation work in North America, however, largely failed, even though in Bahia the work force was primarily Indian until the early seventeenth century and in Spanish America the workforce in Potosí (in Bolivia) was Indian throughout the colonial period.[19]

Indians were totally unused to the sort of labour required on plantations. In addition, their knowledge of the terrain made it difficult to contain them under such a system of land and crop cultivation. There was also a severe demographic problem. Epidemics occurred from time to time in which large numbers of Native Americans in North America were devastated and killed by tuberculosis, pneumonia, influenza, plague, measles, scarlet fever, smallpox and malaria – diseases that spread through contact with people from a different disease environment across the Atlantic.[20] The spread of disease through contact with Europeans had a similar but even more devastating impact on the native Caribs of the West Indies.[21] In North America the Native American groups also resisted European settler encroachment on their lands with fierce armed resistance. They proved difficult to subjugate. This, too, militated against their enslavement.[22] Without the existence of Native Americans, however, the use of enslaved Africans as plantation labourers may well have spread more quickly.[23] In Spanish America, the situation differed: forced indigenous labour via the *encomienda* and *repartimiento* systems was common and, by the late seventeenth century, indigenous men and women and *mestizaje* (mixed race people of joint American-European origin) experienced a positive rate of population growth.[24]

White indentured labourers could also form the workforce for plantations. These were emigrants who had signed a work contract for a specified number of years in order to finance their ship passage to the New World. Such workers could, and did, undertake plantation work, but were not a permanent solution to the labour problem.

They became independent at the end of their usual contracted term of service (typically four, five or seven years). Possession of legal rights enabled them to negotiate their contractual position in local courts. Moreover, in the case of England, their supply dwindled in the late seventeenth century when the English population underwent a static period and domestic economic conditions improved. The costs of coercing Africans into staple crop production were lower than attempting to discipline an unwilling white servant labour force to carry out the same tasks. Transitions from the use of servants to the deployment of slaves on plantations nevertheless took a matter of years in different colonies. The pace of the shift varied considerably. In Barbados the change in the composition of the slave labour force occurred relatively swiftly in the 1640s, whereas the same transition in the Chesapeake occurred over the four decades between 1680 and 1720. Various explanations of the variation in the timing of the transitions can be adduced, but a crucial factor was the availability of the supply of slaves to particular territories.[25]

SLAVE DEMOGRAPHY

The demographic composition of the slave population shaped the parameters of slave life. Sex ratios, age structure and the relative proportion of African and Creole slaves influenced reproductive rates, family formation and black culture. Though the relative proportion of males and females in the Atlantic slave trade varied over time and by region, generally there was a demographic imbalance. Males outnumbered females, often by a ratio of two-to-one. This was because women were prized in Africa as workers and as vital for reproduction and were therefore retained in African societies. Buyers across the Atlantic primarily demanded adult male slaves, especially young, healthy, strong workers. It was not until after 1800 that the rapid growth of sugar cultivation increased the demand for additional labour, leading to a significant growth in the number of African children shipped across the Atlantic.[26]

Apart from the unbalanced sex ratio, several other factors affected the reproductive capacity of Africans taken to the Americas. Many of the enslaved disembarked ship in the Americas already in a debilitated state from the sickness and stresses experienced during the

Middle Passage. The epidemiological shock experienced by people entering a new continent and new disease environment tended to produce above-average mortality rates. A significant proportion of adult female slaves were already advanced in terms of childbearing years. Reproductive rates among the enslaved population of the Americas were shaped by the proportion of Africans and Creoles in a colony. The predominance of Creole slaves in a colony produced a more balanced sex ratio than in colonies where most slaves were Africans. In the latter case, the greater intake of male rather than female slaves via the Middle Passage created the gender imbalance. Creole slaves had other demographic advantages over Africans: births occurred at an earlier stage of a woman's life cycle, adaptation to a new disease environment was not a problem, and consequently fertility increased while mortality waned. African-born slaves in the New World experienced higher age-specific mortality rates and lower fertility rates than Creole slaves.[27]

Slave societies in the Americas had varied demographic experiences. By 1650 positive reproduction rates for people of full and mixed ancestry had already emerged in Mexico. Natural growth rates were also found among slaves and free coloureds in Cuba during its nineteenth-century sugar boom.[28] The USA was another large-scale slave system where the slave population grew in large numbers through natural reproduction.[29] At the outbreak of the American War of Independence only 20 per cent of the slaves in the thirteen British North American colonies were African-born. The demographic increase of US blacks from the late eighteenth century onwards was therefore based mainly on reproduction among Creoles.[30] The situation was different in other parts of the Americas. High mortality rates among imported Africans meant the slave populations in many Caribbean islands and Brazil depended on the continuing influx of newly imported slaves. Thus, for example, a Creole majority did not appear in Jamaica until 1840.[31] Throughout Spanish and Portuguese America the number of slave deaths exceeded slave births, especially on plantations, and child mortality was invariably high, amounting to between 25–30 per of all slave children under the age of eight born in the countryside of Brazil by the early 1870s.[32] High death rates, especially among infants and young children in the Caribbean and Brazil, made natural growth among slave populations difficult to achieve. African-born children lacked the immunological responses to diseases that Creole children inherited from their parents.[33]

Space precludes a discussion of the different demographic experiences of all slave societies in the Americas, but a comparison between the positive growth of the North American slave population and the declining demographic levels of many sugar-producing Caribbean colonies is instructive. The North American disease environment was less harsh than Caribbean tropical conditions. Work regimes on tobacco and rice plantations, and even more so on scattered black communities to the north of Maryland, were less oppressive than the demands of sugar cane cultivation. The possibility that Creole slaves in North America adopted European practices of nursing may have aided reproduction among blacks in the Chesapeake and the lowcountry. Such practices encouraged a maximum length of one year for breastfeeding compared with two or three years among African slave women in the British Caribbean. Shorter breastfeeding periods for babies, it is argued, would have aided the resumption of lactation and contributed to more closely spaced births in North America than in the West Indies.[34] Reproduction was aided by another factor. As the slave population began to reproduce itself in the Chesapeake, the Carolinas and Georgia by *c.* 1750, Creole slave women often formed sexual relationships at earlier ages than their African-born counterparts. This gave them more childbearing years than African-born women, who tended to begin and end reproduction over a shorter time span.[35]

The nutritional status of slaves in North America appears to have been a crucial factor leading to increasing levels of slave fertility. Most slaves in the Chesapeake and the lowcountry had maize as a staple part of their diet, supplemented by vegetables, some meat, water and rum rations, and food foraged by slaves from the fringes of plantations.[36] During the nineteenth century, the dietary intake of slaves in the cotton South was more nutritious than that found among many of their counterparts in Latin America and the Caribbean. Better diets accounted for a higher birth rate among slaves in the United States than elsewhere in the Americas, and to higher birth weight and healthier babies. Slave infants in the US South therefore stood a much better chance of surviving the vulnerable early months of life than was the case for babies in Cuba, Jamaica or Brazil. Studies of adult slave heights among slaves

Fig. 9: Sugar plantation, Port Maria, Jamaica, 1820–1

in the United States have shown that they were taller on average than elsewhere in Africa or the British Caribbean. This is another sign that US slaves benefited from nourishing diets.[37] There is no agreement among historians about whether planters in the American South practised systematic slave-breeding to boost their enslaved population.[38]

The demographic experience of many Caribbean sugar colonies, by contrast, was a continuous struggle for survival. Throughout the eighteenth century the slave population in those islands was heavily dependent on new imports. Slaves on sugar plantations experienced a higher mortality rate than slaves working in any other type of staple crop production. Thus the death rate on early nineteenth-century Jamaican plantations was significantly higher than on coffee plantations or livestock pens.[39] In Trinidad during the same period, nearly three times as many adult males died on sugar as on cotton plantations.[40] High mortality was also common among slaves involved in sugar cultivation in Louisiana, Cuba and Brazil. Planting

Fig. 10: African slave family from Loango, Surinam, 1770s

and harvesting sugar cane was the most physically demanding manual work associated with plantations. Whether the link between sugar cultivation and heavy mortality resulted primarily from the environmental setting for growing sugar or whether intensity of labour was a more critical factor is still, however, a debated issue – the two factors are, of course, not necessarily mutually exclusive.[41]

Slave reproduction was linked closely to the material and working lives of black captives. Slaves were required on most West Indian islands to cultivate their own provisions to feed themselves rather than rely on masters' rations. Daily calorific estimates indicate that Caribbean slaves received less than the energy required for heavy work in the cane fields and around the processing plant on estates.[42] Slave working conditions exacerbated the nutritional problem. Hard field work took a heavy toll on female slaves in particular, because women outnumbered men in the field gangs that carried out the most strenuous work. Pregnant women working in the cane fields customarily did so until six weeks before delivery; they invariably resumed field work, accompanied by their infants, three weeks after the baby's birth.[43] A lethal combination of poor dietary intake, strenuous physical work and reduced ovulation and hormonal imbalance among fertile women came together in sugar-producing areas such as Louisiana, Brazil and the Caribbean to reduce reproduction.[44]

Mortality was also an important factor in the demographic problems of the British Caribbean slave population. Fetal, neo-natal and infant mortality were notably high; not enough slave children survived into adulthood. Many serious diseases affected the chances of infant survival, including tetanus, lockjaw and beri-beri. Tetanus could possibly have accounted for one-fifth of total slave mortality.[45] Disabilities and diseases were also common among adult slaves in the Caribbean. Many slaves suffered from dysentery, dropsy, fevers and diseases of the digestive and nervous systems. Yaws, a non-venereal form of syphilis, left its mark on slave bodies in swollen lumps.[46] The one major disease brought under control in the early nineteenth-century Caribbean was smallpox. Empirical knowledge of quarantine, inoculation and vaccination helped to contain outbreaks of smallpox, but only Jamaica (in 1813) and Trinidad (in 1819) among the British sugar colonies set up vaccine establishments before slave emancipation.[47]

SLAVE FAMILY LIFE

Family life was a central way in which slaves took care of their survival. It gave slaves one of the few means through which they could establish a private existence independent of their masters. But family life was difficult to sustain because many aspects of transatlantic slavery were inimical to the creation of families. Africans were not imported in family groups. Many slaves had experienced a sequence of fractures in their personal lives, having been wrested often from families within Africa, taken against their will to the African coast, and then sold in the Americas without attention paid by merchants to whether those slaves had prior or current family attachments. The lack of power and capital among plantation slaves, long and hard working conditions and white brutality also hindered slave family life. There was also a deliberate disruption of slave families by white estate officials and overseers taking black mistresses, practising miscegenation, and separating households from time to time through hiring out or selling slaves to other plantations. Interracial mating began soon after the first Africans arrived in America. Over time it has been the major contributor to the hybridity of the African-American population.[48]

Modern studies have shown that the nuclear family was the type of household unit most favoured by British West Indian slaves. The proportion of slaves living in such a unit varied across individual islands. In 1813, a census for Trinidad showed that 53 per cent of the slaves lived in nuclear families. In 1796, 80 per cent of the slaves on Newton estate, Barbados lived in nuclear families; so too, did 70 per cent of the slaves at Montpelier estate, Jamaica in 1825. In 1821 and 1822, 54 per cent of Bahamian slaves lived in simple nuclear families. The remaining slaves in these and other Caribbean islands lived in various family groups, but relatively few – less than 10 per cent of slaves in Jamaica and Trinidad, for example – lived in extended family households.[49] Without firm evidence, it is safe to assume that the individual household was equivalent to a family grouping rather than a polygynous compound.

In North America many slaves formed settled family lives, but this was not attained without a struggle. During periods of substantial African migration to the southern colonies, family formation proved difficult to achieve. Male slaves had to find wives away from their plantations. These features of slave family life were transformed as Creoles became more prominent among the enslaved black population. Creole slave families in the Chesapeake were predominantly two-parent and extended households; little evidence survives of polygynous practices stemming from African practices. Slave marriages had no legal sanction but slave men and women had partners who were effectively husbands and wives. Sometimes these relationships were conducted on specific plantations where both partners worked, but it was not unusual for intimate slave relationships to be based on cross-plantation connections.[50]

Family life among South Carolinian slaves was fragile at the beginning of the eighteenth century. Males and females changed their partners frequently. But as the mortality rate declined among South Carolinian slaves and sex ratios became more even from the 1740s onwards, the possibilities for family formation increased.[51] By the antebellum period sometimes as many as a third of slaves on South Carolina's plantations lived in cross-plantation partnerships and households. Despite difficulties of movement and limitations of time spent together, such liaisons were often permanent and firmly guarded by slave men and women.[52] More broadly, throughout the antebellum South family ties were highly valued by slaves. Slaves forged very close bonds in families under the headship of cohabiting or married partners; they had multigenerational extended families and kinship networks.[53]

Slave marriage and family connections were pervasive throughout colonial Brazil. As befitted a nation imbued with the spread of Catholicism, slaves and free blacks had close ties to parents, grandparents, sons, daughters, cousins and godparents. Though some historians have argued that female slave fertility and rates of marriage were low in Brazil, more recent research has made a strong case for the opposite situation: high fertility among slaves and extensive evidence of marriage.[54] Nuclear and extended families predominated on large Brazilian plantations largely because marriage rates increased with the size of the slaveholding. Larger units, by their very nature, offered greater opportunities for permanent intimate liaisons and marriage than smaller slaveholdings.[55] A case study of a large plantation in Brazil for 1791 has shown that most slaves lived in separate family units built around husbands and wives.[56] In Brazilian cities, such as Rio de Janeiro, the formation of slave families was much more difficult to achieve owing to unbalanced sex ratios created by the transatlantic slave trade, masters resisting slave marriages, and difficulties for slaves to find lodgings for married people.[57]

The situation in Cuba has not been researched very fully, but there is evidence of nuclear families and kinship networks prevailing among slaves as they did throughout the Americas.[58] Cuban slave family life was complicated, however, by the fact that liaisons were common between slaves, freed men and women, and the white population, so that families were often not entirely slave households or free domestic regimes. Cuban families in the final decades of slavery frequently had shared members across racial boundaries. Thus Afro-Cuban social reproduction followed racial rules but never in a rigid way. The construction of Cuban families in the slavery era left a legacy of racially mixed Cuban identity based on acceptance of African descent.[59]

PLANTATION WORK

Productive work for white masters was the chief *raison d'être* for importing and employing enslaved Africans in the New World. Most of the waking hours of slaves, on at least six days of the week, were spent toiling for their owners without any wages. Plantation work involved a wide variety of tasks, with various levels of skill. Field workers predominated. They were usually under the direction of a white overseer, who organized the work shifts and routines, ensuring that productivity levels were maintained. The overseer reported directly to the managers of estates, who in turn informed owners or, in the case of absentees, their attorneys about the patterns of work. Beneath the level of the overseer, black slave drivers controlled the hourly work of slaves; they acted as go-betweens between the white elite personnel on an estate and the field slaves. Some slaves had positions as carpenters or fishermen; others had specific skills connected with mills and other manufacturing plant on a plantation. Though in all locations slaves were continually worked hard, the nature of the work varied by crop type.[60]

Tobacco cultivation involved regular, monotonous work over a seasonal cycle that lasted from the beginning of the year until the

Fig. 11: Plantation slaves going to work, Surinam, *c.* 1831

autumn. Gang labour characterized most work done on Chesapeake tobacco plantations. Under this system, slaves worked in units of commonly nine to twelve workers. Their pace of work was determined by the leader of the gang, a black foreman, under the watchful eye of a white overseer. Gang labour maximized productivity for planters. But work on tobacco plantations for slaves was burdensome for two reasons. One was that tobacco was a crop that regularly exhausted the soil. Usually it could only be grown on the same land for three consecutive years before slaves had to clear new land. The second reason was that, as tobacco cultivation moved from the tidewater to the interior, hilly, piedmont areas of the Chesapeake, slave work intensified to clear forest areas, hoe land, and plant fresh crops.[61]

Slave work on lowcountry rice plantations followed a different pattern. The normal method of work on South Carolina and Georgia estates consisted of task work supervised by either a white overseer or a black foreman, known as a driver, or both. Task work operated as follows. An owner or manager assigned specific tasks to slaves for completion on a daily basis. When the task was completed, slaves could quit work for the day and follow their own pursuits on a plantation. This system had the advantage for masters of being able to identify the quantity and quality of work performed as part of the daily task.[62]

Task work was followed at each stage of rice production. For slaves, task work had several benefits. They could carry out their allocated daily portion of work at their own pace. Industrious workers could hope to complete their tasks by early afternoon. Slaves became self-reliant at work and able to adapt their work practices without too much direct interference. Yet rice cultivation was an arduous, unhealthy form of labour that was carried out in swampy areas inhabited by insects, especially mosquitoes, and reptiles. Hot and humid subtropical conditions, with blistering sunshine and plentiful rainfall, made South Carolina and Georgia's climate oppressive in the summer. Slaves exerted great effort in constructing dams across irrigated fields, building embankments, clearing ditches and constructing canalized links between rivers and swamps. Disputes frequently arose between slaves and their white superiors over the time needed to complete certain tasks.[63]

Cotton plantations in the US South had an annual work routine that kept slaves constantly busy. In January and February the picking of cotton was completed and bales of cotton pressed and hauled in wagons to places of shipment. New cotton seeds were sowed in March and April, when adjacent corn fields were ploughed and hoed. Between May and August dirt was scraped away from the cotton with ploughs; hoes were used to eliminate weeds and grass; new ground was cleared and repairs made on plantations; and blades were stripped from corn stalks. From September to December the cotton was picked, put through a cotton gin, pressed and shipped; ditches were cleared and fences repaired; wood was cut and hauled; and more new ground was cleared for the next year's production cycle. Many planters combined the use of the gang and the task systems in cotton production. The choice between these two types of labour organization depended on the nature of the work. Thus it was common for plough-hands to work in gangs but for hoe-hands to be given a specified number of cotton rows to hoe each day. Many slaves had experience with both systems of work routine in the cotton fields.[64]

CUSTOM HOUSE NEGROES, RIO DE JANEIRO.

Fig. 12: Slaves hauling a wagon, Brazil

Work on sugar plantations in the Caribbean and Brazil mainly comprised gang labour, but a certain amount of task work eventually became available. This was particularly the case in the British West Indies after the British government implemented policies of amelioration from 1823 onwards. Usually a sugar estate had three gangs. The first gang (sometimes called the great gang) undertook the heaviest physical work. Slaves working in this gang dug the cane holes, cut the matured sugar cane, loaded the cane onto carts, and took it to the sugar factory works. This was arduous labour in a tropical climate. The second gang was responsible for lighter tasks such as clearing away the trash from the cane fields, chopping and heaping manure, cleaning young canes and threshing light canes. This was a mixed gang of men and women, with some adolescent help. The third gang (or weeding gang) comprised mothers with children. The third gang helped to clear up refuse in the cane fields and to throw dung into the cane holes. The gangs worked in military precision in parallel rows under the supervision of a black driver and a white overseer. Supervisors extracted the maximum productivity from slaves during the cane harvest.[65]

SLAVERY AND THE LAW

Slaves were heritable property in the Americas and their status was therefore encapsulated in legal codes. Different nations drafted laws according to their own priorities and implemented them in varied ways, but all of the legislation was aimed at defining the position of slaves in transatlantic societies and circumscribing their rights. Most laws relating to slaves in Spanish territories originated in Castile and applied there, as well as to Spanish America. Many of these laws forbade slaves from holding arms, travelling at night without a pass, or engaging in trade. It was legal to hold slaves in Spain before the Spanish colonization of South America; it was accepted that slavery was passed at birth from a slave mother to her children. But Spanish slave law laid down that masters had certain duties towards slaves; the condition of slavery was seen as unfortunate and as one in which slaves should be offered protection against ill treatment. In 1680 King Carlos II consolidated Spanish colonial law regarding slaves to provide consistency throughout Spanish America. A dominant theme in Spanish slave laws was the insistence on preserving public order: slaves were forbidden from carrying arms, they had to observe curfews in cities, and there were regulations to prevent, defeat and punish slave risings.[66]

Portuguese slave legislation was often more local and authorized by town councils. It was based on the *Ordenações Filipinas*, originally dating from the fifteenth century but revised in 1603 during the reign of Philip II. This remained the main law dealing with slaves and slave regimes in Brazil until slavery ended.[67] The Catholic Portuguese made little attempt to regulate slavery apart from ineffective edicts intended to protect slaves from vicious treatment. The reforms instigated by the Marquis of Pombal in Portugal between 1761 and 1773 were meant to include humane legislation for slaves, but it is unclear whether such legislation was followed in Brazil. Dutch colonial slave law evolved gradually; it included a ban on marriages between blacks and whites and aimed to preserve a social distance between slaves and masters. Dutch

Flagellation of a Female Samboe Slave.

Fig. 13: Whipping a slave, Surinam, 1770s

laws respecting slavery were much harsher in Suriname, which had a sizeable slave population, than in Curaçao, which had relatively few Africans.[68]

Piecemeal slave laws issued by royal and local officials in the French colonies were systematized under Louis XIV as the *Code Noir* (1685). Based on Roman slave law, this included sixty articles dealing with the treatment and oversight of slaves, the nature of slaves as heritable and commercial property, and the passages of slaves to free status. Details from the *Code Noir* illustrate the comprehensive nature of this legislation for the French colonies in the New World. The regulations under the code placed no limits on the slave's workday, but Article 6 precluded slave owners from working the enslaved on a Sunday or on specified holidays. Article 11 prohibited priests from marrying slaves without their owners' consent. Article 35 forbade owners from marrying slaves against their will. Article 44 declared that slaves were chattel; as such, they could not testify on criminal or civil matters, according to Articles 30 and 31. Article 36 prescribed that slave runaways who remained at large for a month should have their ears cut off and be branded on the shoulder with the fleur-de-lys.[69] The *Code Noir* was the work of the metropolitan government; it was not intended to justify slave owning but to define the power of white masters over the slave community.[70]

Legal codes reflected the repression involved in relations between masters and slaves. Statutes enacted by colonial legislatures after 1660 in British America and the range of punishments that white people meted out to blacks support this sombre view of master–slave relations. Virginia's first major slave code was passed in 1680 and strengthened in 1705. South Carolina had a series of slave codes, including detailed legislation enacted in 1712 that was tightened up in 1740 after the Stono Rebellion had alarmed the low country planter class (see Chapter 4). A statutory law of race and slavery existed in all thirteen British North American colonies by the middle of the eighteenth century. These acts singled out slaves as a caste. On paper they were draconian, allowing for a wide range of physical punishments including branding on the cheek or thumbs, amputation of body limbs, splitting noses, castration, and the death penalty, each one applied according to the nature of wrongdoing by slaves. Under these laws, slaves lacked various rights: the right to marry, the right to testify in court, the right to challenge the hereditary nature of slavery.[71]

Slave laws passed in Barbados and Jamaica in the second half of the seventeenth century began to consolidate racial slavery by singling out Africans for more severe treatment than white servants.[72] This was subsequently carried out more comprehensively. British West Indian slave laws of the eighteenth century were considerably less liberal, for instance, than the Spanish slave laws of the sixteenth and seventeenth centuries. Masters were given unlimited power over their slaves, who were regarded as a special type of property rather than as a subject. Protective clauses for slaves were relatively few. Every British West Indian island passed laws for the capture, suppression and punishment of runaway slaves. Severe penalties were enforced by law on any slave striking or insulting a white person; they included whipping, mutilation and execution. Slaves had special forms of trial and relatively few clauses in laws that offered them protection against unjust, brutal treatment by masters. 'The primary function of the British West Indian slave laws', Elsa Goveia has succinctly concluded, 'was directly or indirectly repressive.'[73] A certain amount of liberalization in slave laws occurred in the British Caribbean, however, as humanitarian sentiment arose with the growth of abolitionism in the later eighteenth century. These changes in slave codes promoted amelioration in the treatment of slaves in order to perpetuate slave regimes confronting an assault on their *raison d'être*.[74]

The United States introduced many new laws regarding slavery. The formation of a federal nation included the introduction of the US Constitution as the supreme law of the land that included a proslavery stance in its clauses. It forbade any federal tampering with slavery unless decreed in a constitutional amendment and guaranteed states' rights in relation to slavery. Between the ratification of the Constitution and the coming of the Civil War (1788–1860), there were frequent debates in US states about whether changes involving slavery were constitutional.[75] In the South, laws were amended to safeguard the rights of slave owners and to withstand abolitionist pressures.[76] In the North, various states introduced gradual emancipation laws, beginning with Pennsylvania (1780) and continuing through New York (1799) and New Jersey (1804).[77] The federal government was wary of any tampering with slavery,

RED SET-GIRLS, and JACK-in-the-GREEN.
Kingston Jamaica   June 1837

Fig. 14: John Canoe dancers, Jamaica, 1837

given the highly charged political and social atmosphere in which that institution was debated (see Chapter 6).[78] It was not possible to emancipate slaves in the United States until after a bloody civil war had been fought over slavery and sectionalism and the Constitution was changed by the 13th Amendment.

CUSTOMS AND BELIEFS

Slave customs and cultural beliefs testify to a rich blend of African practices and adjustments to life on a new continent. They provided a focal point for black communities to organize their own activities in their limited leisure time. Slaves enjoyed music and dance, playing a wide range of musical instruments ranging from fiddles to horns and percussion. They sang at work to ease the boredom and rigours of the labouring routine. Slaves told folk stories often linked with memories handed down from African oral traditions. Often the tales had significant implications for slave action. One common story, for example, was that of Brer Rabbit, a trickster figure based on Anansi stories from West Africa, who managed to outwit many people. Brer Rabbit stories emphasized the need for slaves to use guile in order to cope with the slave system and gave prominence to the underdog. They thus had a cultural meaning for slaves, enabling them to imagine themselves as able to outwit their masters.[79]

Festivals and parades at Christmas, the New Year, Easter and after the crop harvest were times for slave celebrations. These were often public performances, such as the Jonkanoo celebrations held over the Christmas holidays in the Caribbean. During this street parade one slave wore a mask and was dressed in as many rags as he could carry; he then paraded along the street with other slaves following him, singing and making noise for his worship 'the John Konner.'[80] Spiritual values were an essential part of slave communities. A belief in spirits often seemed mere superstition to white observers, but it was bound up with a commonly held black belief that spirits cast spells that could harm or cure – something that was linked to medicinal treatments for ailments by the use of herbs. Slaves carried charms, amulets, bracelets and idols as objects that represented their spiritual beliefs.[81]

Hybrid religious beliefs, combining cosmologies brought from Africa with the spread of Christianity in the Atlantic world, added complexity to slave religion in the Americas. Africans shared a belief in a spiritual world overseen by a Supreme Being, supported by other deities and cults. Ancestral spirits were an essential part of this cosmology. Revelations were the means through which people knew about the spiritual world. These could be communicated by dreams and by augury, divination, visions, hearing voices, spirit mediums or possessed objects. Observation of the course of time was one form of augury. It was reported from the Gold Coast, for example, that a calendar of lucky and unlucky days existed and that Africans avoided doing business on unlucky days. Divination was another form of augury. A well-known African form of divination was known by its Yoruba name of Ifa. This involved spreading cowrie shells on a board and the diviner asking the other world to influence the outcome of an event so that the diviner could answer questions. Gold Coast priests interpreted dreams and visions. Spirit mediums were common in Angola, where the *xingila* would enter a trance state arising from clapping, drumming or dancing, often in the presence of the physical remains of an ancestor. These diverse African practices facilitated embracing Christianity when slaves arrived in the New World, because revelations and belief in the Holy Spirit were an important part of interpreting the Bible. Revelations from African practices and Christianity could fuse to form African-American religious practices.[82]

Christianity and Islam were carried to parts of Africa before the transatlantic slave trade began in earnest. Senegambia was one area where Islamic beliefs spread, while Portuguese Angola was an area where Catholic Christianity was embraced. Though most Africans adhered to their indigenous beliefs before they were trafficked across the Atlantic, elements of Islam and Christianity permeated the mental universe of a good many slaves. Roman Catholicism had made significant inroads through the work of Jesuits in Kongo and Angola, for example, in the seventeenth century, with interactions made between Christianity and African customs.[83] Africans and their descendants adopted certain elements of Catholicism in Brazil, but not at the expense of their own cosmologies.[84] Whether slave indigenous religious rituals and elements of Christianity intersected and led to some whites and blacks on plantations participating in each other's worship is possible in some locations, but has not been found on a wide scale.[85]

One major component of slave spiritual beliefs in the British Caribbean consisted of the practice of Obeahism, a form of witchcraft or sorcery. Obeah is a term probably derived from Igbo-speaking slaves from the Bight of Biafra that can be translated as 'master.' It could be used positively or negatively, involving the use of artefacts, substances and spells either to poison enemies or to heal the wounded. Many slave communities included an Obeah man who would be consulted for these purposes. Planters and their supporters were wary of the influence of these slaves, castigating the superstitiousness associated with Obeah practices and believing they promulgated dangerous magical practices connected with sorcery and witchcraft. As a result, many prosecutions were brought into courts to regulate Obeah practices.[86] In Trinidad Obeahism was closely associated with Roman Catholicism; black converts to

Christianity in that island sometimes consulted Obeah practitioners without any contradictory feelings about their actions.[87]

Life's major staging posts – birth, baptism, marriage, death – were all steeped in spiritual significance for slaves.[88] Funerals, in particular, were observed with a high degree of ritual and ceremony because many blacks believed that death marked a return to Africa.[89] In Brazil a Central African practice known as the *tambo*, an elaborate funeral ceremony, was often used to ensure the comfortable passage of a person's soul to the other world.[90] Slaves claimed the right to bury their own dead in the Americas. They conducted funeral ceremonies that celebrated the lives of their ancestors with clapping, singing and drumming. Plantation food such as chicken, pork and cassava was left in calabashes at the grave and often thrown over the corpse with rum and other victuals. Funerals were followed by feasts at specific times afterwards; in Jamaica, these took place on the ninth and fortieth nights after the funeral. On these occasions the dead were treated as guests.[91] In the US South slave funerals were often held at night, with processions lit by torches, eerie music and graves marked with broken belongings of the deceased.[92]

It was recognized long ago that the Catholic Church was closely involved in converting slaves in Latin America for centuries.[93] Iberian efforts at spreading Roman Catholicism among slaves were relatively large and fairly successful. An important reason for this lay in the insistence of the Spanish Crown from the outset of colonization in South America that Africans should be converted to Catholicism. The Emperor Charles V supported the Christianization of slaves, and the Jesuits, on arriving in Mexico, took a keen interest in the spiritual life of slaves.[94] A strong clerical tradition existed in the Spanish New World colonies from the sixteenth century onwards. Jesuits paid great attention to converting slaves to Christianity in locations such as Cuba and Cartagena in the seventeenth century.[95] Roman Catholicism could also be filtered through the law to influence slave life. In 1785, for instance, a complete Spanish slave code named the *Código Negro Carolino* was written for Santo Domingo that was concerned with conversion to Catholicism and slave participation in the church's rituals.[96]

The spread of Catholicism had a major impact on slaves throughout Latin America. Slaves worshipped Catholic saints and deities, brought priests to their communities to conduct services and administer the Christian sacraments, and followed Christian practices such as baptism and the last rites before death. In the seventeenth-century viceroyalty of Peru, the ecclesiastical authorities defended the ability of slaves to be married in the Catholic Church. Africans in Peru could assert their status as Catholic vassals to claim protection from abusive slave owners.[97] In the first half of the nineteenth century, the Catholic Church in Lima wanted to maintain marriages among slaves and often intervened to prevent the relocation of a married slave from one place to another. The sale of a slave often proceeded only with the approval of an ecclesiastical court.[98]

Slaves in Brazil linked Jesus Christ's qualities to those found in *Oxalá*, an embodiment of the sun and the sky worshipped in Africa, and revered both figures as deities.[99] In Brazil the baptism of slaves was considered a responsibility of all slave owners as a main justification of enslavement was the conversion of the heathen into Christianity and the salvation of their souls.[100] Not all Brazilian slave owners favoured slaves becoming observant Christians, because allowing slaves to practise their religion freely could be inconvenient and expensive, but slave owners were not systematically opposed to slave baptism.[101]

Efforts to Christianize North American slaves were carried out from the beginning of the eighteenth century, but it was not until the 'Great Awakening' of the 1740s and the religious revivalism that swept parts of the South in the 1750s and 1760s that large numbers of slaves were converted to Christianity. These evangelical stirrings of the soul were associated largely with the Presbyterians, Methodists and Baptists, who favoured itinerancy, extempore preaching, minimizing doctrinal differences, conversion as a result of God's saving grace, open-air gatherings, fervent hymn singing, and the prospect for all who joined the Christian faith and maintained their faith to live in the hope of everlasting peace in the life hereafter. Such evangelical exhortation had a widespread appeal to blacks as well as the ordinary white population.[102]

The growth of Christianity among the North American black population became more pronounced after the War of Independence as African-Americans, especially in the northern states, began to form their own churches and chapels.[103] Emotional ecstasy lay at the heart of the black Christian experience. In the conversion to Christianity, slaves and free coloureds in the early nineteenth-century

US South combined Protestant songs, lined out on paper for all in the congregation to read, with the call-and-response character of traditional West African music. At Methodist revival meetings the ceremonies were based on the ring shout, an ecstatic religious ritual in which worshippers moved in a circle while shuffling and stamping their feet, clapping their hands, and spontaneously singing or saying prayers aloud.[104]

Christianizing efforts among slaves (among other groups) was also an important part of the work of the Society for the Propagation of the Gospel in Foreign Parts (SPG), an Anglican organization that flourished particularly in the eighteenth century. It supported the work of schoolmasters and the building of new churches in the colonies, and acted as a counterweight to Roman Catholicism. In Barbados a philanthropic bequest aided its work in the evangelization of slaves at Codrington College and plantation.[105] Missionary work also gradually assumed importance in slave communities from around 1750 onwards. The Moravian Church urged its missionaries to learn the Creole language of the slaves to aid communication. It proved popular among slaves in islands such as Antigua.[106] Baptist, Presbyterian and Methodist mission stations were established throughout the British Caribbean after the end of the Napoleonic Wars. Most of them were concentrated in Jamaica, the largest British sugar island. Missionaries played a significant role in fostering Christianity and literacy among slaves. They were exhorted by the parent societies to obey the planters' wishes but on a daily basis they found this difficult to follow when confronted by the harsh realities of slavery.[107]

Religious practices from Africa combined with Catholic Christianity in non-Anglophone transatlantic slave societies. This led to the creation of neo-African religions such as *Santería* in Cuba, *Calundus* and *Candomblé* in Brazil and Uruguay, and *Vodun* in Saint-Domingue/Haiti. *Santería*, a syncretic religion developed by slaves in Cuba in relation to Roman Catholicism, was centred around *orishas* or saints who are involved in various ritual ceremonies and healing practices designed to help slaves cope with their oppressed position. The liturgical language of *Santería* is lucumi, a dialect of Yoruba. Its practice involves rituals that take place in a *casa de santos* (house of saints). Participants communicate with their ancestors and deities via divination and trances, through animal sacrifice, and through drumming and dance.[108] *Santería* practitioners in Cuba adhered to guidelines called the *regla de ocha* (the rules of the deity).[109]

Calundus flourished in seventeenth- and eighteenth-century Brazil. It took the form of a religious gathering based an African practices connected with spirit possession. Drumming and dancing brought participants into a state of trance. Jesuits often condemned *calundus* because its dances seemed to represent demonic possession.[110] *Calundus* was absorbed into *candomblé*, which yoked together Yoruba, Fon and Bantu beliefs in another syncretic religion based on oral traditions. It made much use of music and dance, with worshippers protected by deities or *orishas*.[111] Participants in *candomblés* included people of different legal status, such as slaves and freedmen, and different racial identities, including Africans, Creoles, Mestizos and whites.[112]

Vodun (more commonly voodoo) was related to the *Candomblé* religion. Practised widely in Saint-Domingue (Haiti), *Vodun* stemmed from Yoruba culture and involved the worship of a senior God and minor spirits through the offering of gifts and animal sacrifices in the hope of better food resources and better health in return. *Vodun*, regarded as subversive by the authorities in Saint-Domingue because of its connections with sorcery and profanation, nevertheless survived as an important cultural practice long after slavery ended in

Fig. 15: Afro-Brazilian dance, Rio de Janeiro, 1820–4

Haiti.[113] *Vodun* and the other African-American religions discussed here combined beliefs brought from Africa with the conditions under which slavery was practised. They all had deep spiritual and ritualistic elements and enabled slaves to exercise agency in the choice of their beliefs beyond the influence of white masters.

Another practice known as *candombe* (not to be confused with *candomblé*) involved a more extrovert expression of Afro-American culture originating in slavery. Practised mainly in Uruguay, and to a lesser extent in Brazil and Argentina, it involved singing, drumming and dancing in a celebratory way. Elders and spiritual leaders, musicians and dancers emphasized their roots in Africa, and performed in a jubilant, festive way that had a visceral aural and visual impact on audiences. *Candombes* were held on Sundays or religious holidays, and were powerfully spiritual events. They eventually spread beyond the slave population to become a popular form of entertainment: by the 1850s and 1860s in Montevideo, for example, *candombes* were the most heavily attended form of public entertainment, attracting 10 per cent of the city's population.[114]

4

SLAVE RESISTANCE

Slaves resisted bondage frequently, as one might expect in a situation where unequal power relationships defined the position of masters and unfree labourers. The harshness and brutality of the slave system on many plantations was bound to lead to slave resistance of one sort or another. Collective revolts were the most dramatic form of resistance, but slaves also challenged their masters through individual acts of defiance. For slaves, unwillingness to perform work adequately, either because their condition stimulated opposition or because they were badly treated, was common. This could be done by working below levels of expected productivity, arriving at work late, failing to complete tasks, breaking tools or sabotaging work routines. Slaves could feign ignorance about learning to use new implements. They could pretend to be careless and sometimes simulated illness. When disenchanted or alienated from their lot, slaves downed tools and stopped work. All these forms of non-violent resistance to slavery interrupted the smooth functioning of the plantation.[1]

Opportunities existed to damage a master's property, to steal food and to interrupt seasonal work routines. Thus sometimes slaves picked tobacco leaves too early, flooded rice fields or stole sugar cane. Disruptions to crop production were a nuisance to planters, but they were to be expected in the circumstances and could usually be contained without serious damage to work regimes. Attacks on the customary rights of slaves could lead to concerted resistance.

This happened in Antigua in 1831, when thousands of slaves marched to Government House in St John's, the island's capital, and protested against the British government's attempt to abolish the slaves' Sunday markets.[2] Conversely, slaves could resist passively by refusing to eat rations after they had been punished.

Sabotage and arson were further tactics that lay at slaves' disposal to disrupt plantations and attack owners' properties. They were major weapons used by slaves against oppressive masters.[3] Setting fire to houses, torching sugar cane or burning storehouses could often be carried out anonymously and under cover of nightfall. In 1740 over 300 houses were burned in Charleston, South Carolina just a year after the Stono Rebellion alarmed white planters. This outbreak of arson was attributed to slaves. South Carolina's lawmakers responded with alacrity to the attack by including in the colony's Negro Act of 1740 execution as the punishment for slaves, free blacks, mulattoes or Indians found guilty of wilfully burning property and crops.[4] In New York in 1741 slaves were accused of starting several fires.[5] Rumours and incidents of arson played a part in the last major slave revolt before slave emancipation, in Jamaica in the early months of 1832.[6] Sabotage by arson frequently occurred in the first half of the nineteenth century in Cuba.[7] Arson was a component in nearly all slave revolts even though it was a felony punishable by death.[8]

Resistance did not necessarily have a political content; in fact, usually this was not present in acts of defiance. Nor did resistance always have the ulterior aim of securing full freedom, though that was clearly the intention of many slave rebellions. Pragmatic considerations usually outweighed ideology in slave resistance and revolts. Often slave resistance was intended to provoke changes in the management of the slave system rather than to abolish slavery.[9] Slaves exercised considerable agency in negotiating and renegotiating the boundaries of power and compulsion and the racial polarities associated with them. Far from being docile recipients of whatever their masters doled out to them, slaves determined or effected when and where cooperation should be suspended.

This is not to suggest that all slaves, throughout their period of bondage, were actively and continuously impelled by a spirit of opposition to their owners. The reality of life on slave plantations was more complex. Inequalities of wealth and status existed among slave plantation workforces. Drivers, skilled manual workers and trusted slaves were often in a much better position to provide for themselves and their families than field slaves. For privileged slaves, there was no compelling reason to resist the system. Because of these realities of slave work and life, it is historically inaccurate to suggest that an entire slave plantation population could be motivated to oppose their masters.[10] Moreover, long-term runaways were the exception to the norm among slave fugitives because ties to a place or plantation and family networks provided a sense of belonging, even under conditions of duress, to restrict the incidence of permanent escape among captives.[11]

Besides overt resistance, there were ways of offering silent resistance or gestures which opposed slavery. An offer of potions or herbal remedies from slaves to white drivers, overseers or managers could lead to poisoning. This may have been a widespread tactic carried out by slaves. Between 1740 and 1785 in Virginia, for instance, more slaves were charged with poisoning than with any other crime except stealing.[12] There could also be verbal or oral resistance by hurling abuse at white personnel on estates. This might involve spitting in overseers' faces, threats to strike managers or swearing at drivers. Acts of insubordination, for instance, along with running away, under-performance, insubordination and symbolic challenges to authority, accounted for over 90 per cent of the offences committed by slaves in Demerara and Essequibo in 1828.[13]

To oppose white masters was a courageous act, for penalties could be severe. Some punishments focused on slave entitlements; others were brutally applied to slave bodies. Fines, whippings, confinement in dungeons, placing iron clamps on feet, occasional mutilation and removal of privileges are just some of the punishments that met determined acts of resistance. All of these are vividly displayed in the diary and actions of Thomas Thistlewood, a cruel white overseer on a Jamaican slave plantation in the mid-eighteenth century. Thistlewood combined constant surveillance of his slaves with no compunction about flogging or abusing those who resisted his control. His repertoire of punishment combined the infliction of psychological and physical pain, often intended to catch unsuspecting slaves off guard.[14]

SLAVE RUNAWAYS

If rebellions represented the ultimate act of collective resistance by bonded labourers, other types of resistance were more prevalent, none more so than attempts to escape bondage through stealing away from masters. This was a common way in which slaves attempted to combat slaveholders' restrictions on their movements.[15] Thus, runaway slaves were common everywhere in the Americas. Slave fugitives usually ran off singly or in pairs; they were often disguised; sometimes they took the tools of their trade to aid their flight. Their aims were diverse. Some wished to escape from coastal neighbourhoods, usually by jumping aboard ship. Others slipped away for brief periods of time to visit friends or relatives in rural areas. Still others headed for the relative anonymity of towns and cities. In Brazil fugitives known as *mocambos* hid out in forests near to towns and farms.[16]

Many fugitives fell into the category of *petits marronages*, effectively truants, who hoped their actions would obtain small privileges or concessions from masters before returning to their plantations.[17] Permanent runaway communities among slaves were fairly uncommon. Some could be found in the backwoods of the Carolinas or Virginia, where they would raid plantations for food or forage in wooded areas, but the terrain was not as conducive to such permanent maroon communities as the forests of the interior of Suriname or the mountains of Jamaica. The best-known North American maroon hideout was the Great Dismal Swamp, a marshy area stretching from Norfolk, Virginia to Edenton in the Albemarle Sound area of North Carolina. A white traveller commented that this area harboured 'prodigious multitudes of every kind of wild beasts peculiar to America, as well as run-away Negroes, who in these horrible swamps are perfectly safe, and with the greatest facility elude the most diligent search of their pursuers.'[18]

Newspapers in the Americas were full of advertisements for absconders. Rewards were offered for those who collaborated with white masters to find them. Runaways who were caught were subjected to a range of punishments. They could be whipped, placed in iron collars and shackles, or sold. Fugitives described in newspapers were just the tip of an iceberg of bonded workers who took flight in an attempt to secure liberty. Other documents referring to runaway bonded labourers indicate that the number was far larger than those advertised. This is unsurprising given that owners would probably only spend money on an advert in cases where a runaway had been absent for a period of at least a month, or where the fugitive was worth recapturing.[19]

Slaves ran away from their owners for innumerable reasons. Social ties with other blacks were a prime motive for absconding. Some African-Americans had experienced separation from family and friends and wished to rejoin them. Slave runaways sometimes had relatives among free people of colour whom they contacted in order to help their escape. Other reasons why slaves fled included unease about being apprehended after stealing an owner's goods, the desire to escape from cruel masters, the influence of outside agitators, and disappointment at not being freed by their owners. Sudden opportunities to leave hurriedly from plantations tempted numerous slaves to escape without extensive preparations. On other occasions, slaves clearly planned their getaways for particular times of the day or specific locations. Though most slaves absconded to escape their masters, flight was sometimes the result of interpersonal and domestic violence within the slave community arising from inequalities of status, wealth and diet among slave populations.[20]

Slave resistance had both inward and outward goals. Some acts of resistance were an internalized, psychological form of rebelliousness that could either be self-destructive for the slave or an outward action of self-enhancement. Acts of resistance could also be an attack on the plantation world or a movement away from the plantation towards urban centres or out of a particular society altogether. Slaves who had acculturated themselves to the varieties of white people and their ways, and who had gained occupational skills, fluent English and confidence in dealing with situations arising beyond their plantations, were in a better position to cope with being a fugitive than slaves who had not yet achieved those attributes. It is not surprising, therefore, that newspaper advertisements for runaway slaves frequently included comments on their language proficiency.[21]

Some slaves ran away from their masters for a few days and then returned voluntarily. They may have spent time visiting friends or family or they had decided to withdraw their labour for a short period owing to poor treatment. Other runaways, however, aimed to flee permanently. Geographical factors affected their chances of

Fig. 16: A fugitive slave, Surinam, *c.* 1831

success. Fugitive slaves near the eastern seaboard of North and South America or in the Caribbean islands often stole away by boat. If they had been living by the shore or along rivers and creeks or in ports, they had often picked up skills that might help them to attempt a maritime escape. Slaves who lived inland, however, did not have this option available and therefore had recourse to hiding among the throng of people in urban centres or escaping to rugged mountainous or woodland areas.[22]

Ports and towns were a magnet for slave runaways. By the late eighteenth century urban centres throughout the Americas had slaves and free black workers in their populations. In South America, cities such as Rio de Janeiro, São Paulo, Buenos Aires and Lima had large free black populations that absorbed runaway slaves with a good chance of their remaining at large. Mingling with the crowds and changing names, runaways stood a better chance of escaping detection in an urban setting than those who remained in and around plantations. In addition, there were always work opportunities in the retail sectors of towns for runaways to support themselves. Skilled slaves, in particular, could find work as carpenters, masons, tailors, cooks and in the maritime trades. A fair amount of urban concentration of fugitives existed in Jamaica by the end of the slavery era: in 1832 Kingston accounted for over a fifth of long-term slave runaways on the island.[23] In the Danish West Indies, towns such as Christiansted and Frederiksted in St Croix and Charlotte Amalie in St Thomas harboured slave runaways in comparative anonymity.[24]

Most slave runaways were male. Females usually comprised between one-tenth and one-fifth of absconders in all locales. This ratio can be explained by the attachment to familial ties found among slave women, notably their reluctance to leave their children. In addition, because more male than female slaves worked as boatmen, ferrymen, labourers on roads and as hired workers, men had greater knowledge of the terrain and more opportunities to escape. The majority of runaways were in their twenties. They were better able to cope with the difficulties of life on the run than older slaves. Moreover, middle-aged slaves were more likely to have forged committed personal relationships, which made them reluctant to move in some cases.[25]

There was a marked seasonal distribution of slave runaways. In North Carolina, for example, the most popular time for African-Americans to quit their masters was either during the harvest season from September to November or between February and April, when the slack season ended and spring planting began.[26] In Virginia more slaves absconded in April, when the seasonal pace of tobacco planting increased, than in any other month. In South Carolina the highest incidence of slave escape occurred in the summer months from May to August, when rice cultivation was particularly rigorous.[27] In Barbados most slaves ran away in July and August. This was just after the sugar harvest ended and when provisions were commonly in short supply. It may be that Barbadian fugitives fled in those months because supervision was more lax than at the height of the sugar harvest, or possibly because hunger drove them to abscond. Innumerable references in runaway advertisements to slaves fleeing with clothes, guns, the tools of their trade, forged passes, and canoes or horses also suggest that plans for freedom were laid before the moment of flight.[28]

Kenneth Morgan

Opportunities for slave flight occurred during wartime. Slaves were widely used as soldiers in the American revolutionary war (1776–83) because of shortages in British manpower, high mortality rates among British troops, and slave immunity to tropical diseases.[29] During the war about 10,000 slaves from Georgia (two-thirds of its pre-war slave population) and 20,000 slaves from South Carolina were lost. The biggest exodus was reserved for 1782 when white loyalists and the British army quitting Savannah, Charleston and St Augustine took about 20,000 slaves with them. Some estimates reckon that the total scale of the flight of blacks from the United States during the war was 80,000 people. These people found new homes in Britain, Africa and parts of the British Empire, including Nova Scotia.[30]

Other wars provided ways for slaves to escape slavery. During the French revolutionary war, Britain could not muster a sufficient number of its own troops to conduct its West Indian campaigns. Thus slaves were purchased by the army on public account to strengthen the garrisons and defences of Jamaica and other British West Indian islands against depredations. Between 1795 and 1808 the British government purchased 13,400 slaves to serve in West India regiments.[31] The most striking example of slaves achieving freedom through military participation in wartime, however, came in the American Civil War, when 250,000 slaves took up arms on the Union side against the Confederate forces. Slaves also contributed significantly to the Confederate war effort in the capacity of servants, teamsters and military labourers.[32] As explained in Chapter 6, the Union army became an army of slave liberation; as it advanced into the South, many slaves fled to join their fellow former captives already serving under arms.[33]

MAROONS

Permanent slave runaway communities were common in many parts of the Caribbean and South America. Such communities were known as maroons, taken from the French word *marronage*, meaning runaway (in Spanish the phrase was *cimarrón*). Areas where maroons flourished were the rugged interior of Jamaica, forested areas away from the coastal plantation fringe in Demerara and Suriname, and remote parts of Cuba, Ecuador, Guatemala, New Grenada, Peru and Brazil.[34] However, smaller maroon communities existed elsewhere – for example, in the woods of Grenada and Dominica. Many maroons lived in inaccessible environments such as jungles, forests and mountain areas. These locations provided relative security from militia trying to track them down, but the pressures of living in such circumstances, often in harsh terrain, made forging viable communities difficult. Only the most tenacious groups survived. Maroons defended their hideaway communities with disguised paths, false trails and, where possible, underwater paths. Fortifications around their villages were built in Suriname and Brazil, where fugitive slave settlements were called *quilombos*.[35] Brazil had hundreds of *quilombos* during the era of slavery, including more than 110 in Minas Gerais alone.[36]

Maroon communities were a potential challenge to European colonization in the Americas, and they were often crushed by various colonial authorities. In 1545 in Peru a bloody battle was fought in which a community of 200 runaways living in a marshy area to the north of Lima was wiped out by colonial troops.[37] In 1795 Spanish expeditions subdued slave runaways in mountain retreats in the Serranía de Coro region of Venezuela.[38] Nevertheless, many maroon communities survived for decades and some became permanent. One historian considers that, with the exception of the Haitian Revolution, which will be discussed below, 'marronage was the only successful overt form of slave resistance in the Americas.'[39]

The generic name for Hispanic maroon communities, *palenques*, came from palisades protecting maroon communities. *Palenques* existed in the thick tropical forests of Colombia. Their members raided and carried out depredations on surrounding areas. The authorities had difficulty in bringing these activities under control.[40] Slave fugitives in Guatemala also made use of *palenques*.[41] *Palenques* were similarly found in the province of Cartagena, New Granada, from the late sixteenth century onwards. They were stable settlements with a clearly defined political and military leadership, and were sometimes organized according to African ethnic origins.[42]

Palenques were common in Cuba by the early seventeenth century. Some lasted for many years. They were still in existence by the middle of the nineteenth century. Cuban *palenques* comprised a series of dispersed huts surrounded by stockades in hidden areas.

They were surrounded by forked poles of hard wood with many sharp points placed at distances from one another. *Palenque* leaders were elected; they recruited maroons and would not allow anyone to leave their hidden settlements who had not spent at least two years there. These maroons raided local communities for gunpowder and weapons and secretly exchanged beeswax and honey with slave communities in exchange for goods and tools.[43]

Maroon communities also survived for long periods in other parts of Latin America. One such settlement called Mandinga on the Vera Cruz–Oaxacan border, in colonial Mexico, survived for nearly a century after 1735.[44] One of the most prominent maroon communities in Latin America was Palmares, in Brazil, a federation of West-African-style villages in the mountains of Alagaos. Palmares had 10–15,000 inhabitants. It had a confederate government led by an elected chief who distributed landholdings, appointed officials, and took charge of fortifications. Palmares survived for almost a century until the 1690s when it was overrun by the Portuguese military authorities.[45]

Maroons survived economically by cultivating gardens and growing crops and by hunting and fishing. They also made utensils. In an account of 1796 John Stedman described how maroons in Suriname preserved game and fish by barbecuing, procured a butter-like substance and wine from palm trees, fabricated pots from clay near their dwellings, made corks and candles, and rubbed wood together for tinder. Maroons had considerable military prowess, becoming expert in guerilla warfare, using bows, arrows and spears, and drawing upon their religious rituals to inspire their opposition to militia or planters. Maroons kept in secretive contact with slave communities in Guadeloupe and Cuba for goods and services.[46] In some localities, the authorities made concerted efforts to track down permanent slave runaways. Nowhere was this carried out more regularly than in Cuba where, in the nineteenth century, professional slave hunters (*rancheadores*), including many free blacks and mulattoes, searched for maroons in the forests and mountains of the island.[47]

Maroons had originally been at the heart of the resistance movement against the whites of Jamaica. They had fought a series of Maroon Wars in the late seventeenth and early eighteenth centuries. These compelled the Jamaican plantocracy to seek accommodation with them through two peace treaties of 1739. These treaties gave the maroons rights to hunt freely throughout unsettled areas of Jamaica, allowed them 1,500 acres of land for cultivation, but obliged them to return fugitive slaves they encountered. Most important, the treaties pledged maroon support to white settlers when slave rebellions broke out.[48] In 1760 maroons joined white forces in putting down the serious slave revolt in western Jamaica begun by Coromantee rebels, from Africa's Gold Coast, and killed the leader, Tacky.[49]

White people in Jamaica suspected maroons were a potential threat to social stability. Despite these misgivings, peace with the Jamaican maroons lasted until 1795 when the English commissioner assigned to Trelawny Town had two maroons flogged for pilfering from plantations. The island's governor feared the maroons and sent troops to capture Trelawny Town. Maroons ambushed the troops but the British army prevailed after laying siege to the maroon towns by surrounding them with military outposts. One hundred Cuban hunting dogs were imported by the British troops and set among the maroons, who were terrified of them. The maroons agreed to surrender in return for amnesty. Over 500 maroons from Trelawny Town were deported. This curtailed the likelihood of further maroon rebellion. In the other Jamaican maroon communities peaceful relations were maintained with whites after the 1739 treaties.[50]

SLAVE INSURRECTION

Resistance to slavery began when captives were taken in Africa. Thus, in the sixteenth and seventeenth centuries, slaves captured by the Portuguese in Luanda frequently escaped before they were loaded on board ship. Captives were terrified about being split up from their own communities and being dispatched across the Atlantic, and they particularly feared the possibility that they would be cannibalized. In the first half of the eighteenth century, so many slaves were running away from captivity in Luanda and its region that several maroon societies were formed. There were other means of resisting enslavement in West Central Africa. Captives could bring cases, with the support of relatives or rulers, before the colonial judicial system; rulers could request that colonial officials intervened to secure the release of captives; and tribunals known as *mukanos* (arising from an African legal system) were held.[51]

Those who did not escape enslavement through these various means were loaded on board ships destined for the Americas, but there was sometimes an opportunity to stage an insurrection while slaves were being held in compounds or on shipboard. The small island of Gorée, situated three kilometres off the coast of Senegal, was the site for several slave rebellions and attempted escapes in the third quarter of the eighteenth century.[52] A larger number of attempted escapes occurred on shipboard. Based on research mainly on the British, American and French slave trades, Eric R. Taylor has identified 493 shipboard insurrections by Africans. Between 75,000 and 100,000 slaves were involved in these risings, of which three-quarters occurred on, or off, the West African coast. Though there are few instances of Africans capturing vessels and successfully managing an entire revolt, slaves regained their freedom on more than 100 occasions. Over 40 per cent of the shipboard revolts occurred at night-time. Favourable conditions for staging an insurrection included being near the African coast, which gave slaves the opportunity to seize a vessel while it was being reprovisioned; access to the upper decks of ships by one or more slaves; indifference by the crew towards Africans or unusually harsh conditions; slaves' access to tools and weapons when the crew was careless about security; and disaffection and mutiny among the crew, enabling slaves to take advantage of the chaos. Successful revolts resulted from careful planning. Unsuccessful revolts resulted from betrayal to the crew and from the help given to captains and the crew by nearby ships and soldiers based ashore. Brutal punishment and reprisals followed, to ward off future rebellions.[53]

The most celebrated slave mutiny on shipboard was a singular event with no similar predecessor or successor. This was the revolt on the *Amistad*, an inter-colonial slaver sailing from one part of Cuba (Havana) to another (Puerto Principe) in 1839. It carried a cargo of Africans from Sierra Leone who had been sold into slavery in Cuba and later taken on board ship for a voyage to the United States. Cinqué, an African slave leader on the voyage, led a mutiny which gained control of the ship. The rebels intended to sail back to Africa, but they were betrayed by two Spanish navigators on board the vessel. Instead of heading towards Africa, the *Amistad* sailed towards Connecticut, where it was intercepted by an American naval vessel. The surviving forty-four Africans were imprisoned as runaway slaves. But they were able to enlist the support of sympathetic lawyers, influenced by abolitionism, who argued in court that the blacks had been illegally taken into slavery and should be treated as free people. The case went to the US Supreme Court, and the blacks were released into freedom. No other slave rebellion in the history of the transatlantic slave trade ever had such a successful outcome for the enslaved.[54]

Slave insurrections were more frequent phenomena after captives had been disembarked in the Americas and sold to plantation owners and their representatives. Such revolts could occur anywhere in the plantation Americas, for many different reasons. The first revolt by African slaves in the Americas occurred on Christmas Day 1521 on Santo Domingo (now the Dominican Republic) where about twenty slaves on the estate of Governor Diego Colón, son of Columbus, staged an insurrection that led to the deaths of several white people. The rebels were quickly defeated. Several of them were either killed or captured and brutally punished.[55]

Eugene D. Genovese argued that certain conditions favoured large revolts.[56] Economic distress – notably hunger – could be a catalyst for slave rebellion. A good example is the large rising on Danish St John in 1733, which resulted from years of drought, hunger and economic depression.[57] Severe drought and problems with provision grounds were evident in Jamaica just before the slave revolt there in 1831/2. The lack of serious deficiencies in food supply in the antebellum United States might be one reason for the lack of slave revolts there between 1831 and 1860. Concentrations of large numbers of slaves on plantations were also more conductive to revolts than areas where most slaves lived on estates of fifty or less. Thus, slave revolts were more common on Caribbean plantations and in the mining districts of Venezuela and Colombia than on estates in the United States, where, apart from South Carolina and Mississippi, blacks did not dominate the overall population. Rebel leadership thrived more easily in areas where significant numbers of slaves were clustered. Slave revolts occurred more frequently in countries that had a high ratio of blacks to whites and slave to free. Jamaica and Saint-Domingue fell into this category, for in each case, slaves comprised over 80 per cent of the population at the time of major revolts.[58]

Wherever slaves lived, the obstacles to challenging white power were formidable and often insurmountable. White militia and planters had great military advantages in terms of weapons, and slave revolts could be compromised by informers, spies and traitors. In the US South, many white people in rural areas had substantial knowledge of, and access to, firearms. Among the slave community, there were always individuals who curried favour with white owners by informing them about any hints of rebellion.[59] Brutality by whites towards blacks was often triggered by rebellions, and it was common for rebel slaves and their leaders to be chased, hunted and captured. Those found guilty of revolt were usually placed on trial, found guilty and sentenced to death. As an example to other slaves not to rebel, the decapitated heads of leaders were often displayed on poles in public.[60]

SLAVE REVOLTS IN NORTH AMERICA

Slave revolts occurred at frequent intervals in the Americas. But there were more aborted risings than actual revolts, more conspiracy scares than actual conspiracies, and few successful rebellions. Why were large risings relatively uncommon in the Americas? Before 1670 there were too few slaves for an effective revolt to take place. The influx of large numbers of Africans to North America in the late seventeenth century coupled with the growth of plantations and the subsequent codification of statutes discriminating against blacks might lead one to expect a more concerted challenge by bonded labourers to their misery. That this did not occur frequently resulted partly from the low density of slaves in North America until about 1750 – Virginia and South Carolina, for example, being much larger geographically than Great Britain. In such circumstances, slaves were accommodated on scattered quarters, which effectively nullified moves to coordinate revolts. Lack of homogeneity among saltwater slaves and the residence of slave owners on their plantations caused divisions among the black workforce and subjected slaves to the constant gaze of white masters.

The main revolt involving slaves in British America during the seventeenth century was Bacon's Rebellion in Virginia. Led by a newly arrived planter, Nathaniel Bacon, the rising attempted to secure land in western Virginia by poorer whites who felt deprived of economic opportunity by the wealthy planters of the tidewater,

led by Governor William Berkeley. These poor white men tried
to wrest land from Native Americans. Over the summer of 1676,
raids against the Indians turned into a rebellion that was almost
a civil war in Virginia. The rising was brief but bloody. Fighting
took place between Bacon's supporters and the Indians, leading to
casualties. The rebels paraded Indian captives through Jamestown in
early September, offering, as they went along, freedom to servants
and slaves who would join Bacon. Bacon caught swamp fever,
transmitted by mosquitoes, and died, probably of dysentery, on 26
October. Without his leadership, the rebellion soon petered out.
Twenty-three of Bacon's supporters were hanged.[61]

Bacon's Rebellion involved disgruntled ex-servants, other
freedmen and slaves joining together to oppose the status quo.
About one in ten of the slaves in Virginia joined in the uprising.
In 1677 an investigation of the causes of the revolt by the king's
commissioners found that a significant part of the rebel force had
been free men who had recently been servants. Historians of the
rebellion have shown how the aftermath of the rebellion led to
moves to tighten slave codes in Virginia and to prise apart any future
armed cooperation between slaves and ex-servants. The measures
were successful, for nothing like the combination of blacks and
unruly whites rebelling against the authorities ever happened again
in North America.[62]

The Stono Rebellion in South Carolina (1739) was the largest
and only full-scale slave revolt in the history of the British mainland
colonies in North America. It began on 9 September 1739 when a
group of slave rebels broke into a store near the Stono River in a
coastal parish twelve miles south of Charleston. Led by an Angolan
called Jemmy, the rebels beheaded two white men, seized weapons
and alcohol, and headed southwards towards Florida. Gathering
between fifty and a hundred recruits along the way, they marched
with drums and banners, and destroyed plantation houses and farms.
By the afternoon they had reached the Edisto River where they
paused, hoping extra black recruits would flock to their cause and
make them invincible. This gave the white militia time to organize
an attack on the rebels, to muster quick support from local planters,
and to erect pickets at strategic crossroads and ferry crossings. By
the evening, most of the black resistance had been quelled. However,
some slave rebels escaped and the whites concentrated their efforts

on hounding them down. During the rising at least twenty white people and forty-four blacks died.[63]

The causes of the revolt remain speculative. Harsh conditions probably played a part. South Carolina had suffered from a bout of epidemic disease in the summer of 1739. That the Spanish garrison of St Augustine had offered freedom to Carolinian slaves shortly before the uprising broke out was perhaps of greater significance, owing to the proximity of South Carolina to the Spanish border and the fact that the Stono rebels headed south in that direction. This happened when Anglo-Spanish hostilities had spilled over into the War of Jenkins's Ear, a largely colonial conflict caused by tensions over the safety of English and Spanish ships plying the Atlantic trade routes. This was a rising shaped by African tactics. Most rebels, including the leader, were Africans rather than Creoles. Many were of Congolese extraction. Their actions exhibited notable features of resistance associated with ethnic martial traditions in Africa. For instance, the initial decapitation of the two white men at the start of the revolt mirrored the common resort to displaying severed heads in African societies as trophies of military prowess. The use of banners and drums as the Africans marched south from Stono was integral to fighting methods followed in west-central Africa. It may be that some rebels had experienced war within Africa; this, after all, was how many slaves had been taken as captives before they were shipped across the Atlantic.[64]

The response of South Carolina's politicians to Stono reveals the importance they attached to dealing effectively with the aftermath of the uprising. South Carolina went to war with the Spanish in St Augustine to try to block an obvious avenue of escape for their slaves. The South Carolina Assembly introduced a prohibitive import duty on slaves, which reduced the introduction of African slaves into the province for most of the next decade. Most important, South Carolina passed a comprehensive slave code in 1740. Drawing on previous statutes, this tightened up the control over slaves and became the basis of the colony's slave law for virtually the next century. The 1740 code laid down larger fines than previously for planters who failed to control their slaves.[65]

Slave revolts could also occur in situations where Creole slaves were the norm and whites were more in evidence. A prominent uprising of this sort occurred near Richmond, Virginia in the summer of 1800. Known after its leader as Gabriel's conspiracy, this was a planned attempt to overthrow white control and gain freedom for enslaved blacks. Gabriel Prosser, the leader, was a young, literate Creole slave working as a blacksmith on a plantation in Henrico County, Virginia. He was familiar with the rhetoric of black insurgence that had informed the massive Saint-Domingue slave revolt (on which see below). The revolt was planned to occur in the harvest season so that slave supporters would not starve. Elaborate plans were laid to attack Richmond, the capital of Virginia, with three columns of black rebels. Advance meetings were held by the conspirators to coordinate strategy. After Richmond was taken, Gabriel hoped that the surrounding environs would capitulate to the black insurgents and that he would end up as the king of a black-led state.[66]

Gabriel's revolt failed to live up to its careful organization. Bad luck and lack of unanimity among slaves who knew of the rising in advance contributed to its swift demise. Planned for the night of 30 August 1800, the rising was delayed for a day because of severe storms. Gabriel gathered about 1,000 blacks to march on Richmond but this was far fewer than he had anticipated or needed. Gabriel appears to have had political motives. He marched with a banner entitled 'Death or Liberty.' The rising was aborted by division among his followers. Some deserted; others informed the local authorities of the rising. The information relayed by black turncoats and the day's delay enabled Virginia's governor to call up 600 troops, search out the conspirators, and punish them. Gabriel was caught, placed on trial, and hanged after refusing to name his co-leaders. Another thirty-five rebels were captured and executed. An 'Easter Plot', led by one of Gabriel's followers, broke out in Halifax County, Virginia two years later, but that also failed.[67]

The last significant slave revolt in the United States also occurred in Virginia. This was the Nat Turner Rebellion that took place in Southampton County, Virginia on 22 August 1831. The leader, Nat Turner, was a literate slave who was deeply religious and who had suffered under the harsh labour regimes of several white masters. He styled himself as a Baptist preacher, and described mystical visions he had experienced to slave congregations at Sunday prayer meetings. Turner believed the visions drew him towards seeking to free black people from slavery. He planned an insurrection for 22 August 1831.

Nearly sixty men moved swiftly from one house to another, killing whites with axes, guns and clubs as they proceeded. Fifty-five white people were killed. Armed groups of whites, federal troops and the militia killed or captured most of the insurrectionists. Turner evaded apprehension for more than a month but was eventually captured, tried, found guilty and sentenced to death. He recited his *Confessions* as an explanation of his actions and was hanged on 5 November 1831.[68]

The suddenness of Turner's Rebellion and the loss of life sent shock waves through the Virginian white community. The aftermath of the uprising led to the most public and sustained discussion of slavery and emancipation ever held in Virginia or any other southern state. Citizens met in county courthouses to consider the insurrection and to draft petitions to their legislators. Some petitions favoured gradual emancipation; others advocated the removal of free blacks from the state in order to protect slavery. The outcome of the debate was a victory for Virginians who opposed slave emancipation, for the legislature refused to consider any emancipation scheme. This was the last time that this issue was debated publicly in Virginia before the US Civil War. Discussions of Nat Turner's Rebellion eventually led Virginia slaveholders to frame a thorough, formal defence of slavery that greatly influenced antislavery thought in the antebellum era.[69]

SLAVE REVOLTS IN THE CARIBBEAN

Slave revolts in the West Indies threatened white masters more directly than was the case in North America. Most plots, revolts and wars which occurred before the turn of the nineteenth century, however, were relatively small-scale affairs that were easily contained by the authorities on the Caribbean islands. The one exception was Tacky's Rebellion in western Jamaica in 1760. This was the second largest slave insurrection to occur on the island. Led by disaffected Coromantee (i.e. Akan) rebels, this outbreak shook the complacency of the Jamaican plantocracy. The uprising began on Easter Day 1760 with slaves plundering the fort at Port Maria, a small town in northern Jamaica. Armed with muskets and gunpowder, they marched south, gathered recruits and engaged in guerrilla warfare.

Fig. 17: Toussaint L'Ouverture, Saint-Domingue, 1800

The leader Tacky was captured and executed and his own band of rebels was broken up fairly soon. Fighting continued, however, for several months. Firm reprisals were put in place to quell the rebels. Over 400 slaves were killed during the revolt, 100 were executed and about 500 transported to British Honduras. Some sixty whites and sixty free people of colour lost their lives in the conflict.[70]

Tacky's revolt was a combination of three uprisings in Jamaica that demonstrated the slaves' capacity for thorough planning to cause the maximum disruption to the plantation regime.[71] Jamaica's legislators were deeply worried about the impact of Obeah on slave behaviour, whether or not it could be linked to resistance. After the revolt Obeahism was suppressed and greater limits placed on slave meetings and slave access to weapons.[72] White Jamaicans sought to separate racial intermixture in the aftermath of the revolt, and intensified efforts to consolidate white solidarity. The casualties, property loss and population displacement caused by Tacky's Rebellion led white colonists in Jamaica to promote Creole labour among slaves, rather than further imports of Africans; but this goal was not realized for over forty years, arising only after the British abolition of the slave trade in 1807.[73]

Throughout the plantation Americas the only slave rebellion that ever resulted in the overthrow of white power occurred in 1791 in Saint-Domingue (the western half of Hispaniola), where a massive, planned upsurge of 400,000 blacks, led by the free black Toussaint L'Ouverture and inspired by the French Revolution's ideals of liberty, equality and fraternity, saw the overthrow of French overlords and the creation of a black republic. Saint-Domingue was a major plantation colony. By the late 1780s it produced more than half the world's coffee and exported as much sugar as Jamaica, Brazil and Cuba combined.[74] Sharp rises in slave prices occurred in Saint-Domingue in the 1770s and 1780s, testifying to the viability of the plantation system in the leading French West Indian colony.[75] The massive slave revolt of the 1790s shattered Saint-Domingue's economic prosperity.

Whites in Saint-Domingue had failed to apply the French National Assembly's rule of 15 May 1791 that all financially qualified men of colour could be enfranchised and become full citizens. This gave impetus to violence between whites and free people of colour. The confrontation gathered momentum to become a large slave revolt. During the uprising, several bands of maroons terrorized the ports and towns of Saint-Domingue, inciting slave unrest and challenging the French army. Toussaint became commander-in-chief of semi-independent African and 'mulatto' warlords, many of whom had led guerrilla bands before he joined the revolution.[76] Sustained *petit marronage* and secret meetings among slaves and free coloureds preceded the revolt. Leaders of the insurrection included those from the higher ranks of the slave system and those with the semi-free status of *liberté de savanne*.[77]

Worried that the revolt would influence slave behaviour in Jamaica, the British government dispatched troops to occupy Saint-Domingue between 1793 and 1798 in an attempt to restore slavery. The rebellion was highly complex, with different regional reactions throughout Saint-Domingue. Some slaves fought for the rebels while others supported the British forces. Free coloureds adopted highly varied political positions along the spectrum from royalism to republicanism. Many slaves fought for improvements to their working lives rather than embracing an overarching desire for emancipation. Diplomatic manoeuvres by Britain and the United States led to the removal of the British occupying forces in 1798 after more than 30,000 soldiers, seamen and foreign regiments in the British expeditionary force had died during the campaign in Saint-Domingue.[78]

Over the next few years the Haitian slaves won their freedom against 50,000 French troops. Many slaves who fought for freedom had a military background in Africa. They had used muskets and swords in wars in regions such as Lower Guinea and Angola, and had acquired tactical skills in fighting, before they arrived in the Caribbean. This background was of vital importance in their combining with Creole slaves to challenge the French forces.[79] Black troops occupied Spanish Santo Domingo (the eastern half of Hispaniola) by the end of 1800 and in the following year Toussaint was named governor general for life by his supporters. He restored plantation labour with payment for workers, and drafted an autonomous constitution for Saint-Domingue in 1801. Celebrated as a hero in a sonnet by Wordsworth and regarded by progressive reformers as a symbol of resistance, Toussaint ruled Saint-Domingue and negotiated the withdrawal of British troops from the island.[80] He professed loyalty to France at this point in proceedings, and made peace with the white planter class in order to get plantations working again.[81]

Napoleon decided he must restore Saint-Domingue to French control. The arrival of a French revolutionary force in the colony in February 1802 began the most violent phase of the Haitian Revolution. French forces massacred blacks who resisted them fiercely to prevent the restoration of white rule. This military force tricked and arrested Toussaint, who was sent to France, where he died in a dungeon in April 1803.[82] The freed blacks led by Jean-Jacques Dessalines, a former slave, fought back ferociously against Napoleon's troops and eventually achieved success. Two-thirds of the French soldiers died of yellow fever. The French were forced to evacuate the colony before the end of 1803 and on 1 January 1804 Dessalines proclaimed the colony's independence under the name of Haiti.[83] His supporters inflicted systematic massacres on most of the remaining whites in Haiti.[84] Tumultuous changes therefore occurred as the slave colony of Saint-Domingue metamorphosed into the free territory of Haiti. The sheer scale of the success of former slaves overthrowing their French masters led C. L. R. James to call the revolt 'a crucial moment in world history.'[85]

While this was happening, Bonaparte's troops were involved in bitter fighting in Guadeloupe between 1799 and 1802. This was an attempt to restore slavery there. Louis Delgrès, a mixed race colonel born in Martinique, led a slave army in Guadeloupe against the French forces. He and his supporters confronted a superior, well-armed French army. Delgrès and his slave army were defeated at the Battle of Matouba on 28 May 1802. He determined to commit suicide rather than be captured, and set fire to gunpowder barrels distributed among his supporters. When the gunpowder exploded, Delgrès and 500 of his army were killed.[86] Slavery was restored in Guadeloupe, but twenty years after Haiti became independent, planters in Martinique and Guadeloupe still feared that free coloured Haitians would inspire slaves to rebel.[87]

Further slave revolts occurred in the French Caribbean. A rising occurred in February 1831 in St Pierre, Martinique, in which restless, insubordinate slaves tried to set fire to the town and pillage white property. Governor Jean Dupotet of Martinique declared a state of siege and gained support from the militia, the police force, troops and marines to put down the revolt three days after it started.

Another rebellion broke out in St Pierre on 22 May 1848 when the anticipated emancipation of slaves in French colonies failed to materialize. Twenty houses were burned, two men were killed and thirty-two people, mainly whites, were burnt alive. On the following day the provisional governor of Martinique announced slave emancipation, which was declared officially on 4 June 1848.[88]

Curiously, when the ideas and impact of the French Revolution were at their height and the Saint-Domingue slave rebellion was in progress, few slave disturbances happened in Jamaica, which was only a few days' travel by sea from the site of the French rebel slaves' action. There was little overspill from the antislavery success in Saint-Domingue into nearby Jamaica. Moreover, a strong British military presence in the Caribbean during the wars with revolutionary and Napoleonic France helped to maintain order in Jamaica. British garrisons deterred Jamaican slaves from staging a rebellion during the turbulent 1790s. Libertarian ideas stemming from the French revolutionary call for liberty, equality and fraternity, and the revolt in Saint-Domingue, probably influenced free coloureds in Jamaica more than the enslaved population.[89]

The major outbreak of slave discontent in the British Caribbean during the 1790s occurred in Grenada in Fédon's Rebellion in 1795/6. This involved a distinctive Francophone mix of planters, slaves and free coloureds led by the free coloured planter Julien Fédon against Anglophone whites, who had settled in the island after it was ceded to Britain in 1763. Bloody fighting marked this revolt. By January 1796 Fédon's forces controlled all of Grenada save for the capital, but British settlers were helped by armed reinforcements who enabled them to prevail in the struggle. Fédon escaped from the clutches of his enemies and his fate is unknown. The British quashed the rebellion with executions and deportation of captives to foreign territories along the Bay of Honduras. This was the biggest challenge by slaves and their supporters to British authority in the Caribbean in the French revolutionary era. Though it ended in Britain retaining control of Grenada, it caused about £2.5 million damage in property and limited the future expansion of sugar cultivation there. Black Caribs in St Vincent rose up against the plantocracy in the wake of Fédon's revolt and controlled the island for six months before General Sir Ralph Abercromby's expeditionary force, sent from England, defeated the insurgents in early June 1796.[90]

Between January and March 1812 a large slave revolt in Cuba comprised a series of connected uprisings collectively known as the Aponte Rebellion. Slaves and free coloureds combined to seek their freedom after widespread rumours occurred indicating that emancipation was about to happen. An early stage of the uprising in Puerto Principe was easily intercepted; the leaders were caught and publicly executed in the town's central plaza on 29 January 1812. A planned revolt in the eastern town of Bayamo ended on 7 February when a slave informed his master of the insurrection. Revolts erupted on plantations outside Havana on 15 March. Acts of arson occurred on plantations. Slaves and people of colour were armed with machetes and knives, but the government immediately called on the local militia who arrested hundreds of insurgents and suppressed the revolt a day after it had begun. It is unknown whether these were three different rebellions in different places or one unified revolt. In each case, however, slaves and free blacks combined to attack the property of their white masters after coming together by rumours circulating of emancipation, stories of the Haitian Revolution, and the desire for political liberty.[91] After the rebellion was put down, nearly 400 people were convicted of participating in the rebellion; thirty-four leaders were executed; and almost 200 others were flogged in public ceremonies.[92]

Cuba experienced regular slave revolts after 1825. These included attacks on plantations in the western district of Guanajay in August 1833 and insurgencies on a number of estates in Matanzas province in 1839. Uprisings in 1843 and 1844 were the most prominent of these rebellions. Estate owners feared for their lives and livelihoods, and argued that the government should protect them by establishing either a permanent militia or billeting troops in rural areas. The government discarded the idea of positioning a permanent militia in the countryside, owing to the political risks involved, but regular troops were deployed to areas affected by unrest. The planters were not pleased to find, however, that they had to share the cost of deploying troops with the government. In early 1844 rumours spread of a major slave conspiracy in the Salvanilla sugar district of western Cuba. A frenzy ensued. Slaves were beaten gratuitously by government agents, suspects captured and tortured, and persecution was common. By the end of 1844, the conspiracy, known as La Escalera from the ladder to which slaves were bound before being flogged, had led to many punishments and the executions of thirty-nine slaves, thirty-eight free coloureds and one white person. This was not a conspiracy concocted by the authorities but a fully fledged outbreak by slaves. After the revolt was put down, the free coloured leadership in Cuba was severely reduced and Spain tightened its grip on Cuba for several decades thereafter.[93]

In the last phase of slavery in the British Empire, three large revolts broke out in the British Caribbean. They were in Barbados (1816), Demerara (1823) and Jamaica (1831/2). The geographical diversity of these uprisings and their different timing makes it difficult to discern common threads that incited slaves to rebel in each colony. Economic factors may have played some part in two of the rebellions. Barbados in 1816 experienced falling prices and an economic slump in the immediate aftermath of the Napoleonic Wars. Jamaica in 1831 was similarly in the midst of a downturn in economic fortunes. The maturity of the three settlements and the composition of their slave populations appear not to have been influential factors in stimulating revolt.[94]

The spread of information about possibilities for freedom for slaves seems to have provided impetus for these revolts. Rumours of William Wilberforce's attempt to steer a registry bill through Parliament in 1815 were rife before the Barbados Rebellion of 1816.[95] Some slaves thought this was the first step towards their freedom. The Demerara revolt of 1823 occurred several months after the Anti-Slavery Society in London announced its policy of gradual emancipation and the Bathurst circular ushered in a government policy of amelioration (see Chapter 6). For slaves in the colonies, this seemed the first step towards granting freedom. In Jamaica in 1831–2 it was widely known that the British Whig government intended to legislate in favour of slave emancipation as soon as Parliament passed the Great Reform Bill. [96]

The role of missionaries and the emergence of a Creole leadership also helped to stimulate these revolts. Nonconformist missionaries were instructed by their parent bodies not to incite slaves to rebel but to teach them obedience, piety and temperance. Often, however, missionaries on the spot opened their eyes to the iniquities of slavery and found considerable tension between what they were instructed to preach and what they privately felt about the institution of slavery. They also had to cope with planter hostility.[97] Many planters attributed the outbreak of the Jamaican slave revolt of 1831/2 to missionary influence. The planters overreacted in their view of missionaries inciting slaves to rebel. Nevertheless, the mission schools established by nonconformist preachers spread the gospels through a network of literate black deacons, who liaised with the mass of black workers. Thus, in the case of Jamaica, the Baptist missionary William Knibb was stirred to condemn slavery as a result of his sojourn in the western parishes of the island. He became intimately involved with the 1831/2 revolt – known as the Baptist War – and was brought to trial for supposedly inciting the slaves to rebel.[98]

Each of the three late slave rebellions in the British West Indies attracted strong black leaders. Bussa, an African-born slave who was head ranger at Bayleys plantation, St Philip parish, rallied slaves from all over Barbados to join him in a revolt. Though very little is known about him as an individual, he appears to have been a brave military leader who was killed in the final battle of the revolt. Nanny Grigg, a literate domestic slave, also played an important role in urging slaves to rebel.[99] Quamina, senior deacon at Bethel Chapel, assumed the role of figurehead in the Demerara revolt. Though he himself did not bear arms, he was hunted down, shot dead, and his body hung in chains outside Success plantation where the rebellion had begun.[100] Samuel Sharpe, a black deacon in the Baptist church, was the leader of the slaves in the Jamaican insurrection. He symbolized the literate Creole leadership that informed and organized slaves. He liaised with other literate blacks after prayer meetings; addressed his fellow slaves with impassioned commitment; and showed organizational capacity once the revolt began.[101]

The rebellions in Barbados and Demerara lasted for one and two weeks respectively. They involved work stoppages, damage to sugar estates, fighting with the militia, and, after their end, severe reprisals. Around seventy sugar plantations were affected in Barbados and over fifty in Demerara. In both territories around 100 slaves (but only two whites) were killed during the fighting. Captives were tortured. Public executions took place after which heads were displayed on poles. One hundred and seventy blacks were deported from Barbados.[102]

The Jamaican Baptist War was a much larger affair. It broke out suddenly on 27 December 1831, after slaves had had time to rest and plan their activities over Christmas, and it continued until March 1832. Beginning in St James parish, it spread to five other parishes in the western half of the island and involved around 60,000 slaves. The slaves torched sugar estates, engaged in guerrilla warfare and hid in the rugged terrain of the interior. The British military garrison in Jamaica had been reduced by 30 per cent in the two years leading up to the rebellion. The rebel slaves knew this was therefore an opportune time to strike back at the plantocracy. Nevertheless, the militia put down the revolt with great brutality. Over 200 slaves were killed and 312 were executed after trials. More than 300 others were imprisoned or transported. Sam Sharpe, the leader, was captured and hanged at Montego Bay on 23 May 1832.[103]

The three late slave rebellions left varied imprints. Bussa's Rebellion made only a small impact on Barbados. Order was restored. No further slave outbreak on the same scale ever occurred in Barbados. The aftermath of the Demerara revolt was more controversial. This was because the congregational missionary, the Reverend John Smith, was thrown into jail in Demerara on the grounds that he incited the slaves to rebel. He died while imprisoned and this provoked a furore in the British press. Public opinion in Britain was inflamed by the maltreatment of a white clergyman, but abolitionist commentary concentrated on the victimization of rebel slaves. The Jamaican revolt coincided perfectly in its timing with the later stages of the Reform bill struggle in Britain. That continuing tussle in Parliament and throughout the political nation gave considerable impetus to the slave cause because it was widely known that the Great Reform Act would pave the way for slave emancipation, as the Whig government had pledged to carry this out.[104]

SLAVE REVOLTS IN BRAZIL

Slave revolts occurred frequently in early nineteenth-century Bahia – in 1807, 1809, 1813, 1816, 1826, 1827, 1830, and especially in 1835.[105] Very few of these uprisings owed anything to the political ideology of resistance projected by the Haitian uprising and its connection to French revolutionary ideas. Nor were the uprisings influenced by abolitionist campaigning, which was largely absent in

Brazil when they occurred.[106] On the contrary, the revolts were more inspired by African traditions, ideas and symbols that slaves had brought with them to Brazil. During the nineteenth century, a large preponderance of African-born slaves lived in Brazil owing to the continued existence of the transatlantic slave trade to Rio de Janeiro, Pernambuco and other ports until the 1850s. Though some Creoles participated in Brazilian slave uprisings, most people engaged in the insurrections were African-born, especially in Bahia and northeast Brazil. A fair number were African Muslims with military experience from their homelands in Benin. Creole slaves in Brazil had more opportunities to seek manumission than recent African arrivals, and they had more experience in negotiating with the existing authorities. These are among the reasons why revolt was not a major strategy for Brazilian Creole slaves to improve their position.[107]

African-born Muslim slaves (known in Brazil as Malês) played the central role in the major uprising of 1835 in Salvador da Bahia. The leaders planned the uprising to coincide with a religious holiday when police would be diverted to control religious processions away from the main city centre. Rebels took to the streets wearing clothes peculiar to practitioners of Islam. There was an attack on a gaol where a black Muslim leader was being held, but this was suppressed by the firearms of the prison guards. The slaves were overcome by cavalry outside a military barracks and quickly fled. The police found Muslim amulets and papers with prayers and passages from the Koran on the bodies of the fallen rebels. Some rebels wore necklaces inscribed with the name of Dessalines, the leader of the Haitian Revolution. The rebels found little support from Creole slaves or even from the free coloured population, who distanced themselves from the more militant Africans. This divisions of potential rebels enabled the central authorities to overcome the revolt and for slavery to continue in Brazil. Some of the leaders were deported to Africa. The 1835 uprising in Salvador was probably the best-planned urban slave uprising in the history of the Americas, but it was crushed – as nearly all slave uprisings were – by the superior arms and organization of the white authorities.[108] There were no further significant slave revolts in Brazil. The defeat of nearly all slave revolts is a major explanation for the lack of connection between such uprisings and the process of slave emancipation: Saint-Domingue is the one exception to this rule.[109]

5

THE ABOLITION OF THE SLAVE TRADE

Slavery was accepted in many societies from the ancient world to the late Middle Ages without there being major disputes about its legitimacy. Far from being an aberrant status for people, slavery was common in many societies, whether among the city states of ancient Greece and Rome or medieval Russia and the Ottoman Empire.[1] Slaveholding in Europe and the Middle East, unlike transatlantic slavery, did not usually involve racial subjugation. Nor did it require the labour of slaves to cultivate staple crops. In those respects, earlier forms of slavery differed from the dominant form of racial slavery found on plantations that dominated the transatlantic slave experience. But the fact that slavery was already widely condoned before slavery began in the Americas, often with reference to biblical examples, made it easier for European colonizers to make extensive use of Africans throughout the Americas from the sixteenth to the nineteenth centuries.[2]

Though antislavery views were expressed before the period of the European Enlightenment in the mid-eighteenth century, they were few and far between. For the most part, slavery was condoned before c. 1750. Theologians and philosophers generally supported slavery. Thomas Hobbes, for example, in his influential *Leviathan* (1651), argued that slaves were a normal part of human societies, which he regarded as based upon a pyramid of power ranging from slave owners near the top of a vertical hierarchy to enslaved people at the bottom.[3] Antislavery ideas only started to gain wider currency – and they did so fairly rapidly – with the onset of Enlightenment philosophical ideas in the three decades between 1750 and 1780. Such views spread into legal thought and literature. From the American revolutionary era onwards, proslavery and antislavery advocates were locked in a war of ideas and words as they set out their respective views on either the need to retain or overthrow slavery and the slave trade.[4]

Proslavery advocates were dominated by the planters and merchants with direct involvement with slavery and the slave trade. Often they could call upon sympathetic political support from various assemblies, parliaments and monarchs. In Britain the proslavery lobby was dominated by the West India Interest. This was the collective name given to the merchants and planters who were engaged in transatlantic slaving to the Caribbean. Many of these men had made fortunes from their West Indian slave properties and had returned to live in Britain as absentee owners. They were well connected to the political elite.[5] They drew up petitions, wrote pamphlets and lobbied in and out of Parliament to support their case. The planter class repeatedly emphasized their economic importance to the British Empire and countered arguments made by their opponents that free trade and free wage labour should replace protectionism and slavery.[6]

Slavery apologists in Britain influenced proslavery thought in the United States. Writers, preachers and speakers emphasized the servile historical status of black slaves, their degraded life in Africa before enslavement, and the need for slaves to be Christianized and educated before they could be considered for freedom. In keeping with arguments by political economists, proslavery sympathizers viewed slavery as an example of divine trust backed by biblical precedent.[7]

Antislavery ideas first made important headway in the 1750s as a result of Enlightenment ideas spreading notions of human progress and viewing slavery as a regressive institution. The circulation of antislavery ideas occurred rapidly via international networks of thinkers. The key text that began to advance such attitudes was Montesquieu's treatise *L'Esprit des Lois* (1748). This offered an oblique attack upon slavery by suggesting it was morally wrong to keep people in a position of bondage.[8] Montesquieu's work was widely read as an important philosophical work. Scottish philosophers soon took up the lines of argument against slavery that Montesquieu had articulated. Francis Hutcheson and others produced a stream of pamphlets and tracts in the 1750s that extended these views. Antislavery ideas also spread to the realms of law and economics. William Blackstone, the leading British jurist and a conservative commentator, stood out against slavery and the slave trade in his *Commentaries on the Laws of England* (1765-9).[9] Even more important, in the long run, were the arguments of Adam Smith, who offered a strong case for the economic advantages of free wage labour over slave work in *An Inquiry into the Nature and Causes of the Wealth of Nations* (1776). This was based on his view that slave work was relatively unproductive because it was based on coercion of unwilling workers whereas free labour offered wage incentives that could increase productivity.[10]

Antislavery ideas had begun to make some headway in North America by 1776 and their impact escalated in the following quarter-century. Apart from changing philosophical views, condemnation of slaveholding increased among religious groups, especially Protestants. Methodists such as John Wesley and Francis Asbury exhorted against the immorality of slaveholding.[11] Quakers, who were harsh critics of handling stolen goods, from which they could extrapolate to the condition of slaves, denounced slavery and the slave trade as wicked.[12] Evangelicals in the Church of England attacked slavery and the slave trade from the 1780s onwards, viewing the traffic as one that was sinful and in urgent need of cleansing. These groups believed in spreading the Christian concept of benevolence in relation to slavery and the slave trade. They advocated the Pauline injunction to treat other people as one would wish to be treated oneself and applied it to slaves. Two other themes were also frequently put forward. One was an emphasis on God's Providence, explaining that God would reward righteous societies and punish wicked societies. The other was an emphasis on God's progressive revelation, the main idea here being that peace and plenty for societies that eliminated slavery and the slave trade was the earthly sign of providentialism.[13]

Many of these ideas circulated throughout the transatlantic world via correspondence, the spread of printed literature, visits to North America, speeches, sermons and lectures. The Quakers, in particular, played a crucial role in spreading the antislavery message through their strong transatlantic links. Prominent American Friends such as John Woolman and Anthony Benezet publicized the cause both at home and on visits to Britain.[14] The Religious Society of Friends believed in pacifism and condemned warfare; they opposed the capture of slaves in conflicts in West Africa. They believed in the equality of all people in the eyes of God, whatever their skin colour and worldly status. Quakers banned their members from engaging in the slave trade and disapproved of Friends owning slaves. Yet even for the Quakers, the crusade against slaveholding did not come easily. In the American heartland of Quakerism – Pennsylvania and New Jersey – Friends strived for generations until about 1770 before it was accepted that slaveholding among their members should end.[15]

Dissemination of antislavery ideas was a necessary preliminary step for nations considering whether to abolish their slave trade, but the influence of such attitudes on individual acts of abolition varied considerably. In some countries, the protests taken against the slave trade led to the growth of lobby and pressure groups, usually influenced by Christian principles. These groups played an active part in persuading governments that humanitarian concerns about the immorality of the slave trade should lead to abolition. In other countries, such pressure groups were of much more limited significance and had little to do with slave trade abolition. This was the case even though all countries with a flourishing slave trade in the age of the French Revolution had widespread channels of influential communication, through meetings, correspondence, speeches and petitions, many of which emphasized international concerns about the continued existence of slavery and the slave trade.[16]

Networks of anti-slave trade sympathizers and strategies for circulating their ideas proliferated from the late 1780s onwards, inspired initially by Anglo-American cooperation against the slave trade by Quakers and evangelical Anglicans. The humiliation of Britain's loss of her American colonies in 1783 appeared to provide an ideal context for anti-slave trade sympathizers to promote their activities as an atonement for national sins and to attack a vulnerable political establishment in Britain.[17] But the work of Quakers and Anglican evangelicals in the years immediately after the American revolutionary war (1783–6) does not suggest that they could exploit any loss of confidence in Britain's economic stability and superiority. On the contrary, Britain in 1788, when the first slave trade enquiries arising from abolitionist agitation were heard in Parliament, had many signs of imperial confidence and continued attachment to slavery and West India trade.[18] Thus it was difficult for opponents of the slave trade to secure their aims swiftly; strongly entrenched pro-slave trade supporters resisted arguments put forward by abolitionists and organized their own groups to uphold the status quo. Those opposed to the slave trade soon realized it was best to campaign against the slave trade rather than combine that with an abolitionist thrust against slavery at the same time. In most cases, abolition of the slave trade preceded slave emancipation by roughly a quarter of a century.[19]

DENMARK

Denmark, a relatively minor player in the Atlantic slave trade, became the first nation to abolish its slave trade permanently. Antislavery literature circulated in Copenhagen by the late 1780s, mainly in periodical articles translated from English and French, but it had relatively little influence on the decision to end the Danish slave trade. Ruled by the monarch of Denmark-Norway and without a parliament, Denmark's slave trade was ended by a royal edict of 16 March 1792 that was intended to come into effect on 1 January 1803. The abolition arose largely from economic reasons. A Great Negro Trade Commission was established in Denmark in 1791 to consider whether the Danish slave trade could be abolished while ensuring that sugar production in Danish Caribbean colonies, notably in St Croix, could continue. Its conclusion was that allowing between 30,000 and 45,000 slaves to be imported into Danish territories during the 1790s would increase the labour force of the sugar plantations sufficiently to enable an abolition of the Danish slave trade to occur. The commission was influenced strongly by the ideas of Ernst Schimmelmann, a wealthy and influential German-born politician, who argued that slaves in Danish territories could survive by natural reproduction without the need for a constant flow of saltwater Africans.[20] Schimmelmann and other statesmen thought Denmark could attempt to develop plantations in Africa that were free of slave labour. This argument also influenced the decision to abolish the Danish slave trade because such attempts would render the slave trade superfluous.[21]

The Danish Negro Slave Trade Commission was aware of the agitation that had placed consideration of the slave trade on the British parliamentary agenda in 1788. It met and debated the clauses encapsulated in the royal edict of 1792 with the expectation that Britain was about to abolish its slave trade. Details of the horrors of the Middle Passage, taken from writings by Thomas Clarkson and Alexander Falconbridge, informed the discussions, but there was no strong impetus to end the Danish slave trade on humanitarian grounds. Instead, there was an agreement that Denmark should continue with slavery and sugar plantations for the foreseeable future, and that slave trade abolition needed to be calculated in terms of the projected number of slaves for Danish plantations to maintain productivity. This consideration lay behind the time lag between the royal edict of 1792 and implementation of the policy in 1803. In Britain, William Wilberforce, addressing the House of Commons on 2 April 1792, noted that Denmark 'had already rejected the foul intercourse. It was a noble achievement, and should make Britons blush to have missed the opportunity of leading the glorious example.'[22] Denmark, however, never benefited fully from the intentions of the 1792 ordinance because self-reproduction of its slave population was never achieved.[23]

BRITAIN AND THE UNITED STATES

The abolition of the British and US slave trades were two separate proscriptions of transatlantic slaving that occurred proximately in time. In less than a month in the spring of 1807, Britain and the United States independently agreed to legislate against the continuing importation of African slaves to their territories. In Britain, the statute to abolish the slave trade was passed by both houses of Parliament on 25 March 1807. In the United States, the House of Representatives voted on 2 March 1807 by 113 to 5 votes to end slave imports to the United States. This was approved by the Senate, with the blessing of President Thomas Jefferson. The American act of abolishing the slave trade became effective on 1 January 1808. The British act to abolish the slave trade stipulated that no vessel could clear (from customs) after 1 May 1807, and that no slaving vessel could land in the British West Indies after 1 March 1808.[24] Britain and the United States were aware of each other's political progress towards abolition. There was a degree of competition to see which nation would have the honour of being first in the race.[25]

These twin abolitionist measures were important landmarks in the history of abolitionism. Britain and the United States were the first major slave trading nations to end their transatlantic slave trades once and for all. In both cases, the slave trade would have continued, perhaps indefinitely, if the bans had not taken place, for there was always a demand from the Americas for more slaves. Statistics show the continuing significance of the British and US slave trades when abolition occurred. Between 1800 and 1808, British ships delivered 288,000 slaves to the Americas, principally to the Caribbean. Some West Indian destinations were British colonies; others were territories captured by the British from the French and the Dutch during the Napoleonic Wars.[26] In the first decade of the nineteenth century, when slave imports to the United States were confined exclusively to the Lower South, nearly 67,000 Africans arrived in the Carolinas and Georgia.[27]

The different political traditions of Britain and the United States had a significant bearing on the process of slave trade abolition. In Britain, the parliamentary tradition ensured that an end to the slave trade could only come about by a law passed within the context of a unitary state based on parliamentary sovereignty and a constitutional monarchy. In the federal and republican United States, individual states could enact laws against slave importation to their own jurisdictions, but a total ban could only happen with congressional approval based upon the constitutional decision (effectively preserving states' rights) that no interference could take place with slave imports until twenty years after the US Constitution was ratified in 1788. From 1794 onwards Congress passed a series of laws aimed at restricting Americans from participation in the slave trade, but it was not feasible to produce a bill to eliminate all American involvement in the trade until *c.* 1807.[28]

Despite these differences, commonalities existed in the processes that led to abolition. The humanitarian morality of the fight against the slave trade in both countries was a notable point of contact between the two abolitions. Both slave trades needed to find political mechanisms to enable protests to be mobilized both at the extra-institutional level through speeches, petitions, lobbying and other forms of pressure, both at grassroots level and through the enactment of laws. Both Britain and the United States needed major spokesmen to protest about the inhuman aspects of bondage and the ethical need to end slave trafficking. Both countries took account of how abolition of the slave trade related to the wider issues of the persistence of slavery in the United States and in the British Empire and the ultimate goal of slave emancipation in both nations. In both cases, activists realized they were involved in pursuing 'a mighty experiment.'[29] Britain and the United States experienced abolitionist arguments formulated over several decades, a struggle against the slave trade that was hard-fought and countered by strong vested interests, and a need to find a way in which the timing of abolition would work.[30]

Britain had a more nationally organized abolitionist movement than the United States at the turn of the nineteenth century. This occurred despite the fact that many abolitionist ideas were first aired in North America before they spread to Britain and despite the further fact that the American Revolution broadcast the themes of republicanism, liberty and natural rights, while Britain avoided the implementation of revolutionary principles and republicanism. Slaves were, of course, a visible presence in North America, whereas there were none in England. The reason for the divergent abolitionist thrust in both countries did not result from differences in moral ideas, for they were very similar in both cases; it lay in mobilization and organization. Put simply, American abolitionism flourished at the local and colony/state level for the most part and experienced considerable fragmentation, whereas British abolitionism found a national direction through the work of the Society for Effecting the Abolition of the Slave Trade, established in London in 1787. Though this drew upon provincial opinion, its regular meetings in London gave it a strong focus in the nation's capital.[31]

The Society for Effecting the Abolition of the Slave Trade was close-knit and dominated by Quakers. It met regularly and focused on mobilization of public opinion against the slave trade, leaving campaigns against slavery to the future. The Society distributed many tracts through a network of booksellers. It campaigned vigorously up and down the length and breadth of Britain, notably in 1787–92, the years when abolitionism first made a significant impact in Parliament. The Society could point to the humanitarian scandal caused by the crew of the Liverpool slave ship *Zong* throwing 132 slaves overboard to drown when potable water ran out during the Middle Passage, and then trying to claim insurance against their loss when the vessel reached Jamaica. The owners took the case to court, but Lord Chief Justice Mansfield ruled against them on the grounds that the captain and crew were at fault. The Society gathered evidence on the conduct of the slave trade from Thomas Clarkson's indefatigable gathering of oral information from leading British slaving ports. It marshalled this evidence effectively and swiftly so that the evils of the slave trade – the cruel treatment of slaves, the separation of families, the abundant mortality, the horrors of the Middle Passage – were brought before parliamentary committees. A vigorous petitioning campaign and the use of symbolic emblematic material – notably the widely circulated engraving of the Liverpool slave ship *Brookes* – had a vital impact on bringing home the abolitionist message to Britain's parliamentarians and the British people.[32]

American abolitionism in the 1780s had nothing like this effect. There was no national organization for the movement, which is not surprising in a new nation still to work out an effective national government; abolitionism mainly existed at the regional or state level and was heavily concentrated in the northern states.[33] In addition, American antislavery and, to a lesser extent, moves towards slave manumission were a stronger thrust than abolitionism during the 1780s when anti-slave trade campaigning first became prominent in British public life. Rather than having a strong, organized group of abolitionists in the nation's major city, as Britain did from 1787 onwards, Americans had societies with names that indicated they were not entirely concerned with agitation against the slave trade but focused more generally on opposing slavery. This is true of the Pennsylvania Abolition Society (which, however, did expend energy on anti-slave trade petitions) and the New York Manumission Society. In the late eighteenth century Americans favouring liberty on racial grounds focused their energies more on enacting anti-slavery legislation, such as the gradual emancipation laws in Pennsylvania, New Jersey and New York, rather than coordinated attacks upon the slave trade.[34]

Americans concentrated more on the inequity of slavery than on the evils of the slave trade because slavery existed on American soil and was an unavoidable part of life there, especially in the South, whereas British slavery existed three or four thousand miles away from home, in the Caribbean, and was therefore out of sight. Some American laws nevertheless included bans on the slave trade at state level. This is true, for example, of Virginia's ending of the slave trade in 1778 or Pennsylvania's gradual abolition law of 1780.[35] By the late 1780s, however, the United States had a greater emphasis on limiting slavery in a gradual way rather than focusing on slave trade proscription as such.

Abolitionist organization had by the turn of the nineteenth century registered some notable achievements in Britain and the United States. In the North American sphere, several northern states, including New York and New Jersey, had banned slave imports by the time the US Constitution was ratified. By then, only two American states – Georgia and North Carolina – still allowed slave imports, South Carolina having banned slave imports in March 1787. A decade later, when Georgia closed its slave trade in 1798, only South Carolina was left as a state that still imported Africans.[36] In the British case, abolitionist pressure in Parliament led to the passing of Dolben's Act (1788), which restricted the number of slaves who could be carried in relation to the tonnage of a vessel; to a vote by the House of Commons in 1792 that the British slave trade in principle should end in 1796, though that did not happen then; and to further restrictions on slave carrying by ships in a statute of 1799.[37]

In both the American and British cases, however, abolitionist pressure was only partly responsible for these achievements. Some American states banned slave imports mainly for economic reasons. Thus Virginia's ban on slave imports in 1778 was driven by an economic need to protect a regional economy that already had a surplus of slaves.[38] Economic depression lay behind South Carolina's prohibitory act dealing with slave imports in 1787.[39] In Britain, a more direct connection can be traced between abolitionist campaigning and restrictions on the slave trade, such as Dolben's Act and the Slave Carrying Act of 1799. It might be argued, however, that the restrictions were an attempt by Parliament to improve the conditions on board slave ships in order to keep the slave trade in operation on a more humane basis.[40] Abolitionism itself could not end the slave trade from Britain or to the United States. It was necessary instead for abolitionist ideas and pressure to coincide with political campaigning and with appropriate timing to achieve success.

The political agitation concerning slave trade abolition was, at first sight, quite different in the United States and Britain, though there was congruence in the timing of abolitionist legislation in both nations. In the United States, the first Continental Congress was the first body (in 1774) to state that slave imports should be ended to the British North American colonies. This decision was bound up with the non-importation of British goods as a result of the Coercive Acts of 1774. But it carried no threat of action because the Continental Congress lacked powers of enforcement.[41] The slave trade was omitted from the Articles of Confederation (1781), which would not in any case have had the political power to force the new US states to comply.[42]

It was not until the Constitutional Convention of 1787 that political manoeuvring to secure a slave trade ban first became important at a national level. Delegates were divided about what to do, constitutionally, about the African slave trade because the differing views of individual states had to be accommodated. The end result was a compromise between the New England states and the Lower South over slave imports. This unlikely set of bedfellows came about through the economic needs of the respective states. New Englanders wanted protection for their commodity imports, while Georgia and South Carolina wanted to retain the option to open or close their ports to slave imports depending on their economic situation. The result was an agreement to insert Article 1, Section 9 in the Constitution (supported by Article V) banning federal interference with slave imports for twenty years – until 1808.[43]

At both the constitutional convention and during the ratification process in the states, delegates and other interested parties put forward various views in favour or against the slave trade clause in the Constitution.[44] Virginians, in particular, were divided over the issue. Some leading Virginian planters, such as George Mason and James Madison, would have been happy to see the slave trade closed. William Livingston of New Jersey and other delegates realized, however, that the slave trade had to remain open for South Carolina and Georgia to agree to join the American Union.[45] It has been suggested that the threat by the South Carolinians and Georgians to secede from the Union unless they got their way over the slave trade clause was a bluff, though in other respects politicians and voters in both these states knew they would benefit from ratification.[46] But if one looks at the language used by the delegates from South Carolina during the Philadelphia debates, it is explicit and not at all equivocal: the words do not sound like a bluff.[47]

Political action over banning slave imports to the United States was effectively stymied in the twenty years after 1788 by Article 1, Section 9 of the Constitution. The matter of the slave trade continued to be raised in a national context, but only to have hopes dashed for abolitionists. In 1790, for example, the first federal Congress dealt with petitions opposing the slave trade. The petitions were dismissed and reference was made to the constitutional clause as the reason why the matter was considered untouchable.[48] During the 1790s the question arose about the importation of slaves to federal territories. This was something on which Congress could act because the territories, unlike the states, were under federal control. Thus in 1798 Congress forbade slave importation from abroad into the Mississippi Territory. This was extended in 1804 to a congressional ban on slaves imported to the Orleans Territory and to the rest of the Louisiana Purchase, a vast territory of 828,000 square miles then just bought by the United States from France.[49] This did not resolve the fact that South Carolina and Georgia could not be forced to close their slave trades. Georgia, in fact, closed slave imports in 1798, as already mentioned. But South Carolina wanted to retain its states' right over this matter, and accordingly it opened and closed its slave trade as its House of Assembly decided.[50]

While progress over eradicating the slave trade was impeded by the US Constitution's protective clause, the British drive to abolish the slave trade had more scope for political pressure at the national level. Abolitionists had established substantial 'moral capital' for attacking the slave trade.[51] Beyond Parliament, grass-roots campaigning by abolitionists made significant advances in the late 1780s and 1790s. By 1792 over a fifth of the adult British male population – a higher proportion than those who were enfranchised – had signed anti-slave trade petitions calling for an end to the British slave trade.[52] Many tracts and pamphlets criticized the slave trade. Artefacts publicizing the abolitionist cause were widely circulated. These included the medallion sponsored by the pottery manufacturer Josiah Wedgwood, with the inscription 'Am I a Slave and a Brother?' placed above the figure of a kneeling slave with his hands in chains – an iconic emblem of the anti-slave trade campaigns.[53] The outbreak of war between Britain and France in 1793 and its long gestation into the early nineteenth century made it difficult for parliamentarians to conceive of slave trade abolition. British statesmen found more pressing matters to deal with, and the bloodshed caused by the Saint-Domingue slave rebellion (1791) and attempts to restore civil order there made tampering with the slave trade seem foolhardy.[54]

In both the British and American cases, however, there was no indication by 1803–4 that slave imports would be ended legally in the near future. In the United States, the prospects for a total ban on slave imports seemed to fade with the reopening of South Carolina's slave trade in 1803, which had the varied purposes of bringing in Africans to maximize cotton production, to eradicate illegal slave shipments from the Caribbean, and to extend slavery to the Louisiana Purchase.[55] Yet within four years, both Britain and the United States had enacted laws proscribing the slave trade in their respective jurisdictions. The timing of these moves is significant. Though the processes operated differently, the interplay between abolitionism, political manoeuvring, and the political and economic context in each nation illuminates the decisions for abolition.

In Britain the movement against the slave trade was transformed by parliamentary recognition that at least two-thirds of the Africans taken in British vessels were sold in foreign and conquered territories in the Caribbean – primarily Dutch, French and Spanish settlements – after 1800. The reason for this lay in the higher slave sale prices gained there at this time than in the British Caribbean. Parliament considered it a dangerous practice in wartime for Britain to be supplying slaves to enemies who would thereby increase their own slave populations and plantation output at Britain's expense. After Britain had gained naval command on the oceans after the defeat of France at the Battle of Trafalgar (1805), the time seemed ripe for action.[56] Measures against the slave trade occurred swiftly. After the House of Commons in 1805 rejected the abolitionist call for an end to the British slave trade, Wilberforce explained to Prime Minister Pitt that abolitionism could not sustain another similar setback. Pitt, taking note of this view, issued an order-in-council of 1805 to end the British slave trade to foreign and conquered colonies. This was confirmed in a parliamentary act of 1806.[57] These twin, related measures transformed the prospects for abolition. Only Jamaica, Trinidad and British Guiana of the British Caribbean colonies had a buoyant slave market by 1805.[58]

With the death of Pitt in 1806 and the installation of a new coalition ministry sympathetic to abolition, and the depleted state of the British slave trade, it was relatively straightforward for a final assault on the British slave trade in Parliament. Roger Anstey once referred to the timing of this particular politico-economic juncture being favourable to abolition because of the number of abolitionist sympathizers in the 'Ministry of all the Talents.'[59] The arguments made in Parliament in 1806–7 against the slave trade combined an abolitionist thrust with emphasis on the poor state of the British sugar market. Parliament voted overwhelmingly in favour of slave trade abolition in 1807. Historians have long debated contentiously where the final push for abolition was mainly owing to abolitionist pressure on Parliament or by parliamentary recognition that the slave trade was economically redundant. Eric Williams and Seymour Drescher's arguments best represent the opposing poles of these arguments, though many other historians have contributed to the debate.[60]

It seems to me, however, that it is a false dichotomy to set up abolitionism on the one hand and economic deficiencies on the other: there were elements of both in the 1807 decision to end the slave trade. What seems more important is that Parliament responded to a wartime situation involving geopolitical matters and rival slave and sugar economies with a strong dose of national patriotism to end the slave trade, and to do so in the three stages mentioned: the order-in-council of 1805, the act against supplying slaves to foreign and conquered colonies of 1806, and the final act of abolition in 1807. These achievements effectively snuffed out the development of plantation economies in Trinidad, Demerara, Essequibo and Berbice until after British slave emancipation in 1834. Abolitionism had created an intellectual and moral climate in which the slave trade seemed unenlightened and regressive, but it was a mixture of political manoeuvring and considerations of the geopolitical position of Britain's slave trade that led to abolition. Abolitionism itself could not achieve this result.

In the United States, the reopening of South Carolina's slave trade in 1803 was influenced by a coalition of upcountry planters needing unfree workers to meet the cotton boom and lowcountry planters recognizing business opportunities.[61] This influx of saltwater Africans into South Carolina was not strictly needed economically, however, because an interstate slave trade, with its base in the Upper South, had been supplying slaves to the southwest and expanding areas of slavery since the late 1780s. In addition, good demographic conditions for the growth of American-born slaves existed.[62] Not all South Carolinians wanted the slave trade reopened, but attempts to close it, even with governor's support, failed in 1804, 1805 and 1806, largely because a lucrative market for slaves in New Orleans was available.[63]

The only way in which the South Carolina slave trade could be proscribed once and for all was to invoke the constitutional clause that lapsed in 1808. Jefferson did so in his annual message to Congress on 2 December 1806 when he indicated that the day was drawing near when a federal ban on slave imports could take place.[64] His call to action over a total ban of foreign slave importations to the United States proceeded uncontroversially. As Robin Blackburn notes, it was a 'quiet abolition.'[65] Political negotiations occurred during the congressional debates, with a different bill introduced by each house, but a clear-cut decision was reached to end the trade.[66] No southerner in Congress was willing to defend the international slave trade at this juncture.[67] Abolitionism was noticeably absent from the congressional debates. This was unsurprising given that moral views on the slave trade had not been expressed seriously in Congress from its first meetings in 1789–90 until 1807.[68] Congressional debates over ending the US slave trade in 1807 focused not on ending the trade as such but rather on the status of blacks illegally imported.[69] The American end of the slave trade succeeded because it compartmentalized a specific part of the problem of slavery that could, in 1808, lead to federal action on constitutional grounds.

INTERNATIONAL ACTION AGAINST THE SLAVE TRADE

After the dual abolitions of their respective slave trades in 1807–8,

Britain and the United States exercised influence on further prohibitions of the traffic. But the sheer growth of the slave trade for over forty years thereafter, largely to Brazil and Cuba (as Chapter 1 has shown), suggests that the influence of the dual abolitions on the abolition of the slave trade by other powers was somewhat limited.[70] Britain nevertheless undertook the role of controlling the continuing transatlantic slave trades after 1808 by maintaining a West Africa Squadron in the Atlantic to intercept suspected illegal shipments of slaves. This preventative body increased the numbers of its vessels over time.[71] Courts of Mixed Commission and Vice-Admiralty courts in Sierra Leone and Cape Town were established in which British, Portuguese, Spanish, Dutch and Brazilian judges heard cases. British diplomacy, in particular, proved influential in securing the formal abolition of the Dutch, French, Spanish and Portuguese slave trades between 1814 and 1830. Only the newly independent republics in Venezuela and Argentina ushered in abolition on their own, between 1810 and 1813, partly because they wanted British recognition of their new status. In few cases of abolition after the British ending of the slave trade were grassroots anti-slave trade movements important for influencing the course of action. Of greater importance was the example set by Britain and the demonstration that nations with flourishing slave trades could bring transatlantic slaving to an end.[72]

Britain, in particular, expended a great deal of effort to eradicate the international slave trade. These initiatives ranged widely in geographical terms. They included the writings, speeches, lobbying activity and petitions of abolitionists; various organizations that served as foci for these initiatives; diplomatic pressures and negotiations between government officials, abolitionists, and representatives and statesmen of other nations; the efforts of the Royal Navy to suppress slave trading off the West African coast; the contribution of the Mixed Commission and Vice-Admiralty Courts in freeing Africans who had been illegally forced into the transatlantic slave trade; and Britain's contributions to international treaties and conferences. The Mixed Commission Courts, resulting from bilateral treaties between Britain and Portugal, Spain, the Netherlands, Brazil and the United States (1817–62), were most active when in the hands of British commissioners.[73] Some British measures to suppress the Atlantic slave trade focused on West Africa. The Royal Navy, for example, staged a naval blockade of Ouidah, the main port for the Kingdom of Dahomey, and intervened militarily in Lagos, both in 1851–2.[74] The British took nearly 90 per cent of all captured slave ships in the nineteenth century. Nearly 200,000 slaves were liberated from those vessels.[75] Nevertheless, there were strict practical and strategic limitations to the use of force to achieve an international abolition of transatlantic slaving. In the 1840s and 1850s Britain had no legal authority to search slave ships sailing between Angola and Brazil. Operational and diplomatic impediments also hampered attempts to curtail that branch of the trade. The United States refused to join the system of mixed commissions until Abraham Lincoln became President in 1861.[76] The United States did not accept mutual rights of search with the British and by the late 1830s the American flag was often used as a cover for Spanish and Portuguese slave traders.[77] Britain itself could not command total acquiescence from its own citizens in relation to slave trade suppression. While Britain was acting from a morally high position to seek to close the slave trades of other powers, some British merchants continued to provide capital, credit, goods and insurance to foreign slave traders. Sometimes this happened because new supplies of slaves were needed for British-owned enterprises in South America, such as gold mines in Brazil and copper mines in Cuba.[78]

THE NETHERLANDS

The Netherlands cast aside its slave trade quietly. The Dutch slave trade had already dwindled substantially before the onset of the French Revolutionary and Napoleonic Wars. Britain had captured Dutch colonies on the 'wild coast' of South America during that conflict. Demerara, Essequibo, Berbice and Suriname were dominated by British planters in the latter stages of the wars, and were still in British hands in 1806 when the British Parliament passed an act to end the supply of slaves to foreign and conquered colonies. Thus, ipso facto, the Dutch slave trade ended at that time. Suriname, the most thriving of the Dutch plantation economies, ceased to import slaves legally. The ending of the Dutch slave trade was characterized by political pragmatism rather than humanitarian motives. The new king, Willem I, had spent several years living in exile in Britain; he agreed to abolish the Dutch slave trade to please the British and gain their support for the return of conquered colonies to the Netherlands at the Congress of Vienna in 1814/15. This occurred without abolitionist pressure in the Netherlands.[79]

Formal acceptance of the abolition of the slave trade was one condition under which Britain returned Suriname to the Dutch king in 1814. Shortly after the formation of the new kingdom of the Netherlands, on 15 June 1814, an order-in-council made slave trading from Dutch ports illegal. An Anglo-Dutch treaty signed two months later included an article to abolish the Dutch slave trade. On 4 May 1818 Britain and the Netherlands signed a separate bilateral treaty to end the slave trade. This was largely observed by Dutch merchants, though some illegal trafficking of slaves continued. To ensure compliance with the agreements, Anglo-Dutch courts were established in Sierra Leone and Suriname. Curtailment of the Dutch slave trade was therefore achieved without controversy through executive and diplomatic action rather than through the activities of abolitionists.[80]

FRANCE

French attempts to abolish the slave trade were poorly supported by abolitionists and were protracted for political reasons. France abolished slavery, but not her slave trade, during the French Revolution. An abolitionist movement known as the Société des Amis des Noirs, supported by British abolitionist literature, had been formed in 1788 under the leadership of the journalist Jacques Pierre Brissot. Concentrating its activities on legislative change rather than appealing to public opinion, this society was banned by Robespierre and his supporters during the Terror of 1793. The French Convention emancipated slaves in the Caribbean in 1794, effectively ending the French slave trade, but Napoleon restored slavery in 1802 while fighting unsuccessfully to regain the rebellious colony of Saint-Domingue. While Napoleon remained in power, abolitionism was suppressed effectively.[81] In 1814 Napoleon abdicated as Emperor of France and in the following year, returning from exile on Elba, he abolished the French slave trade. This was an attempt to gain British support during his last 100 days as emperor. The tactic did not work. At the end of the Napoleonic Wars, however, the restored Bourbon regime of Louis XVIII was persuaded under British pressure to maintain the ban.[82]

France took further measures against the slave trade in 1817–18, but these failed to stop illegal supplies of enslaved Africans reaching the French Caribbean. The French government, aware that its planters had been denied access to a new supply of slaves by the British occupations during the Napoleonic Wars, made little effort to curtail the slave trade.[83] Patrols against the French slave trade emerged slowly but became operational in late 1823. Further significant action against the French slave trade took place after the Revolution of 1830. In the following year the July monarchy passed a law that sanctioned the seizure of French slave ships and the imprisonment of their owners, and finalized negotiations with Britain in two treaties providing for the mutual right of search of suspected slaving vessels off the West African coast. This treaty of suppression of the slave trade was consolidated in a further treaty of 1833. Though French abolitionist organizations existed at this time, these developments owed more to direct French government action and British pressure than to French enthusiasm for abolitionist ideas and activities.[84]

PORTUGAL AND BRAZIL

Ending the slave trade to American territories connected with the Iberian powers was a lengthy process. Both Portugal and Spain agreed to abolish the slave trade under British diplomatic pressure. Courts of Mixed Commission were established at Sierra Leone and Havana to intercept prizes taken. But this proved ineffective because Spain and Portugal proved unwilling to take action against their own nationals. The Portuguese government in Lisbon came under pressure from Britain to abolish their slave trade between 1807 and 1834, but successfully resisted demands for abolition.[85]

Diplomatic pressure eventually delivered a more decisive attack against the Iberian powers' continuing involvement in transatlantic slaving. In 1835 Britain persuaded Spain to sign a convention that allowed for proper right-of-search clauses. In 1839 the British foreign secretary Lord Palmerston gained parliamentary agreement that the Admiralty could capture any slaver bearing the Portuguese flag as if it were a British vessel. The Aberdeen Act of 1845 placed ships carrying Brazilian colours in the same category as Portuguese vessels.[86] These measures eliminated some of the slaving traffic, but the demand for slaves in Brazil was so large that the prospects of fully enforcing anti-slave trade measures seemed unpromising by the late 1840s.[87]

The long-drawn-out negotiations by which Britain tried to pressurize first Portugal and then Brazil (after its independence in 1822) to curtail the slave trade are testimony to the limits of diplomacy in relation to anti-slave trade measures. In 1815 British diplomatic pressure gained the assurance of Portugal that its slave trade north of the Equator should be made illegal. This ended the delivery of slaves to some parts of Brazil – Bahia, Pernambuco and Maranhão – but left open the larger slave traffic from Angola to southern Brazil. This underscored the point that slave trade prohibition was not equivalent to slave trade suppression. For many years after the end of the Napoleonic Wars, the greater part of the Brazilian slave trade was sheltered from interference by the British navy.[88] Nevertheless, for nearly half a century Britain pursued a moral crusade against the Brazilian slave trade that cost £12.4 million between 1816 and 1865.[89]

Newly independent Brazil had no interest in an immediate abolition of the slave trade. But after protracted negotiations, an Anglo-Brazilian anti-slave trade treaty was agreed in 1826 by which Britain recognized Brazilian independence in return for a guarantee that Brazil would abolish its trade. Though an official end to the trade occurred in 1830, illegal slave trading continued for the next two decades. Successive Brazilian governments proved ineffective at limiting the flow and Britain did not have the naval capacity to patrol Brazil's extensive coastline. British attempts to exert further diplomatic pressure on the Brazilian government to introduce more effective anti-slave trade legislation came to nothing during the rest of the 1830s. By 1840 no workable Anglo-Portuguese anti-slave trade treaty had been signed and the British navy had only limited ways in which it could suppress the illegal slave traffic to Brazil. The British West African and South American squadrons lacked the necessary numbers and speed of ships to prevent this trade.[90]

Between 1839 and 1844 the British government persisted in its efforts to strengthen the Anglo-Brazilian anti-slave trade treaty of 1826. Lord Aberdeen's Act of 1845 instructed British warships to seize all Brazilian ships engaged in the slave trade and to use British Vice-Admiralty courts to adjudicate the vessels confiscated. This unilateral action involved abandoning the official joint efforts of previous diplomacy. In the late 1840s the British navy captured unprecedented numbers of ships taking enslaved Africans illegally to Brazil. By late 1849 the Brazilian minister of justice, Eusébio de Queirós, began to enforce existing laws against the slaving traffic in the waters near Rio de Janeiro.[91] In 1849–50 Britain deployed naval vessels to arrest slave vessels in Brazilian rivers and ports even though such action violated the sovereignty of an independent state.[92]

The abolition of the Brazilian slave trade in 1850 was a sudden action that did not result from internal abolitionist pressure in Brazil. It is unclear whether slave resistance in Brazil created sufficient fear for the authorities to implement slave trade abolition, or whether the yellow fever epidemic in Bahia in October 1849 played a role in suppression of the traffic.[93] But it is clear the slave trade abolition arose through diplomatic and political pressure from Britain and from the willingness of the Brazilian cabinet to sanction the measure. Britain's naval patrol of Brazilian waters attempted to demonstrate the effectiveness of intervention at a time when free trade supporters were placing pressure on Parliament to abandon the naval squadron as being ineffective and as an impediment to the free exchange of goods with Brazil – a major market for British exports. Ignoring Brazilian sovereignty, British vessels seized and destroyed slaving vessels in Brazilian waters. In one notable attack, in 1850, HMS *Cormorant* burned two ships at Paranaguá that had landed 800 slaves. Brazil proved unable to resist the seizures.[94] Palmerston took advantage of the freedom given under acts of 1839 and 1845 for the Royal Navy to intervene against Portuguese and Brazilian slavers without territorial restrictions. Brazil protested against such actions, but the objections were ignored by the British Foreign Office.[95]

The Brazilian legislature became alarmed at the threat posed by Palmerston's gunboat diplomacy backed by the world's most powerful navy. It therefore initiated debates about whether to abolish the slave trade. Brazil's politicians wanted to avoid a commercial blockade of their ports by the British navy and also to avoid war. The Royal Navy ceased its depredations for six months to allow the Brazilians to sort out their own policies that might lead to ending the slave trade, but resumed the attacks when action failed to materialize. Brazil's government decided that it was time to act: their decision was accelerated by British pressure.[96] Without any strong anti-slave trade sentiment in Brazil and the inclination to avoid armed conflict with Britain, but also with the clear sense that ending the slave trade would have little effect on the status of slavery in Brazil, the Brazilian government acted swiftly to terminate slave imports. It helped the Brazilian government that considerable hostility existed against the Portuguese, who dominated the slave trade to Brazilian ports. There is little firm evidence to suggest that it was in the economic interests of Brazil to curtail her slave trade because the sugar and coffee sectors of her economy still had a demand for enslaved Africans.[97]

SPAIN AND CUBA

British attempts to persuade Spain to curtail its slave trade lasted for half a century after the end of the Napoleonic Wars. An Anglo-Spanish treaty of 1817 ended the Spanish slave trade from May 1820 in return for £400,000 in British compensation. But implementation of the treaty was difficult to achieve as the two main colonies affected, Cuba and Puerto Rico, were adamantly opposed to ending the slave trade. Royal Navy vessels patrolled in Cuban waters during the 1820s, but there were too many other tasks in the Caribbean for the warships to deal with rather than concentrating on capturing illegal slavers. Moreover, Spanish officials in Cuba gave protection to the illegal suppliers of enslaved Africans. British pressure on Spain and Cuba with respect to the slave trade increased in the 1830s. A treaty of 1835 with Spain provided for the seizure and condemnation of ships carrying equipment specifically intended for the slave trade. Nevertheless, Spain and Cuba were determined to continue their protection of transatlantic slaving because the Cuban plantation economy demanded supplies of Africans. A new penal law of 1845 was enacted after considerable British diplomatic pressure, but the Spanish government reassured Cuban planters that existing slave properties would be protected even if they bought newly imported slaves.[98]

The penal law of 1845 was the only official measure that aimed to counteract the Cuban slave trade for a further twenty years, but it was widely regarded as a failure. Cuban merchants circumvented it partly by using the many available US ships. This was an astute move, as no right of search agreement existed between Britain and the United States. The United States regarded the Caribbean as lying within their sphere of influence, and was opposed to British naval vessels intercepting ships flying the US flag and asking to check their credentials. Britain was worried that the Americans might annex Cuba, but was careful not to antagonize the US government over the continuance of the Cuban slave trade. The reluctance of the American government to interfere over the slave trade to Cuba may have been influenced, to some extent, by the fact that US captains, crews and ships played a vital part in supplying slaves to Cuba.[99]

In 1858 Britain resolved to stop the Cuban slave trade by implementing a gunboat patrol of Cuba but these vessels were soon withdrawn to avoid confrontation with the United States. By 1860 there was still no remedy to the continuance of the Cuban slave trade. Cuba remained a colony of Spain and therefore lacked a government of its own that could determine whether it continued its slave trade. Palmerston, now prime minister, was unwilling to deploy naval vessels against Cuba, on similar lines to the attack on Brazil, because he feared it might foment a slave rebellion and a return to the Spanish absolutism of the 1830s or American action to annex Cuba. He was not in a position to make this an issue over which war would be declared.[100]

Matters changed significantly during the American Civil War. Lincoln's administration fretted that the Confederate states might intervene to control the Cuban slave trade. An Anglo-American slave trade treaty of 1862 brought additional British vessels to Cuban waters in search of illegal slave imports. This measure, known as the Lyons-Seward Treaty, after the British ambassador in Washington, DC and Lincoln's secretary of state, was the first time there had been a combined Anglo-American agreement against the Cuban slave trade. Britain now felt able to strengthen its West Africa Squadron to combat illegal trafficking of Africans on vessels bound for Cuba. In 1863 Britain and the United States increased their naval presence in Cuban waters and targeted suspicious vessels more aggressively. Economic factors helped the Anglo-American pressure on Cuba. In particular, plummeting sugar prices in Cuba by the 1860s coupled with the high prices for African slaves led to a sharp drop in demand from Cuba for imported slaves.[101]

Towards the end of the American Civil War, Britain realized that the final steps to end the Cuban slave trade would need to come from Spain itself. Politicians in Spain regarded the Southern Confederacy as a support for the continuance of slavery in Cuba, but the Union triumph at the end of the war led the Spanish government to fear that the military strength of the American northern states might lead to annexation of Cuba. Spain's reformist government wanted to end the Cuban slave trade as a stepping stone for further reforms. In Cuba itself there were calls in 1865 for the end of slavery, partly inspired by the granting of slave emancipation in the United States. The governor of Cuba, Dulce y Garay, argued that the Cuban slave trade should end in order for Spain to improve the system of Cuban slavery. Spain took the initiative. Its politicians drew up a comprehensive bill to abolish the Cuban slave trade. This was supported by a royal decree in September 1866, followed by a law in May 1867. It was accepted in Cuba three months later. Britain played a minor role in influencing this legislation. The Cuban authorities did not need to play an active role to support these changes. Thus the ending of the slave trade to Cuba arose from a mixture of diplomatic and political issues, especially the collapse of the Southern Confederacy; abolitionism played relatively little part in its demise.[102]

Surveying the complex reasons for the abolition of the slave trade by different powers during the nineteenth century indicates that the British abolitionist campaign left an important legacy but was insufficient in itself to persuade other countries to follow suit. Britain expended naval resources, abolitionist propaganda and diplomatic pressure in large measure on the continuing slave trades of other nations. Curtailment of the slave trade by various powers, however, followed a distinctive path. Denmark was the one nation to implement a royal decree to finish its transatlantic slaving activity. Britain ended its slave trade, after much abolitionist pressure, in response to humanitarian and economic priorities. The United States, caught up in the momentum leading towards British abolition of the trade, had to wait to ban slave imports until the constitutional ban on non-interference with the slave trade had elapsed. The Netherlands, a dependent ally of Britain, abolished its slave trade without controversy virtually thirty years after it had ceased to operate. France ended its slave trade through introducing a law authorizing abolition and signing treaties with Britain to this effect. The abolition of the slave trade to Brazil was the one example of belligerent intervention (by British blockading vessels) that prompted a government to speed up its own slave trade legislation. In the case of Cuba, British and American naval cooperation in the aftermath of the US Civil War, along with serious action on the part of Cuban and Spanish authorities, played an important role in slave trade abolition. Abolitionism therefore only directly influenced the ending of various branches of the slave trade in the Anglo-American trading sphere; it operated indirectly elsewhere in connection with internal political decisions.

6

SLAVE EMANCIPATION

The routes to freedom for slaves were varied. One way of becoming free was to run away permanently from slave masters, but, as Chapter 4 showed, this was not easy to achieve. Apart from laws dealing with slave emancipation, only two other ways existed for the enslaved to gain their freedom. One was self-purchase. This was relatively infrequent in North America and the British Caribbean as most slaves never had funds to buy their freedom.[1] But in Cuba and other parts of Spanish America, legal mechanisms (*coartación*) existed whereby slaves could demand to be valued at a just price and then to work towards self-purchase and freedom.[2] A Cuban slave law of 1842 guaranteed slaves the right to initiate and fulfil the purchase of their freedom via *coartación*.[3] The Portuguese equivalent to this practice was known as *coartaçao*, which involved a slave's purchase of freedom through instalment payments, as negotiated with a master; this was widely adopted in the Minas Gerais area of Brazil.[4]

The other method widely used to secure freedom for slaves was through a process of manumission. The usual way of carrying this out lay in specifications to free slaves by deed or in a slave owner's will. Various motives lay behind manumission. In some cases slaveholders decided to free trusted slaves who had served them loyally; the arrangements for manumitting such slaves represented a reward for faithful service. In other circumstances, manumission

141

resulted from a need to shed surplus slaves where work requirements changed to the extent that fewer slaves were needed for agricultural work. It is no surprise, in this context, that the transition from a tobacco monoculture to more grain production in the Chesapeake in the late eighteenth century led to slave manumissions: fewer workers were needed to cultivate grain than tobacco, and work on cereals was not confined to plantations and could be undertaken by a mixed white and black labour force.[5]

Studies of manumission in different slave societies offer insights into the manner in which this form of slave freedom was achieved. In seventeenth-century Barbados, manumission was effected through will or testament, deed, and legislative or court action. Documents were needed to prove that the manumission had been granted. The proportion of manumissions to the total slave labour force was minute, however, in seventeenth-century Barbados. Most African-Americans set free by this method resulted from action by a small number of testators in wills. The majority of those manumitted were slaves working in domestic households or children. Bequests of money and sugar, and sometimes land and clothing, were included as part of the process. Freedom by this means did not automatically occur on the death of the testator but some time afterwards. The median length of time for manumitted slaves to become free in seventeenth-century Barbados was five-and-a-half years. Most wills do not specify a reason for manumission; when they do, the reason usually given is loyal and conscientious service.[6]

In late seventeenth- and early eighteenth-century Bahia, manumissions were usually drawn up in a charter known as the *carta del alforria* or *carta da Liberdade*. A common reason given in these documents for freeing slaves lay in surrogate paternity. In other words, slaves regarded affectionately by masters after they had been raised as children in a master's household were favoured in the manumission process. Insufficient evidence survives to determine whether the majority of such slaves were the biological offspring of masters. Manumission could be carried out gratis in Bahia, but a considerable number of slaves purchased their manumission through raising money by themselves or through relatives. The fact that almost half of the slaves achieving manumission in Bahia between 1684 and 1745 did so by purchasing their freedom testifies both to the possibilities of slaves gaining money in a market economy and regarding freedom as a desirable goal.[7] Purchasing manumission among slaves was also common in Buenos Aires, the capital of the Viceroyalty of Río de la Plata, between 1776 and 1810.[8] The reasons for manumission changed over time in relation to shifting social, economic and demographic contexts.[9]

Slave manumission was much more common in Brazil than in the United States, where several states restricted this method of freeing slaves in the nineteenth century.[10] In the US South, for example, courts refused to enforce contracts where slave owners had offered manumission to the enslaved; statutes and court decisions restricted owners' rights in their wills to manumit slaves; high levels of proof were required for slaves to show their ancestors were free; and routes to slave freedom through owners bringing them into free states or free territories were pared down.[11] Where manumission was granted, as in early national Baltimore, it was frequently stimulated more by the economic self-interest of owners than by republican ideology or humanitarianism.[12] In Brazil, by contrast, the use of various methods for freeing slaves, outlined above, led to an expanding free coloured population in the nineteenth century. By the time of its first national census in 1872, Brazil had 4.2 million free coloured people as opposed to 1.5 million slaves. Brazil, in fact, had the highest number of free coloureds in any major American slave society.[13]

In the French Antilles most manumitted slaves were women and children, especially those who were of mixed race. The most common type of manumission was undertaken on a conjugal basis. This included *libre de savane* and *libre de fait* manumissions, which were unofficial, incomplete acts of freedom that slave owners granted to mixed-race slave women.[14] In these and other cases, in all transatlantic slave societies, manumission was an individual reward to a slave from a master or judge granted through their discretion; it was not intended to lead to general emancipation and was not undertaken to alter the status quo of slavery. Manumission was therefore an act that could not, by its nature, enable large numbers of slaves to achieve freedom within a short time period.[15]

Apart from the tumultuous overthrow of slavery by slaves and free coloureds in Saint-Domingue in the 1790s (discussed in Chapter 4), the main way in which slaves were freed arose from legal acts of emancipation by individual nations. In most cases, this was an extended process. Slave emancipation did not follow the abolition of the slave trade swiftly in any major country that engaged in transatlantic slaving. In most countries a process of gradual emancipation was the norm, with only a shift to immediatism in the later stages of the movement towards emancipation. The reluctance to free slaves swiftly arose usually from the insistence by white politicians that African-Americans needed to be prepared for freedom through the spread of literacy, moral education and Christianity. Any attempt to free slaves overnight, as it were, without careful preparation for their freedom, was perceived by white masters as likely to lead to social chaos and a labour shortage. The timing of emancipation depended upon a carefully calibrated intermixture of abolitionist campaigning and political opportunity, but it was accompanied by delays, sometimes a loss of direction, and the need to fight against entrenched planter interests. In two cases – Saint-Domingue and the United States – the quest for slave emancipation involved a long and bloody civil war.

BRITAIN AND THE CARIBBEAN

Most successful campaigns for slave emancipation occurred in the half-century between 1830 and 1880. Britain was at the forefront of such movements, but slave emancipation in the British Empire was not easily achieved. The British abolitionist movement, which was committed to gradual emancipation, experienced a lull in its activities immediately after 1807. For some years, the campaign against slavery seemed to lose direction. The Society for Effecting the Abolition of the Slave Trade was wound up in 1807, its work completed, and replaced by a new organization, the African Institution, which drew on a similar membership. The aims of the African Institution were to ensure the laws against the slave trade were properly enforced; to encourage commercial expansion through direct commodity trade between Britain and Africa; and to persuade other European powers to follow the British lead in abolishing their slave trades. The first two of these objectives were pursued, if sometimes with difficulty. The Royal Navy dispatched vessels to patrol the Atlantic sea lanes from Africa to intercept illegal vessels. Direct trade to and from Africa, especially in palm oil, was conducted from British ports. The third aim was taken over by British diplomacy (as discussed in Chapter 5).

To the Friends of NEGRO EMANCIPATION, this Print is Inscribed.

Fig. 18: Commemoration of slave emancipation in the British Empire, 1834

Unfortunately, the African Institution never aroused much popular enthusiasm, possibly because it delayed a direct assault on slavery as an institution in the British Empire. It soon concentrated its activities on trying to run the British Crown territory of Sierra Leone as a progressive colony rather than the broader remit outlined above.[16] The major abolitionist achievement of the period 1807–23 was to secure slave registration by parliamentary act. The leading figure behind this measure was James Stephen, a Colonial Office lawyer. He acted from the premise that a system of recording the main characteristics of slaves could determine whether planter amelioration was, in fact, taking place, leading to improved slave reproduction and better treatment of blacks; and also to ensure that the slave trade laws were enforced, especially the ban on the intra-Caribbean movement of slaves. It was hoped that the findings would indicate demographic growth over time from increased fertility. A slave registration act was passed in 1817, though the practice was imposed by the Colonial Office on the Crown colony of Trinidad in 1813. Slave registration took place every three years and served four purposes. First, it provided data on the size of slave populations on individual plantations, enumerating blacks by age, name and skills, to determine whether illegal slave imports were still occurring. Second, it provided accurate statistics on slave fertility and mortality, which enabled the British government to gauge whether planters were treating their slaves better and promoting slave breeding. Third, the census data publicized living and working conditions for slaves throughout the British Caribbean. Finally, slave registration served as a platform for further reforms connected with slavery. Faced with hard statistics, it was hoped that planters would have no option but to pursue ameliorative policies towards their slaves; if they failed to do so, government intervention to amend the situation would be justified.[17]

A new wave of abolitionist zeal began with the establishment of a central Anti-Slavery Society between 1821 and 1823. Heavily backed by the Quakers, this society was led by Zachary Macaulay, a philanthropist who had been at various times a bookkeeper and estate manager in Jamaica, governor of Sierra Leone and editor of the *Christian Observer*, a leading abolitionist publication. The official title of the new society was the Society for the Mitigation and Gradual Abolition of Slavery Throughout the British

Commonwealth. This encapsulates the rather mild intentions of its founders. The society aimed to pressurize Parliament for an improvement in the lot of slaves, with gradual emancipation as its eventual goal.[18]

The brewer and abolitionist Sir Thomas Fowell Buxton announced the intentions of the society in a parliamentary speech in May 1823, in which he outlined plans to free slave children at birth and stated that slavery was 'repugnant to the principles of the British Constitution and of the Christian Religion; and ... ought to be gradually abolished throughout the British Colonies with a due regard to the well-being of the parties concerned.'[19] This cautious statement sought to appease planters; it was vague about the timing of gradual emancipation, but this helped to allay alarm among the West India merchants and planters and their supporters. Government policy was swiftly announced by George Canning, the foreign secretary, just a few days after Buxton's speech. Canning stated that it was necessary for 'decisive measures' to be taken to ameliorate the condition of slaves in the British Caribbean. Such measures would be enforced, leading to 'a progressive improvement in the character of the slave population.'[20] In some respects the abolitionist emphasis on gradual emancipation was similar to the government's espousal of amelioration, with the major difference being that a different outcome was envisaged: freedom for slaves, on the one hand, and a continuation of slavery on the other. Both the Colonial Office and the abolitionists anticipated the evolution of slaves into a hard-working, respectful free labour force.[21]

Soon afterwards Lord Bathurst, the colonial secretary, sent a circular to the governors of the Crown islands in the Caribbean outlining a detailed government programme of amelioration. This had been drafted in close connection with the views of the Society of West India Merchants and Planters in London. Bathurst's proposals emphasized the need for Christian instruction to improve the slaves' character, and requested that local assemblies ban Sunday markets to keep the Sabbath for religious observance. Other proposals included offering slaves the right to present evidence in courts of justice; the removal of obstacles to manumission; the prohibition of the sale of slaves from an estate in order to meet proprietors' debts; the setting up of savings banks for slaves; and changes to the laws on punishment. Bathurst's circular also requested the removal of the whip from slave drivers and banned corporal punishment for female slaves. The circular was given greater weight by an order-in-council of 1824 which required Trinidad to implement these reforms and which advocated compulsory manumission for slaves.[22]

Planters in the Caribbean were reluctant to implement the proposals suggested by the Colonial Office and many island assemblies saw the ideas put forward as interfering with their legislative autonomy. The West India Interest conducted a propaganda campaign in the mid-1820s to convince the British public that most slave owners were humane Christians who recognized the need for good treatment of slaves, and that proselytization of Christianity had made great progress in West Indian slave communities.[23] Their views were undermined by evidence coming back from the West Indies about the poor treatment by planters of some missionaries there. Accounts of the persecution of the Reverend John Smith in Demerara in 1823 made a strong impact. A congregational minister sent out by the London Missionary Society, Smith spent seven years in Demerara. He was caught up in the slave revolt there partly because one of his black deacons, Quamina, was the leader of the insurgence. Accused of inciting the slaves to rebel, Smith was found guilty of complicity and sentenced to death. He was reprieved by the monarch but died in jail of a fever. His death gained wide publicity in the British newspaper press. He was held up as 'the Demerara martyr' – someone who had died because of the brutality of the slave system in the British West Indies.[24]

Smith's death and the obstructive methods of West Indian assemblies over amelioration encouraged an upsurge in abolitionist activity. Antislavery benefited from extensive newspaper coverage, especially in its own publication, *The Anti-Slavery Reporter*, first issued in 1825. Abolitionists printed and circulated vast numbers of shorter publications. Between 1823 and 1831 the Anti-Slavery Society published 2.8 million tracts, distributed throughout the nation. There were sermons, speeches and meetings. Lecture tours were undertaken by prominent campaigners. Petitioning of Parliament resumed. Between 1828 and 1830, for example, some 5,000 petitions calling for the gradual abolition of slavery were submitted to Parliament. Probably more than one-fifth of all British males aged over fifteen signed the antislavery petitions of 1833.[25] Ladies' Anti-Slavery Associations were formed in different British cities, in which middle-class women used their energy and spare time to distribute leaflets, cajole people to sign petitions, and publicize antislavery meetings. They provided an important outlet for political participation by women at a time when they were excluded from Parliament and public office. They drew heavily on nonconformist congregations, in which women had always been prominent in numbers and leadership.[26]

Stronger links were forged between nonconformist groups and abolitionists in the late 1820s. The Methodists, in particular, were virtually unanimous in their condemnation of slavery on moral grounds: over 229,000 Wesleyan Methodists (95 per cent of the membership) signed antislavery petitions presented to Parliament in 1833.[27] Missionaries were active in virtually all the Caribbean islands by this time. They were mainly Wesleyan Methodists but included a fair number of Baptists, Congregationalists and Moravians. The missionaries' presence and their pastoral and evangelical work among the slaves filled a gap left by the relative indifference of the established church and its representatives to the plight of slaves. Dissenting missionaries and abolitionists were imbued with a firm sense that God's Providence upheld the moral order in the world. In order to achieve salvation, redemption was necessary, and this could only be achieved as far as slavery was concerned by the destruction of physical bondage.[28]

The election of a Whig government in 1830 gave great impetus to the campaign to emancipate slaves in the British Empire. Abolitionists sensed that political opportunities now existed to present their case vigorously because the Whigs, unlike the Tories, were seen as a reforming party. Abolitionists substantially increased their pressure on Parliament in the three years after 1830. Petitions were organized very efficiently. Large public meetings were held throughout the country to publicize the abolitionist message. The establishment of the Agency Committee in 1830 was instrumental in changing the pace of abolitionist attack and also the urgency of the arguments deployed. It was a group of radical, often younger, campaigners tired of the procrastination associated with gradual emancipation. The Agency Committee organized paid, professional lecturers to tour Britain and promote the abolitionist message, and was responsible for the shift from long-held traditions of gradual emancipation to immediatism. Underpinning this change in policy was a strong evangelical sense that slavery was a grave sin and that for an individual to be at ease in his or her conscience, or to hope for redemption, an immediate cleansing of sin was necessary. William Wilberforce and many other abolitionists, however, still favoured gradual emancipation. In 1832 the rift between gradualists and immediatists came to a head and the Agency Committee broke away from the Anti-Slavery Society to form the Agency Anti-Slavery Society.[29]

The abolitionists needed patience in the first eighteen months of the new Whig administration because the government was dominated by the drive to secure parliamentary reform. The Great Reform Act was achieved by June 1832. It enfranchised significant numbers of the middle classes, among whom were many people sympathetic to antislavery. The push for emancipation was helped by the large slave rebellion in Jamaica that broke out after Christmas 1831. The persecution of white missionaries in Jamaica, the burning of their chapels, and the savagery with which rebel blacks were tracked down, brought to trial and either executed or imprisoned, came just at the right time for abolitionists make the most of the oppression.[30] The Agency Committee's immediatist arguments also gained force from the emerging view that free waged work was superior to slave labour. Adam Smith had famously posited this argument half a century before in *An Inquiry into the Nature and Causes of the Wealth of Nations* (1776). During the final years of British slavery, economic thought was shifting significantly away from protectionism and the inefficiency of slave labour was increasingly claimed.[31]

The final debates on emancipation began in Parliament on 14 May 1833 when Edward Stanley, the new colonial secretary, announced a scheme for slave freedom. Stanley announced that immediate measures would be taken to end slavery in the British Empire: the emancipation scheme provided for all slave children aged under six to be freed and for adult slaves to become apprentices for a period of time before attaining full freedom. The system of Apprenticeship was to be overseen by 132 special (or stipendiary) magistrates sent out from Britain to ensure that the new temporary arrangements for blacks worked smoothly. The government would offer a loan of £15 million to planters in compensation for the loss of their slaves' labour.[32]

Buxton led the abolitionist attack in the Commons on the government's emancipation scheme, which was not the type of legislation on freedom that antislavery campaigners had anticipated. A compromise was worked out. The amount of compensation paid was increased to £20 million. Moreover, it was an outright grant, not a loan; the government, at the eleventh hour, was convinced by the planters' call for recompense for the loss of their property. In addition, the planters argued that slave registration had conferred title on their slave chattels. Apprenticeship was to run for six years for field (or praedial) slaves and for four years for domestic slaves, with blacks working on an unpaid basis for 40–45 hours a week. Apprentices were to be remunerated for additional work undertaken beyond these set hours. After their terms were completed, the apprentices would become free blacks. An exception to this was that all slave children aged under six were immediately set free by the 1834 Emancipation Act.[33]

After minor amendments in the Lords, the emancipation bill was passed by a comfortable margin in the Commons on 31 July 1833, a month after the death of Wilberforce. At midnight on 31 July 1834, around 775,000 slaves in the British West Indies then became free.[34] The credit for achieving slave emancipation in the British Empire must be given to the continued pressure of the abolitionists inside and outside Parliament; to the greater involvement of nonconformist groups in a moral and humanitarian struggle; to the good fortune of a sea change in the political climate after the Tory Party fell into disarray in the late 1820s; to the election of a Whig government determined to legislate on slave emancipation; to the effective work of the Agency Committee lecturers; and to the role played by missionaries and slaves in the Caribbean, notably in the Jamaican slave revolt in 1831, in demonstrating the urgency of the need for slave emancipation. These various facets of the antislavery movement coalesced in the five years after *c.* 1828 to produce the momentum necessary for the rapid demise of slavery in the British Caribbean. Britain maintained a broad-based antislavery commitment well into the Victorian period.[35]

SWEDEN AND DENMARK

Slave emancipation in the small colonial possessions of Sweden and Denmark began in 1846–7. The moderate Swedish Abolition Society rejected public petitioning on the subject but instead made a private appeal to the monarch. This resulted in the king granting slave emancipation in 1846 and providing funds to ensure this happened. As a result, just over 500 slaves in the tiny colony of St Bartholomew were freed. The Danish case was a little more protracted. The Danish government had been influenced by British abolitionists in the 1830s to introduce ameliorative measures with regard to slavery in their Caribbean colonies. Most of these schemes, aimed at improving the working conditions and education of slaves in the Danish West Indies, were implemented by the long-serving governor-general, Peter von Scholten.[36]

Gradual emancipation was introduced in the Danish Caribbean 1847 with a period of projected transition from slavery to freedom. But slave action in the Danish West Indies speeded up the move towards freedom by extensive popular mobilization, spurred on by slave emancipation in the French colonies (discussed below). Slaves in St John rose up against planters and destroyed much property there in 1848, just as their predecessors had done in a slave revolt in late 1733. On 3 July 1848, 8,000 slaves gathered in front of Frederiksted fort, St Croix, demanding their freedom. Later that day von Scholten declared by gubernatorial fiat that all slaves in the Danish West Indies were free. No blood was spilt. The order forbade future enslavement and declared all children born to slaves as free, but required that slaves should remain on their plantations until 1859.[37]

FRANCE AND THE CARIBBEAN

France had initially acted much earlier than Britain to free slaves in her Caribbean colonies, but this was a short-lived phenomenon that was overturned. It then took almost another half-century for the French to bring about a second emancipation. The first emancipation happened on 4 February 1794, an act carried out by the revolutionary convention. This was a *fait accompli* created by the massive slave rising in Saint-Domingue in 1791. The act of emancipation fitted the Declaration of the Rights of Man of 1789, one of the hallmarks of French revolutionary ideology. The turmoil of the 1790s in Saint-Domingue was followed by further fighting in the years from 1801 to 1804 (all discussed in Chapter 4), which led to the establishment of the independent republic of Haiti. The Haitian government tried to force ex-slaves to work on plantations as peasants but this policy was eventually abandoned.[38] After 1815 the restored French monarchy of Louis XVIII adamantly opposed abolitionism, which it identified with republicanism. The second emancipation of French colonial slaves had to wait until the February Revolution ushered in the Second Republic in the spring of 1848. French abolitionist campaigning was a slow affair. Before 1830, few initiatives towards slave emancipation occurred in France. Abolitionism continued to operate in a lukewarm context under Louis-Phillippe's July monarchy (1830–48). This was partly because the king feared change and was adamantly opposed to slave freedom. British abolitionists provided ideas, money and support for French abolitionists, but this was not sufficient to stir up effective action in France in favour of slave freedom. French abolitionism reacted to the success of British slave emancipation in 1834 without producing a compelling programme that could be translated into effective campaigning.[39]

The Société de la morale chrétienne, which existed from 1821 until 1861, was a leading French group that focused on gradual emancipation but its lobbying activities were intermittent. Its successor under the July monarchy was the Société française pour l'abolition de l'esclavage. This had a small membership of less than a hundred members, confined to the political and social elite. It met only when the legislative calendar dictated and acted cautiously. Both these societies contended with an entrenched and powerful planter class and a French establishment that supported slavery.[40]

French abolitionism beyond the confines of these societies also had limitations. French abolitionists acted more individually than their British counterparts; they bickered endlessly among themselves, they were poorly organized and, unlike their British equivalents, they largely failed to recruit the Catholic Church, female members or mass public opinion in support of their cause. Whereas female campaigners and Protestant dissenters were central in the propaganda campaign against British colonial slavery, French abolitionists failed to tap female support and the Roman Catholic Church lay quiescent on the evils of slavery. Moreover, mass petitioning to mobilize popular opinion, so effective in Britain, was largely eschewed in France until the 1840s. Even then, memories of the violence that had characterized the first emancipation in 1794 militated against popular mass support for slave freedom. Signs of mobilization for emancipation occurred with the petitions by working-class printers to the Chamber of Deputies in 1844, but these lacked wider support.[41]

This poorly coordinated and fairly weak situation with regard to abolition would probably have continued without a major political upheaval to stir up action. France never had the same degree of popular support for petitioning against slavery that was found in Britain.[42] It took the coming of the Second Republic and the seizure of opportunity by a small group of antislavery proponents in favour of immediatism to bring down slavery in the French colonies in 1848. On 4 March of that year the provisional government formed a Commission for the Abolition of Slavery led by the white French abolitionist writer Victor Schoelcher, who had visited Haiti and had outlined plans for continued sugar production there without slavery. Schoelcher's visit to the French West Indies in 1840 enabled him to witness slavery at first hand. His idealism, combined with the cruelty he witnessed towards slaves and the unhappiness of slaves with their lot, convinced him that slavery must be abolished.[43]

Schoelcher arrived in France from the Caribbean on 3 March 1848 and immediately persuaded François Arago, the new minister of the navy and the colonies, that a decree of immediate emancipation should be issued. Planters in the French Caribbean and their representatives argued against this view, but Schoelcher's promotion of emancipation withstood these attacks. Schoelcher's influence extended throughout the entire French Caribbean. The Commission for the Abolition of Slavery demanded free and unconditional liberation for the quarter million slaves in the French Antilles. The emancipation decree, acknowledged by this request, was dated 27 April 1848. Schoelcher, the author of the emancipation decree, and the black abolitionist Cyril Bissette, a free person of colour, were vital figures in facilitating this outcome. Schoelcher and Bissette were elected to the legislative assembly for Martinique in 1848 and 1849.[44]

THE UNITED STATES

The ending of slavery in the United States was a protracted process.

The six decades between the turn of the nineteenth century and the death of slavery during the American Civil War witnessed the entrenchment of slavery in the Deep South, the spread of slavery across a cotton belt moving into southwestern states, and the creation of a self-conscious southern civilization centrally based around the preservation of slavery in the antebellum period. Those decades also saw the rise of abolitionist sentiment in the North; various attempts to expose the moral bankruptcy of slavery; and the need to eradicate it from a nation founded on libertarian principles. In those decades slavery and its ramifications also assumed an ever-larger role in US politics.

The staple crops grown on North American plantations had always been linked closely to marketing opportunities in Europe. Tobacco was shipped to Britain and Northern Europe to satisfy the growing nicotine habit of consumers there. Rice was sent to the West Indies and across the Atlantic to markets in Germany, the Low Countries and the Iberian peninsula as a substitute commodity

Fig. 19: Emancipation Day, South Carolina, 1863

for grains.[45] But cotton became the staple commodity that served European markets par excellence. The demand of the British textile industry for raw supplies of cotton for clothing manufacture reached considerable heights. Cotton became, in the first half of the nineteenth century, a central cog in an Atlantic economy linking ports such as London, Liverpool, New York and Mobile, Alabama. Annual US cotton production rose from around 3,000 bales in 1790 to more than 4 million by 1860. 'King Cotton' was the spur behind the support of Lancashire cotton producers for the Confederate cause in the American Civil War.[46]

Cotton production spread from Georgia and South Carolina in the early nineteenth century in a southwestern direction into newly settled states such as Arkansas, Alabama, Florida, Texas, Mississippi and Louisiana. Cotton plantations relied on the gang labour used on tobacco plantations; overseers and drivers provided the required discipline. They drew upon an extensive internal slave trade by which slaves no longer needed in the eastern states were transferred and sold at marts such as New Orleans and Natchez. This traffic in slaves helped to created great wealth for merchants and planters in the Mississippi Delta.[47] By 1860, according to the census of that year, around four million slaves belonged to American planters, and most of those slaves were attached to cotton plantations.[48]

Whether the plantations were efficient units of production that maximized or rewarded slave productivity or whether they were remnants of a passing agricultural order that failed to industrialize and modernize are large issues about the economic nature of antebellum slavery that historians still debate. The same is true with regard to assessments of the contribution made by plantations to southern economic development.[49] The Old South became increasingly attached to slavery for economic reasons. Apart from certain areas such as South Carolina, where slaves outnumbered whites as early as 1710, most southern states held about two white people to every black person. Many white southerners owned no slaves at all, and those that did were more likely to own a handful rather than large numbers. But the 'plain folk' of the Old South were just as wedded to the continuance of slavery as the grandee cotton masters.[50]

Slavery was an integral part of life in the South and southerners

Fig. 20: Black soldiers in the Union/Federal Army, *c.* 1863/4

regarded it as indelibly linked to the prosperity of the region, to the right of individuals there to choose their lifestyle without federal interference, and to the continuing social hierarchy of people marked by class and race. Some southern intellectuals defended the plantation world by viewing it through a nostalgic lens in which happy slaves were graciously treated by masters as familial members. Proslavery defenders in the South based their arguments on various grounds, including John C. Calhoun's notion of slavery as a 'positive good', which justified slavery on the grounds of white supremacy, paternalism and the intellectual and racial division between free whites and the enslaved.[51]

The federal government largely set aside the issue of slavery during the Jefferson and Madison presidencies, though in 1808 there was congressional agreement that slave importation should end, as a clause in the Constitution, according to some interpreters, had suggested it should.[52] It was during the Jefferson presidency that the vast Louisiana Territory was purchased – an omen for the future, because when parts of that territory eventually applied for statehood, a federal decision would be necessary about whether they should hold slaves or be free havens. Public anxiety over the spread of slavery to newly settled western territories emerged over the Missouri Crisis (1819–21). The incorporation into the Union of Missouri as a state raised the issue of whether or not it should be allowed to have slaves. After much acrimonious discussion, a compromise was reached whereby Missouri became a slave state and other parts of the Louisiana Purchase were excluded from slavery. To achieve a balance throughout the nation, Maine was admitted as a free state at the same time that Missouri became a slave state.[53] As it happens, Missouri became a border state and only about 10 per cent of its population were slaves by 1860.[54] What mattered to Americans, however, was not the proportion of slaves in an individual state but the principle about whether slavery extension should be allowed at all.

South Carolina emerged at the forefront of the southern protection of slavery in the 1820s. Several slave conspiracies occurred in the Palmetto state during that decade, notably that by Denmark Vesey, a free black who organised a formidable conspiracy among the slaves on Charleston in 1822.[55] In each case, planters supported the view that the planned uprisings were the result of outside interference, mainly by northern abolitionists, rather than the result of deficiencies in their own slave system. Several commentators argued against a broad construction of the Constitution to protect the southern commitment to slavery. Calhoun was the intellectual figurehead for the right of southerners to nullify federal law. He also developed a theory of the 'concurrent majority', that is, the right of a permanent minority to veto numerical majority rule. Nullification, in his view, was based on the assumption that the Constitution was a compact between individual states and individual citizens meeting in ratifying conventions, and that the partners of this compact had as much right to veto laws as the federal government. A nullification crisis occurred in South Carolina in 1831–2 that led immediately to an explicit defence of the institution of slavery by South Carolinians. There was now no conception of slavery in South Carolina being evil. In the next three decades, the rest of the South followed the lead given by South Carolina.[56]

Intense sectional feeling was aroused by the developments regarding American slavery between the admittance of Missouri to the Union as a slave state and South Carolina's decision to approach the brink of withdrawing from the Union in the nullification crisis. Sectional antagonisms emerged with the divergence of southern proslavery advocates from the revival of abolitionism in the North after the launch of William Lloyd Garrison's newspaper *The Liberator* in 1831. The North was not completely united in its opposition to slavery and neither was the South united in its support. In the northern states abolitionists included those in favour of gradual emancipation and those who wanted immediate freedom for blacks. Many abolitionists were willing to dilute their programme for racial justice in order to make it acceptable to a broad range of Americans.[57]

Abolitionists were often treated as marginal outsiders in the North during the Jacksonian era and mobs broke up their meetings.[58] Some northerners were not abolitionists at all but merely opposed to the extension of slavery across the Mississippi River. In the South very few abolitionist sympathisers existed, but many southerners were as much concerned with issues connected with economic development, banking and tariffs as with slavery. This perhaps explains why South Carolina was always an extreme case of a state that defended slavery against all odds in the antebellum South and why secessionism did not emerge as a general movement in the South until after the Civil War broke out in 1861.[59]

Free blacks played an important role in the antebellum United States in their opposition to racial discrimination and to schemes to colonize free blacks in Africa. Between the 1790s and the 1830s free blacks increased their numbers in the northern states, and they became the most rapidly growing segment of the southern population. They were aware of the political rhetoric and ideas of their time, and acquired a finely attuned notion of their legal and political rights. Free black leaders in northern cities, such as Philadelphia and New York, were stirred by the success of the Saint-Domingue insurrection of the 1790s. This inspired them to hope for the spread of antislavery ideas in the United States and the eradication of slavery there. Free black leaders, including James Forten and Frederick Douglass, opposed the moves towards colonization of US blacks overseas: they held protest meetings against the American Colonization Society in the 1820s and 1830s and became active contributors to publications that advocated slave emancipation. By the 1840s free blacks in the United States had a widely articulated set of responses about slavery that informed the complex political and jurisdictional issues that pertained to 'the peculiar institution.'[60]

The annexation of Texas (1845) and the Mexican War (1846-8) received criticism from many northerners who viewed James K. Polk as a southern president prepared to extend the territory of the United States into potential slaveholding areas but not follow through the same policy for acquiring a northwestern Pacific territory, Oregon. A political crisis over slavery ensued between 1846 and 1850, culminating in the Compromise of 1850 and the addition of the Fugitive Slave Cause. The latter compelled US citizens to assist in capturing runaway slaves. The crisis confirmed in the minds of southerners the threat to their section seemingly raised by northern abolitionism. The aftermath of the crisis clearly revealed a process of political and cultural sectionalism in the South. One important aspect of southern distinctness which emerged after 1846 was a self-conscious view of slavery as both legitimate and virtuous. Southerners became increasingly confident that slavery was a permanent feature of their society. All the ingredients for secession were in existence by 1850; only feelings of loyalty and sentimental attachment to the Union delayed secession for another decade.[61]

The crisis assumed a broader cultural dimension with the bestselling publication of Harriet Beecher Stowe's *Uncle Tom's Cabin*, which became a reference point for sectionalism in the 1850s. Stowe's novel presented a case for slavery and slaveholders being un-American and un-Christian. This judgement was widely supported in the North but vigorously contested in the South. In the furore that emerged over the success and meaning of the novel, northerners such as Thaddeus Stevens attacked not only slavery but the planter class as a violation of American democracy. George Fitzhugh and other southerners took the opposite view. They regarded the market orientation of northern society as cruel and inhuman and argued that the personal bond between master and slave elevated the South above northern society. Sectionalism became much more full-blooded after the publication of Stowe's novel and hardly amenable to a compromise such as that of 1850.[62]

During the 1850s American political parties were transformed largely in relation to the sectional crisis over slavery. The Democratic Party survived; the Whig Party disappeared; and a new grouping, the

Republican Party, emerged. The Democratic Party had enormously diverse interests, including strong antislavery, free soil, proslavery and secessionist elements; but it won support and retained cohesion, apart from the Texas and Mexico controversies, by voting together in Congress.[63] The Whig Party, by contrast, lacked cohesion and in the early 1850s lost leaders such as Henry Clay and Daniel Webster; it supported Nativism but in so doing lost much immigrant support; and it seemed in danger of disintegration. It collapsed as a party during the controversy over Kansas and Nebraska (1854–6), which allowed these territories to become states and decide whether they wished to allow slavery on the basis of popular sovereignty. The Whigs were replaced by the Republican Party, which held that openness of opportunity was fundamental to American society. Until after the 1856 presidential election the Republican Party was an insurgent party, fighting on one platform, but by 1860 it had broadened its appeal to win votes. Its continued existence in the late 1850s was guaranteed by turmoil in Kansas, evidenced by the thrashing of Senator Charles Sumner by congressman Preston Brooks of South Carolina after Sumner had attacked South Carolina's entrenched position on slavery.[64]

The controversy over slavery surfaced in the Dred Scott case and the Lecompton Convention in 1857 and in the crucial Lincoln–Douglas debates of the following year. Chief Justice of the Supreme Court Roger B. Taney ruled that Dred Scott, who had lived as a free black in Illinois and Wisconsin, had no right to sue for citizenship because he had moved to the slave state of Missouri. The Dred Scott decision in effect declared the Missouri Compromise unconstitutional, but this had no impact because that compromise had been superseded in 1854 by the Kansas–Nebraska Act. This opened the Kansas Territory and the Nebraska Territory to slavery and future admission of slave states to the Union by allowing white male settlers in those territories to decide whether or not they wanted slavery through popular sovereignty. The Dred Scott decision nevertheless inflamed public opinion.[65] So, too, did the Lecompton Convention (1857), in which the proslavery legislature of Kansas tried to confirm a constitution that fitted their political position.[66]

Stephen A. Douglas split the Democratic Party in 1858 and campaigned in Illinois against Abraham Lincoln for the post of senator. In the Lincoln–Douglas debates of 1858, the destiny of America appeared to be at stake. Douglas tried to brand Lincoln as a radical. In his 'House Divided' speech, Lincoln had argued that the ultimate extinction of slavery was a legitimate aim embedded in the thought of the American Founding Fathers. Douglas attacked this speech as revolutionary. He thought Lincoln favoured black equality with whites, whereas he himself believed that blacks were inferior and possessed no rights. Douglas favoured popular sovereignty and argued that the nation should continue on its present course; there was no need for the extinction of slavery. He also attacked Lincoln because he thought his Illinois rival wanted to strengthen the national government.[67] Lincoln opposed Douglas's view of popular sovereignty by arguing that it gave whites the right to treat blacks as property rather than as people.[68]

Lincoln argued in the 1850s that the Republican Party was a national rather than a sectional party. He had a moral belief in the ideals espoused in the Declaration of Independence and the revolutionary libertarian creed. He vigorously opposed popular sovereignty in the territories because this would give Americans the freedom to choose justice or injustice; and he thought it behoved the federal government to remove injustice. He also argued against popular sovereignty because it was a policy that appeared to break down the power of the federal government. Lincoln called the United States 'the last best hope of Earth' because the Constitution implied that slavery must eventually be extinguished and that the United States should progress towards a more perfect Union.[69] Lincoln constantly attacked the immorality of slavery. The ultimate extinction of that institution was fundamental to Lincoln's belief in America's progressive destiny. Lincoln believed that morality could not be divorced from politics and that in the United States the main political and humanitarian issue to be confronted was slavery. Lincoln sought to preserve the Union: this defined him politically and formed the keystone of Republican Party ideology.[70]

Slavery did not die an easy death in the United States. After the Union attack on Fort Sumter in 1861, various southern states gradually seceded and formed the Confederacy under the leadership of Jefferson Davis. Four years of bloody civil war followed, leaving lasting scars throughout the nation.[71] During the war Lincoln framed his emancipation proclamations, believing this was the only way to win the war and preserve the Union. The Confederacy refused to offer freedom to its slaves in return for military service in defence of southern secession. But the North took a different view. Black troops were recruited into the Union army. In the South, many slaves deliberately sabotaged the plantation system.[72] In these ways blacks can be seen as participating in the war to resolve their own status in American society. Slaves enlisted enthusiastically in the Union ranks. Nearly 33,000 black troops were recruited in the North and 140,000 in the Confederacy. They had to deal with discrimination over wages and combat roles, and served in racially segregated regiments, but they came to see themselves as saviours of the Union and liberators of their own people. By coming into military lines, black troops influenced Lincoln's decision to proceed with slave emancipation.[73]

In 1863 Lincoln's Emancipation Proclamation freed slaves in the Confederacy, but not in the Union or areas occupied by Union troops or in Tennessee (which Lincoln omitted at the suggestion of war governor Andrew Johnson). It allowed northern governors to begin enrolling ex-slaves as troops in their states. By late 1863 Lincoln and his generals were convinced that black troops were essential for northern victory in the war. In 1864 Lincoln urged Congress to pass the 13th Amendment to the Constitution to abolish slavery altogether in the United States, and this was achieved by the end of 1865, eight months after Lincoln's assassination by John Wilkes Booth.[74]

A programme of Reconstruction tried to resolve the problems of the defeated Confederacy and the position of blacks in southern society, but it did so in a largely unsatisfactory, incomplete way with equivocal attention given to black rights.[75] The defeated Confederate leaders could only envisage a post-emancipation world of serfdom and peonage; many Unionists opposed the entry of free blacks into their states; and northern abolitionists were not racial progressives.[76] Discrimination against free blacks continued for nearly a century afterwards, with segregation, lynching, the rise of the Ku Klux Klan and Jim Crow legislation. All these combined to show that the legacy of slavery in the United States cast a long and dark shadow.

THE NETHERLANDS AND SURINAME

After the United States granted slave emancipation, several other slaveholding powers still existed. The Dutch were the last northern European imperial power to implement slave freedom. This occurred in 1863. The lateness of this emancipation largely stemmed from the absence of a significant abolitionist presence in the Netherlands. Even though the Dutch were renowned for their tolerance and humanitarianism, the Dutch government's lukewarm response to British, French, Swedish and Danish emancipations between 1833 and 1848 partly reflected the absence of domestic pressure for abolitionism.[77] When the democratic Dutch constitution was established in 1848–9, only eight out of 1,500 petitions for the new constitution called for the introduction of slave emancipation.[78]

By 1853, however, leading Dutch politicians, whether liberals or conservatives, agreed that slave freedom should eventually be implemented in Dutch colonial possessions, but with no timescale for its enactment. A vigorous abolitionist campaign might have influenced the Dutch government to act on this matter, but abolitionism continued to make little progress in the Netherlands by 1860. Three possible explanations for this state of affairs can be adduced. First, the limited influence of religious groups, whether Catholic or Protestant, on discussions about the morality of slavery did not help the cause of antislavery in the Netherlands. Second, economic arguments that forced labour could only be more expensive than free labour were not made. Third, the artisan class, which had played a significant role in French and (especially) British abolitionism, was not organized on a widespread scale in Holland until the late 1870s.[79] There was also a limited colonial dimension to Dutch abolitionism. Suriname planters were determined to continue slaveholding until the bitter end. When slave emancipation did arrive in 1863, it was influenced by the Emancipation Proclamation issued by Lincoln in the United States. Slave emancipation in the Dutch colonies led to a long apprenticeship of ten years for former slaves in Suriname before they were fully free.[80]

SPANISH AMERICA

Slave emancipation was a slow process throughout Spanish America. But it was achieved more easily in the various polities where slavery was structurally of modest importance than in countries, such as

Cuba and to a lesser extent Puerto Rico, where slavery was either integral to the economy or not easily expendable. Several newly independent states of South America drafted 'free womb' laws under which the children born after the declaration of independence were considered free. This occurred in Chile (1811), Río de la Plata (1813), Colombia, Ecuador, Peru and Venezuela (all 1821) and Uruguay (1825). These laws were either a concession aimed at securing slaves for military service in various South American wars for independence or a reward for wartime service. Full slave emancipation was enacted in Chile (1823), the Central American Federation (1824) and Mexico (1829).[81] The process was more protracted elsewhere in South America. In Ecuador enslaved people used the language of republicanism in petitions submitted for their freedom in the 1820s, but it was not until 1852 that the Ecuadoran Assembly voted to abolish slavery, which came into effect in 1854.[82] Peru formally declared independence in 1821 but an attempt to instal a 'free womb' law was opposed by landowners and slaveholders until slavery was abolished in Peru in 1854.[83]

Cuba and Puerto Rico were still part of the Spanish Empire by 1860. Moves towards slave emancipation in both countries therefore depended upon metropolitan influence and initiatives. In both cases, though rather less in Puerto Rico than in Cuba, few serious moves towards slave freedom had occurred by the outbreak of the American Civil War. Planters in Cuba and Puerto Rico strongly opposed emancipation, and mortgagees, bankers, shipowners and merchants in Spain had strong vested interests in the continuance of slavery. Between 1859 and 1866 the captains general of Cuba tried to ban discussion of the abolition so that slaves did not hear abolitionist discourse. Gradual emancipationists in Cuba argued in favour of reforming slavery and for abolition to occur in the future. The American Civil War and the granting of slave freedom in the United States, however, gave a strong fillip to Spanish antislavery activity.[84] During the war, Spanish politicians looked to the Southern Confederacy as a bulwark against any attempt by the United States to annex Cuba. But the Unionist triumph in the war, along with Lincoln's freeing of slaves in the United States, left Cuba, Puerto Rico and Brazil in 1865 as the last significant bastions of slaveholding in the Atlantic world. Minority liberal elements in Spain by that time expected slavery in Cuba and Puerto Rico would be abolished gradually, but no timescale could be applied to that outcome.[85]

Abolitionism began to make modest progress in Spain in 1865 when a Spanish Abolitionist Society was formed. This aimed to copy the tactics used decades earlier by Anglo-American abolitionists. Petitions, articles in the popular press and public rallies all began to occur in Spain in support of slave emancipation. Abolitionist members were overwhelmingly secular, as the Roman Catholic Church stayed largely aloof from arguments for slave freedom. In Spain there was nothing like the popular support for abolitionism that nonconformist Protestants had supplied in Britain and the United States. Neither Cuba nor Puerto Rico had representation in the Spanish Cortes Generales (a bicameral legislature). Thus there was no parliamentary channel through which abolitionist sympathizers could exert their influence. When the Cuban slave trade ended in 1867, however, Spaniards and Cubans were increasingly aware that consideration of slave emancipation would be necessary to appease Britain and the United States.[86]

Action soon followed. The liberal Spanish government that came to power in 1868 soon turned its attention to slavery. This was partly in response to the Cuban and Puerto Rican uprisings against Spanish rule in 1868. In 1870 the colonial minister Segismundo Moret Y Prendergast drafted and passed the Moret law which secured gradual slave emancipation in Cuba and Puerto Rico. This was an attempt by Spain to win gratitude from freed slaves and freed people of colour in Cuba in an order to ensure that insurgents in the Cuban revolt (1868–78) did not capture the moral high ground. The Spanish government calculated that Cuban slaveholders would accept the new law. The terms of the legislation were to free all slaves aged sixty-five or over and all children born of slave mothers after the law was enacted; but those children had to work for their master under a *patronato* system until the age of eighteen and were then tied to their masters as labourers for a further four years. These terms freed relatively few slaves of working age. Article 21 of the Moret law promised further legislation to curtail slavery altogether after the revolt ended.[87]

Abolitionist forces in Puerto Rico gained confidence from the Moret law. A small group of well-organized, active abolitionists in Puerto Rico capitalized on the fact that some planters recognized the stagnation of the slave population on the island and were willing to consider an indemnified transition to free labour. The new Spanish Republican government abolished slavery in Puerto Rico in 1873. Slaves were required to sign three-year contracts with their former masters. Slave owners received 200 pesos per slave as compensation from the Spanish treasury. Puerto Rico succeeded in achieving emancipation for its 31,000 slaves partly because of abolitionist pressure, but partly also because a transition away from slave workers to contract labour was already in progress. This meant that estate work was not racially stigmatized.[88]

It used to be argued that, during the long anti-colonial rebellion in Cuba in the decade after 1868, Creole rebels called for the gradual abolition of slavery, but there was no rising by slaves to support this goal.[89] This is now known to be incorrect. In fact, thousands of slaves joined an insurrection for Cuban independence between 1868 and 1878. They abandoned farms and estates to join insurgent forces to support their own freedom from slavery as well as Cuba's freedom from colonialism. Military leaders inducted slaves into the abolitionist movement, and deployed insurgents in numerous acts of guerrilla warfare. They attacked plantations, served as messengers, and gradually undertook prominent military positions. By 1878, some 16,000 Cuban slaves had gained their legal freedom by rebelling against Spain.[90] A seepage of slaves into freedom occurred with the dislocations caused by war. Moreover, planters in eastern Cuba, whose economic conditions were worse than in the western half of the island, manumitted slaves and substituted Asian contract workers in their place until 1873, when a Chinese Passenger Act forbade North American and British shipping from continued participation in the trade.[91]

By the late 1870s Cuban slaveholders had 'a diminishing emotional attachment to the formal institution of slavery.'[92] This stemmed from the freedom accorded to certain categories of slaves under the Moret Law and the demographic decline of slavery in Cuba. The number of slaves in Cuba fell from 363,000 in 1868 to just under 20,000 a decade later. But though the rebellion weakened slavery in Cuba, the final push towards emancipation only occurred after it ended. In 1880 the Spanish government enacted an immediate emancipation law. This required former slaves to work for their ex-masters for eight years under a *patronato* or apprenticeship system; they were allowed to buy their freedom under these regulations. The system was curtailed in 1886, two years before it was supposed to expire, as a result of abolitionist pressure. By then, the Cuban labour force had been reorganized: droves of slaves had quit their plantations through absconding and immigrants filled the gap left by slave labour.[93] That this was not a disaster for Cuba's sugar owners arose from the rapid industrial advance in sugar technology after slave emancipation: successful mill owners modernized their facilities, injected capital into their properties, and became planter-industrialists.[94]

BRAZIL

Brazil was the last remaining slaveholding power in the Atlantic world to implement slave emancipation. There were few signs of this happening, however, when slaves in the United States gained their freedom. In 1865 the coffee, cotton and sugar plantations in Brazil still dominated the economy and an extensive internal slave trade transferred black workers from regions where some degree of economic decline had begun to other, more productive areas.[95] By the end of the 1860s, however, many Brazilians realised slavery was becoming a discredited institution and that action against it would soon be required. Slave emancipation in the United States had set an example for remaining slaveholding nations to follow. Moreover, the destruction to property and the loss of life experienced in the American Civil War was a warning that internal divisions over slavery could lead to serious destruction.[96]

Moves towards freedom for slaves in Brazil occurred in two phases. During the 1870s, elite action towards gradual emancipation began. After 1880 more popular mobilization against slavery occurred, with a struggle between gradualists and immediatists. Elite concerns about slavery emerged with doubts over the institution by the second and last Emperor of Brazil, Dom Pedro II. He thought Lincoln's Emancipation Proclamation and the passage of the 13th Amendment to the US Constitution had signalled the changes necessary for other slave-owning societies in the Americas.[97] Dom Pedro II did not face any serious abolitionist agitation in Brazil, but he had an acute sense of moral isolation after these decisive measures.[98] But though he supported the abolition of slavery as a matter for public debate,

Dom Pedro II chose not to act on this belief in 1866 because Brazil was engaged in a war with Paraguay.[99] Dom Pedro II was eventually responsible for ensuring political action ensued against slavery in Brazil. He assembled, with great difficulty, a cabinet willing to consider the question of slavery. After five months of bitter political debate in the Senate and House of Deputies, a gradual slave emancipation law was passed in September 1871. It became known as the Rio Branco law after the statesman Viscount Rio Branco whose conservative government had sanctioned the legislation. This 'free womb' law granted freedom for all slaves born after its passage. Masters were required to raise children until they were aged eight; they could then relinquish their responsibility through indemnification or use the children's labour until they were aged twenty-one. Those remaining as slaves were allowed the option of buying out the value of their labour service. This cautious measure was greeted with little popular opposition from abolitionists, but merchants and planters in Rio de Janeiro and its vicinity voiced their dissent. The law was passed without support from strong antislavery societies.[100]

The 1880s saw more widespread and concerted opposition to slavery in Brazil. An Emancipation Association and a Brazilian Antislavery Society were formed in 1880. Three years later black leaders had emerged in the Brazilian abolitionist movement, notably the accomplished orator José de Patrocinio. Planter incidents of violence against slaves were published in newspapers, which started to print more sympathetic articles against the continuance of slavery. Brazilian provinces with a limited or declining commitment to slave labour, such as Amazonas and Ceará, were susceptible to antislavery influence and ideas. In the large province of Bahia slave activists joined the abolitionists. In Brazil as a whole, censuses showed that the slave population declined by almost one-fifth between 1874 and 1884.[101]

By 1885 women began to canvass in city streets in Rio and São Paulo against slavery, even though strong cultural barriers about women's political involvement in public life existed. Slaves fled from plantations in large numbers. Planters resorted to violence to try to stop slave runaways but could not prevent the majority from escaping to freedom. Dom Pedro II and a new ministry with a Liberal leader reacted to these pressures by decreeing in 1885 that all slaves over the age of 60 should be freed. This did not stop the abolitionist momentum. In 1886 abolitionists were sufficiently organised to visit plantations and to encourage slaves to abandon estates. This occurred on a large scale, as blacks made use of Brazil's extensive railway network to aid their flight.[102]

The flight of slaves from estates, along with the intensification of abolitionist activity, convinced many planters that slavery would soon end in Brazil. They therefore began to import free labourers from outside Brazil to make up for the shortfall. Some estate owners also began a process of voluntary manumission for their slaves. Matters came to a head in 1888 when the Senate and the Chamber of Deputies, with the support of the Regent Isabella, announced simply in a law that slavery had become extinct in Brazil. This was an act of immediate emancipation that was achieved without any violent pressure. Planters expected to claim compensation worth around £20 million for the loss of 725,000 slaves. Isabella's failure to implement such compensation backfired for her politically, as it was a major factor in the coup that overthrew her and the Brazilian monarchy in 1889 and to the creation of the first Brazilian republic.[103]

In the late slave emancipations in Cuba and Brazil, various complex internal economic and political factors divided the classes with a stake in slavery, but the influence of the ending of slavery in the United States played a major role in giving impetus to abolitionist groups in Cuba and Brazil to increase their pressure on their respective governments for reform as well as providing impetus for slaves to influence the road to freedom. Without the pressure exercised on slavery by the Anglophone world, it is likely that slavery in Cuba and Brazil would have continued longer than it did.

THE LEGACY OF SLAVERY

Slavery ended at different times in the Americas between the Saint-Domingue revolt of the early 1790s and the coming of freedom for slaves in Brazil in 1888. In each nation where slave emancipation occurred, there was a long period before freed people acquired full social and political rights. Whether in Brazil, the United States or throughout the Caribbean, ex-slaves had a long struggle in order to achieve voting rights, legal equality, educational opportunities and professional work prospects. Racism, and in many instances colonialism, cast a long shadow over the status of black people. Despite the persistent efforts of abolitionists, the effects of racism continued for many decades after the formal end of slavery in different jurisdictions. The curtailment of slavery required a major adjustment on the part of various white elites and there is no doubt that white politicians in former slave societies found the new treatment necessary to liaise with African-Americans as free people rather than slaves was a considerable challenge. It is not surprising therefore that all societies where slavery had flourished found the white elite searching for a gradual approach towards slave freedom.

The pattern for a gradual transition towards full freedom for former slaves was set by Britain in her Emancipation Act of 1834, which ushered in a transition period from slavery to freedom during which black workers became apprentices. The Apprenticeship was overseen by government-appointed Special Magistrates, who visited plantations to try to secure fair play on both sides. Apprenticeship was practised in nearly all British Caribbean islands, except for a few small territories, such as Antigua, where it was decided that freedom could occur immediately in 1834.[1] The period of Apprenticeship, however, was full of disputes between owners and slaves. In 1838 the colonial secretary Lord Glenelg, under pressure from abolitionist campaigning, announced that Apprenticeship would come to an early end. Thus on 1 August 1838 Apprenticeship was formally ended in the British Caribbean.[2] Former slaves could now decide where they lived and what labour they undertook. But their lack of status, power and education meant that the possibilities of a future free, independent life operated under considerable constraints. Large numbers of freed people left plantations to establish their own holdings on vacant land for peasant settlement. Sometimes this involved squatting. Wage-earning freed people purchased small plots of land on the edge of estates. They were able to sustain their lives at a customary level through working provision grounds and marketing their produce.[3]

Planters maintained their sugar output by importing cheap Asian (predominantly Indian) indentured servants as labourers after the end of Apprenticeship. But these workers and ex-slaves failed to maintain sugar production at internationally competitive levels: the British Caribbean share of world sugar production fell from 40 per cent at the time of slave emancipation in 1834 to 2 per cent in 1900. Despite this declining position for the British Caribbean sugar industry, no alternative to the plantation system had emerged by the beginning of the twentieth century. A strong sense of Creole identity had emerged by then among the black population in British West Indian territories, but this was not accompanied by significant political advances. Blacks in the Caribbean long remained under the shadow of colonialism. Moves towards political rights and social progress for these people largely occurred after World War II and then only in fits and starts. It was not until political independence came to British Caribbean territories, mainly in the 1960s, that these problems could be addressed.[4]

Haiti had a distinctive history after becoming an independent republic in 1804. The end of slavery there was accompanied by violence and social disruption. Jean-Jacques Dessalines, the first ruler of independent Haiti, maintained a sizeable army and ruled with military force; the social divisions brought to the surface during the revolt of the 1790s continued; white Haitians were massacred by 1804; and it took many years to rebuild the shattered agricultural economy. Dessalines tried to keep disgruntled former slaves working on plantations, but they opposed this bitterly. Dessalines was killed by a mob of his own officers in 1806, but the militarization of Haitian society, accompanied by efforts by free blacks to forge new livelihoods in difficult economic circumstances, continued into the 1820s.[5] Haitian blacks offered staunch resistance to working on plantations and to laws introduced by the country's leaders to restrict their autonomy and movements. But, after years of struggle, the leaders of Haiti allowed state land to be broken up and sold to citizens. This led to the dismantlement of plantations.[6] Small-scale farming and squatting was common throughout Haiti by the 1840s and was firmly established as a way of life for most Haitians in rural areas by the 1870s.[7]

Slaves achieved freedom in the United States from 1863 onwards (see Chapter 6). The immediate post-civil war years combined positive moves for black freed people but also continuing racism and prejudice against former slaves during Reconstruction (1865–77) and beyond. Important civil rights gained constitutional approval fairly soon after the end of the civil war. The 14th Amendment (1868), secured after a bitter struggle and opposition from many politicians in the US South, granted citizenship rights and equal protection under the law to all people within its jurisdiction. The 15th Amendment (1870) prohibited federal and state governments to deny all adult citizens the right to vote.[8] Freed blacks enthusiastically participated in politics with these protections in states such as South Carolina and Mississippi where the plantocracy had powerful entrenched interests.[9] In various southern towns, blacks immediately followed the announcement of freedom to hold mass meetings to demand the suffrage and equal rights. Philanthropists in northern US cities made extensive efforts in the 1860s and 1870s to educate and advance the cause of former slaves through numerous Freedmen's Aid Societies and Relief Associations.[10] A Freedmen's Aid Bureau, set up as a federal organization in 1865, helped ex-slaves with legal advocacy over family issues in local and national courts. But much of the funding for the bureau was cut back in 1869 and terminated by Congress terminated in 1872.[11]

Union troops remained in the South during Reconstruction. Together with various aid associations and efforts by northern abolitionists, they worked hard to improve the lot of freed people but faced an uphill struggle to deal with the poverty and illiteracy of blacks and the continuing resentment of many southerners about the loss of their slaves. Northern attempts to aid free blacks waned in enthusiasm, however, by the mid-1870s. In 1877 President Rutherford B. Hayes ended Reconstruction by an executive order to withdraw troops from the South. By then blacks throughout the South were still struggling to achieve economic independence beyond the plantations. Southern planters developed a sharecropping system in order to tie freed blacks to work for their former employers. This farm tenancy system avoided payment of wages. The arrangements were for blacks to sign an annual contract that gave them an advance on the expected crop share. Frequent shortfalls in their crop share, however, led to escalating debts. Numerous planters refused to allow sharecroppers to leave, thereby maintaining a form of peonage on their plantations. As in the Caribbean, full political and civil rights for blacks in the United States did not arise until the 1950s and 1960s, with the rise of civil rights' protests and changes to the US Constitution in favour of black people.[12]

After the end of slavery in Cuba and Brazil, freed blacks faced much prejudice and discrimination from white elites. Some former slaves in sugar-producing areas of Cuba removed themselves to forest areas where they cultivated land as squatters. Ex-slaves on Brazilian plantations sometimes remained on their estates as labour tenants or sharecroppers, growing their own produce for subsistence or sale. But a decline in the profits of coffee production in southeastern Brazil by the early twentieth century forced planters to shed labour, which led many free blacks to renounce their tenancies. By 1900 many former slaves in Cuba and Brazil had migrated to large cities where they became part of an extensive black proletariat, often living in slums. Work opportunities were far from easy to acquire as many employers encouraged large-scale European immigration to Latin America (with many people coming from Italy, Spain and Portugal) to replace free black labour. This changed the composition of the working population of Latin American cities drastically between 1880 and 1930. Buenos Aires, for example, had 780,000 immigrants by 1914 and fewer than 10,000 Afro-Argentinians. In Rio de Janeiro, São Paulo and Buenos Aires, black workers found most of the work available was as day labourers or domestic servants, while Afro-Cubans were often restricted to low-skilled poorly paid jobs.[13]

In recent years, the legacy of slavery in the Atlantic world has been kept alive by campaigns for reparations to make redress for slavery and by efforts to memorialize the slave experience. Reparations are inevitably a highly contentious matter, because they involve recognition by various Western powers of their historic involvement in slavery and of how to address moral and legal arguments that they should offer financial compensation to countries in which slavery and the slave trade flourished. At one end of the spectrum are arguments that former slave trading nations should discharge their debt to the descendants of former slaves by writing an ethical blank cheque; at the other are calls to wipe the slate clean, accept the fact that many different terrible wrongs have happened in the past, and concentrate instead on financial aid to modern nations where there is extensive black poverty. Arguments abound about whether current generations can be held responsible at the state level for the actions of their ancestors over a century-and-a-half ago, and whether one should take account of the African contribution to the exploitation of their fellow Africans. The movement towards reparations appears to be gaining momentum, but no major country involved in slavery and the slave trade has yet agreed to pay reparations or decided to whom cash should be paid and on what scale.[14]

The memorialization of slavery has grown apace in recent years with the opening of slavery galleries at museums such as the Merseyside Maritime Museum and London's Dockland Museum, numerous exhibitions on transatlantic slaving, and the erection of monuments and plaques to notable men and women who were once slaves or who played a significant role in abolitionism. Cities heavily involved with the slave trade, including Bristol and Liverpool, have devised slave trade walks for visitors. Memorialization has to be handled carefully to illustrate the agency of the enslaved while retaining symbols of the oppressed system in which they lived. To erect monuments to former slaves also involves sensitive handling of the use of public space so that multicultural communities feel that public recognition of those who were once powerless, oppressed and racially stigmatized have improved their position in society in the period of well over a century since slavery ended in the Atlantic world. Britain currently has more galleries devoted to slavery and the slave trade than public monuments commemorating transatlantic slavery, but this will no doubt change in the future.[15]

While the memory of transatlantic slavery is handed down from one generation to another through the interpretation and understanding of documents, artefacts and documents, different forms of slavery are still practised in today's world. They often flourish in settings (such as parts of Asia and Eastern Europe) that have no historic connection with transatlantic slavery. They are also frequently more invisible to most people (as is the case with trafficking of vulnerable women and children) than was the case with slaves working on the plantations and in the towns and ports of the Americas. But while these modern forms of slavery differ in significant ways from the types of slavery discussed in this book, they are a reminder that the exploitation of people in a state of complete unfreedom is still a major problem besetting many societies throughout the world – one that is compounded by the greater ease of international mobility than was the case over a century ago, and one that requires continued campaigning, vigilance and action by antislavery activists to be brought to an end.[16]

Further Reading

No single recent book offers an overview of the full range and scope of transatlantic slavery and the nations associated with its development, but the state of scholarship on particular themes and participants can be gleaned from the chapters in David Eltis and Stanley L. Engerman (eds), *The Cambridge World History of Slavery. Volume 3. AD 1420–AD 1804* (Cambridge: Cambridge University Press, 2011). Key debates and important literature on transatlantic (and other forms of) slavery are analysed in Gad Heuman and Trevor Burnard (eds), *The Routledge History of Slavery* (Abingdon: Routledge, 2011). The impact of slavery on European empires is addressed in the essays published in Barbara L. Solow (ed.), *Slavery and the Atlantic System* (Cambridge: Cambridge University Press, 1991).

Several encyclopedias and handbooks offer good introductions to slavery in the New World. Among them are Paul Finkelman and Joseph C. Miller, *Macmillan Encyclopedia of World Slavery*, 2 vols (New York: Macmillan, 1998); Seymour Drescher and Stanley L. Engerman, *A Historical Guide to World Slavery* (Oxford: Oxford University Press, 1998); and Robert L. Paquette and Mark M. Smith (eds), *The Oxford Handbook of Slavery in the Americas* (New York: Oxford University Press, 2010). A handy introduction to documentary sources on slavery and the slave trade is available in Stanley L. Engerman, Seymour Drescher and Robert L. Paquette, *Slavery* (New York: Oxford University Press, 2001).

Important general books on transatlantic slavery are Eric Williams,

Capitalism and Slavery (Chapel Hill: University of North Carolina Press, 1994; originally published in 1944); Robin Blackburn, *The Making of New World Slavery: From the Baroque to the Modern 1492–1800* (London: Verso, 1997); and David Brion Davis, *Inhuman Bondage: The Rise and Fall of Slavery in the New World* (New York: Oxford University Press, 2006). The involvement of individual nations in slavery and antislavery can be followed in Kenneth Morgan, *Slavery and the British Empire: From Africa to America* (Oxford: Oxford University Press, 2007); Peter Kolchin, *American Slavery, 1619–1877*, rev. edn (New York: Hill and Wang, 2003); Stuart B. Schwartz, *Sugar Plantations in the Formation of Brazilian Society: Bahia, 1550–1835* (Cambridge: Cambridge University Press, 1985); and Josep M. Fradera and Christopher Schmidt-Nowara (eds), *Slavery & Antislavery in Spain's Atlantic Empire* (New York: Berghahn Books, 2013).

The most comprehensive statistical estimates on the flow of black Africans via the slave trade to the Americas is available on a website generated by a team of historians and made freely available at the following url: www.slavevoyages.org. This is a revised, expanded edition of a database first made available on CD-ROM in 1999. Covering all nations that participated in the slave trade and providing figures, graphs, maps, and a directory of African names, this website can be utilized to project all manner of calculations connected with transatlantic slaving. The estimates contained in this database form the basis of the maps in David Eltis and David Richardson, *An Atlas of the Transatlantic Slave Trade* (New Haven: Yale University Press, 2010). Still useful for its insights, though superseded in many of its figures, is Philip D. Curtin, *The Atlantic Slave Trade: A Census* (Madison: University of Wisconsin Press, 1969). Historical images of slavery and the slave trade are available online in *The Atlantic Slave Trade and Slave Life in the Americas: A Visual Record* (http://hitchcock.itc.virginia.edu/Slavery/index.php).

A good overview of transatlantic slaving is available in a new edition of Herbert S. Klein, *The Atlantic Slave Trade* (Cambridge: Cambridge University Press, 2010). A more detailed account is provided in James A. Rawley with Stephen D. Behrendt, *The Transatlantic Slave Trade: A History*, rev. edn (Lincoln, NE: University of Nebraska

Press, 2005). Among many good specialized books on the slave trade are the reprinted edition of Roger Anstey, *The Atlantic Slave Trade and British Abolition, 1760–1810* (Farnborough: Gregg Revivals, 1993); Johannes Menna Postma, *The Dutch in the Atlantic Slave Trade* (Cambridge: Cambridge University Press, 1990); Robert Louis Stein, *The French Slave Trade in the Eighteenth Century: An Old Regime Business* (Madison: University of Wisconsin Press, 1979); and Joseph C. Miller, *Way of Death: Merchant Capitalism and the Angolan Slave Trade 1730–1830* (Madison: University of Wisconsin Press, 1988). For the significance of the slave trade at a leading slaving port, see the essays in David Richardson, Suzanne Schwarz and Anthony Tibbles (eds), *Liverpool and Transatlantic Slavery* (Liverpool: Liverpool University Press, 2007). The context of the slave trade out of Africa is explained, with many regional examples, in Paul E. Lovejoy, *Transformations in Slavery: A History of Slavery in Africa*, 2nd edn (Cambridge: Cambridge University Press, 2000). The connections between slaving and capital accumulation are freshly examined in Joseph C. Miller, *The Problem of Slavery as History: A Global Approach* (New Haven: Yale University Press, 2012).

The centrality of plantations to the history of slavery in the Americas is clearly delineated in Philip D. Curtin, *The Rise and Fall of the Plantation Complex: Essays in Atlantic History*, 2nd edn (Cambridge: Cambridge University Press, 1998). The world of the planters of the early English Caribbean is illuminated by Richard S. Dunn, *Sugar and Slaves: The Rise of the Planter Class in the English West Indies, 1624–1713* (Chapel Hill: University of North Carolina Press, 1972). Other studies that include detailed appraisal of planters include Stuart B. Schwartz, *Sugar Plantations in the Formation of Brazilian Society: Bahia, 1550–1835* (Cambridge: Cambridge University Press, 1985); and Richard Follett, *The Sugarmasters: Planters and Slaves in Louisiana's Cane World, 1820–1860* (Baton Rouge: Louisiana State University Press, 2006).

Demographic and cultural aspects of slavery form the basis of Michael Craton, *Searching for the Invisible Man: Slaves and Plantation Life in Jamaica* (Cambridge, MA: Harvard University Press, 1978); B. W. Higman, *Slave Populations of the British Caribbean, 1807–1834* (Baltimore: Johns Hopkins University Press, 1984); Bernard Moitt,

Women and Slavery in the French Antilles (Bloomington: Indiana University Press, 2001); and Vincent Brown, *The Reaper's Garden: Death and Power in the World of Atlantic Slavery* (Cambridge, MA: Harvard University Press, 2010). Slave work is explored in Lorena S. Walsh, *Motives of Honor, Pleasure, and Profit: Plantation Management in the Chesapeake, 1607–1763* (Chapel Hill: University of North Carolina Press, 2010); Philip D. Morgan, *Slave Counterpoint: Black Culture in the Eighteenth-Century Chesapeake and Lowcountry* (Chapel Hill: University of North Carolina Press, 1998); and Justin Roberts, *Slavery and the Enlightenment in the British Atlantic, 1750–1807* (Cambridge: Cambridge University Press, 2013). The most controversial treatment of slave work and productivity in the United States is Robert W. Fogel and Stanley L. Engerman, *Time on the Cross: The Economics of American Negro Slavery* (Boston: Little, Brown and Company, 1974).

Slave resistance involved day-to-day strategies that impeded the production schedules of plantations, runaway tactics and planned revolts. Examples of slave resistance are scattered throughout Ira Berlin, *Generations of Captivity: A History of African American Slaves* (Cambridge, MA: Belknap Press, 2003), while the female dimension is explored in Stephanie Camp, *Closer to Freedom: Enslaved Women and Everyday Resistance in the Plantation South* (Chapel Hill: University of North Carolina Press, 2004). Sophisticated explanations of slave resistance are found in Eugene D. Genovese, *Roll, Jordan, Roll: The World the Slaves Made* (New York: Vintage, 1976). Slaves in flight are described in John Hope Franklin and Loren Schweninger, *Runaway Slaves; Rebels on the Plantation* (New York: Oxford University Press, 1999); Gerald W. Mullin, *Flight and Rebelion: Slave Resistance in Eighteenth-Century Virginia* (New York: Oxford University Press, 1972); and Alvin O. Thompson, *Flight to Freedom: African Runaways and Maroons in the Americas* (Mona, Jamaica: University of the West Indies Press, 2006).

A good general study of slave rebellions is Eugene D. Genovese, *From Rebellion to Revolution: Afro-American Slave Revolts in the Making of the New World* (1979; reprinted New York: Vintage Books, 1981). Specific slave uprisings are analysed in Emilia Viotti da Costa, *Crowns of Glory, Tears of Blood: The Demerara Slave*

Further Reading

Rebellion of 1823 (New York: Oxford University Press, 1994); Laurent Dubois, *Avengers of the New World: The Story of the Haitian Revolution* (Cambridge, MA: Harvard University Press, 2004); and Matt D. Childs, *The 1812 Aponte Rebellion in Cuba and the Struggle Against Atlantic Slavery* (Chapel Hill: University of North Carolina Press, 2006). A lively exchange of views on the extent to which slaves were responsible for abolitionist initiatives can be found in Seymour Drescher and Pieter C. Emmer (eds), *Who Abolished Slavery? Slave Revolts and Abolitionism. A Debate with João Pedro Marques* (Oxford: Berghahn Books, 2010). A rare successful slave revolt is the subject of Marcus Rediker, *The Amistad Rebellion: An Atlantic Odyssey of Slavery and Freedom* (London: Penguin, 2012).

Comprehensive coverage of attitudes towards slavery is provided in a trilogy by David Brion Davis: *The Problem of Slavery in Western Culture* (Ithaca, NY: Cornell University Press, 1966); *The Problem of Slavery in the Age of Revolution* (Ithaca, NY: Cornell University Press, 1975); and *The Problem of Slavery in the Age of Emancipation* (New York: Alfred A. Knopf, 2014). The notion that understanding of freedom is dependent on an awareness of slavery is discussed in Orlando Patterson, *Freedom in the Making of Western Culture* (New York: Basic Books, 1991). Extensive material on attitudes towards slaves is analysed in Winthrop D. Jordan, *White over Black: American Attitudes towards the Negro, 1550–1812* (Chapel Hill: University of North Carolina Press, 1968). The place of abolitionist attitudes in the rise and fall of global slavery is a central theme in Seymour Drescher, *Abolition: A History of Slavery and Antislavery* (Cambridge: Cambridge University Press, 2009).

A learned discussion of the origins of activism against the slave trade in Britain, emphasizing the impetus provided by the American Revolution, is found in Christopher L. Brown, *Moral Capital: Foundations of British Abolitionism* (Chapel Hill: University of North Carolina Press, 2006). The growth of antislavery networks between different countries has recently been investigated in J. R. Oldfield, *Transatlantic Abolitionism in the Age of Revolution: An International History of Anti-Slavery, c. 1787–1820* (Cambridge: Cambridge University Press, 2013). The outlook of planters towards their slave workers is described in James Oakes, *The Ruling Race: A History of American Slaveholders* (New York: Alfred A. Knopf, 1982). The ideological position of planters and their supporters is the subject of Larry E. Tise, *Proslavery: A History of the Defense of Slavery in America, 1701–1840* (Athens, GA: University of Georgia Press, 1987).

A panoramic interpretation of the course of abolitionism throughout the Atlantic world is provided in Robin Blackburn, *The Overthrow of Colonial Slavery, 1776–1848* (London: Verso, 1988). Interesting insights into the ending of the slave trade appear in the essays published in David Eltis and James Walvin (eds), *The Abolition of the Atlantic Slave Trade: Origins and Effects in Europe, Africa, and the Americas* (Madison: University of Wisconsin Press, 1981). The chequered progress of French abolitionism is covered in Lawrence C. Jennings, *French Anti-Slavery: The Movement for the Abolition of Slavery in France, 1802–1848* (Cambridge: Cambridge University Press, 2000). The role of economics in British slave trade abolition is assessed in Seymour Drescher, *Econocide: British Slavery in the Age of Abolition* (Pittsburgh: University of Pittsburgh Press, 1977); and David Ryden, *West Indian Slavery and British Abolition, 1783–1807* (Cambridge: Cambridge University Press, 2009).

The role of international diplomacy in relation to ending the slave trade is central to Leslie Bethell, *Abolition of the Brazilian Slave Trade: Britain, Brazil, and the Slave Trade Question, 1807–1869* (Cambridge: Cambridge University Press, 1970). A comparable work for the Spanish Caribbean is David Murray, *Odious Commerce: Britain, Spain, and the Abolition of the Cuban Slave Trade* (Cambridge: Cambridge University Press, 1980). Further work on the diplomatic aspects of abolitionism can be found in Keith Hamilton and Patrick Salmon (eds), *Slavery, Diplomacy and Empire: Britain and the Suppression of the Slave Trade, 1807–1975* (Brighton: Sussex Academic Press, 2009). The protracted and gradual dismantling of slavery and the slave trade in the United States is the theme of Don E. Fehrenbacher, completed and edited by Ward M. McAfee, *The Slaveholding Republic: An Account of the*

United States Government's Relations to Slavery (New York: Oxford University Press, 2001).

The difficult transitions from slavery to freedom in different parts of the Atlantic world are set down in Rebecca Scott, *Slave Emancipation in Cuba: The Transition to Free Labor* (Princeton, NJ: Princeton University Press, 1985); Rebecca J. Scott, George Reid Andrews, Hebe Castro, Seymour Drescher and Robert Levine, *The Abolition of Slavery and the Aftermath of Emancipation in Brazil* (Durham, NC: Duke University Press, 1988); Eric Foner, *Nothing but Freedom: Emancipation and its Legacy* (Baton Rouge: Louisiana State University Press, 1982); and William A Green, *British Slave Emancipation: The Sugar Colonies and the Great Experiment, 1830–1865* (Oxford: Clarendon Press, 1976). The continuance of slavery beyond the various abolitions occurring throughout Europe and the Americas is surveyed in Suzanne Miers, *Slavery in the Twentieth Century* (Walnut Creek, CA: Altamira Press, 2003).

The public commemoration of slavery is discussed in Gert Oostindie (ed.), *Facing up to the Past: Perspectives on the Commemoration of Slavery from Africa, the Americas and Europe* (Kingston: Ian Randle, 2001); and J. R. Oldfield, *'Chords of Freedom': Commemoration, Ritual and British Transatlantic Slavery* (Manchester: Manchester University Press, 2007). Artistic representations of slavery are placed in context in Marcus Wood, *Blind Memory: Visual Representations of Slavery in England and America, 1780–1865* (Manchester: Manchester University Press, 2000). Exhibitions about slavery are the subject of Douglas J. Hamilton and Robert J. Blyth (eds), *Representing Slavery: Art, Artefacts and Archives* (London: Lund Humphries, 2007). Redress for societies that experienced slavery is the subject of Hilary McD. Beckles, *Britain's Black Debt: Reparations for Caribbean Slavery and Native Genocide* (Kingston: University of the West Indies Press, 2013).

Notes

Introduction

1   David Eltis and Stanley L. Engerman, 'Dependence, Servility, and Coerced Labor in Time and Space', in David Eltis and Stanley L. Engerman (eds), *The Cambridge World History of Slavery. Volume 3. AD 1420–AD 1804* (Cambridge: Cambridge University Press, 2011), pp. 1–21.

2   For a good introduction to these broad themes, see David Brion Davis, *Inhuman Bondage: The Rise and Fall of Slavery in the New World* (New York: Oxford University Press, 2006).

3   Kevin Bales, *Disposable People: New Slavery in the Global Economy*, rev. edn (Berkeley and Los Angeles, CA: University of California Press, 2004).

4   http://www.antislavery.org (accessed 18 March 2015).

Chapter 1: The Flows of the Slave Trade

1   The main compilers of the online database (www.slavevoyages.org), originally published in 2008, were David Eltis, David Richardson, Stephen D. Behrendt and Manolo Garcia Florentino. This compilation expands the first published version available in *The Transatlantic Slave Trade: A Database on CD-ROM* (Cambridge: Cambridge University Press, 1999), documenting 27,233 voyages, for which Eltis, Richardson, Behrendt and Herbert S. Klein were the main contributors. The revised database supersedes earlier estimates of the volume of the slave trade, the most notable of which was Philip D. Curtin, *The Atlantic Slave Trade: A Census* (Madison, WI: University of Wisconsin Press, 1969), a book that is still, however, insightful on the distribution of slaves in time and space. For maps based on the revised database, see David Eltis and David Richardson, *Atlas of the Transatlantic Slave Trade* (New Haven, CT: Yale University Press, 2010).

2   David Richardson, 'Involuntary Migration in the Early Modern World, 1500–1800', in David Eltis and Stanley L. Engerman (eds), *The Cambridge*

World History of Slavery. *Volume 3. AD 1420–AD 1804* (Cambridge: Cambridge University Press, 2011), p. 572.

3   David Eltis and David Richardson, 'A New Assessment of the Transatlantic Slave Trade', in Eltis and Richardson (eds), *Extending the Frontiers: Essays on the New Transatlantic Slave Trade Database* (New Haven, CT: Yale University Press, 2008), pp. 8–9. For slave voyages still to be traced, see Joseph E. Inikori, 'The Known, the Unknown, the Knowable, and the Unknowable: Evidence and the Evaluation of Evidence in the Measurement of the Trans-Atlantic Slave Trade', in Toyin Falola (ed.), *Ghana in Africa and the World: Essays in Honour of Adu Boahen* (Trenton, NJ: Africa World Press, 2003), pp. 535–65. A recent study has identified a further 69,056 embarked slaves from Dutch illegal slave trading voyages that can be added to the database: see Karwan Fatah-Black and Matthias van Rossum, 'Beyond Profitability: The Dutch Transatlantic Slave Trade and its Economic Impact', *Slavery and Abolition*, 36/1 (2015), p. 72.

4   Bernard Bailyn, 'Considering the Slave Trade: History and Memory', *William and Mary Quarterly*, 3rd series, LXVIII/1 (2001), pp. 246–7.

5   Joseph C. Miller, 'A Theme in Variations: A Historical Schema of Slaving in the Atlantic and Indian Ocean Regions', *Slavery and Abolition*, 24/2 (2003), pp. 169–94.

6   James Walvin, *Fruits of Empire: Exotic Produce and British Taste, 1660–1800* (New York: Macmillan, 1997); Carole Shammas, 'The Revolutionary Impact of European Demand for Tropical Goods', in John J. McCusker and Kenneth Morgan (eds), *The Early Modern Atlantic Economy* (Cambridge: Cambridge University Press, 2000), pp. 163–85.

7   Good introductions to the contribution of these nations to transatlantic slaving are Herbert S. Klein, *The Atlantic Slave Trade*, 2nd edn (Cambridge: Cambridge University Press, 2010) and James A. Rawley with Stephen D. Behrendt, *The Transatlantic Slave Trade: A History*, rev. edn (Lincoln, NE: University of Nebraska Press, 2005).

8   Joseph C. Miller, *Way of Death: Merchant Capitalism and the Angolan Slave Trade 1730–1830* (Madison, WI: University of Wisconsin Press, 1988); Roquinaldo Ferreira, *Cross-Cultural Exchange in the Atlantic World: Angola and Brazil during the Era of the Slave Trade* (Cambridge: Cambridge University Press, 2014); Daniel Domingues, 'The Atlantic Slave Trade to Maranhão, 1680–1846: Volume, Routes and Organisation', *Slavery and Abolition*, 29/4 (2008), pp. 477–501; and Mariana Candido, *An African Slaving Port and the Atlantic World: Benguela and its Hinterland* (Cambridge: Cambridge University Press, 2013).

9   Pieter Emmer, 'Slavery and the Slave Trade of the Minor Atlantic Powers', in Eltis and Engerman (eds), *The Cambridge World History of Slavery*, III, pp. 469–72; Per O. Hernaes, *Slaves, Danes, and the African Coast Society* (Trondheim: Department of History, University of Trondheim, 1998); and Andrea Weindl, 'The Slave Trade of Northern Germany from

the Seventeenth to the Nineteenth Centuries', in Eltis and Richardson (eds), *Extending the Frontiers*, pp. 250–71.

10　Pieter Emmer, 'Slavery and the Slave Trade of the Minor Atlantic Powers,' pp. 451–2; Stuart B. Schwartz, 'A Commonwealth Within Itself: The Early Brazilian Sugar Industry, 1550–1670', in Stuart B. Schwartz (ed.), *Tropical Babylons: Sugar and the Making of the Atlantic World* (Chapel Hill, NC: University of North Carolina Press, 2004), pp. 158–66.

11　Recent research has increased the number of slaves taken by the Spanish flag by about 500,000 captives, but these data have not yet appeared in the public domain in line with the quarter-century periods in this table. See Alex Borucki, David Eltis and David Wheat, 'Atlantic History and the Slave Trade to Spanish America', *American Historical Review*, 120/2 (2015), p. 440.

12　For analysis of the size, direction and characteristics of the early slave trade conducted by the Iberian powers, see António de Almeida Mendes, 'The Foundations of the System: A Reassessment of the Slave Trade to the Spanish Americas in the Sixteenth and Seventeenth Centuries', in Eltis and Richardson (eds), *Extending the Frontiers*, pp. 63–94.

13　Miller, *Way of Death*; Manolo Garcia Florentino, *Em costas negras: una história do trafico de escravos entre a Africa e o Rio de Janeiro (Seculos XVIII e XIX)* (São Paulo: Arquivo Nacional, 1997); Eltis and Richardson, *Atlas of the Transatlantic Slave Trade*, p. 39.

14　The licences issued in the early Spanish-controlled slave trade are discussed in Georges Scelle, *La traite négrière aux Indes de Castile: Contrats et traités d'assiento*, 2 vols (Paris: L. Larose and L. Tenin, 1906) and Pierre and Hugette Chaunu, *Séville et l'Atlantique (1504–1660)*, 8 vols (Paris: Editions de l'Ecole, 1955–60). Slaves taken by ships under the Spanish flag are discussed in Borucki, Eltis and Wheat, 'Atlantic History and the Slave Trade to Spanish America,' pp. 440–1.

15　These proportions are based on Shammas, 'The Revolutionary Impact of European Demand for Tropical Goods', pp. 184–5.

16　The main quantitative trends in the British slave trade are summarized in David Richardson, 'The British Empire and the Atlantic Slave Trade, 1660–1807', in P. J. Marshall (ed.), *The Oxford History of the British Empire. Volume 2. The Eighteenth Century* (Oxford: Oxford University Press, 1998), pp. 440–64.

17　K. G. Davies, *The Royal African Company* (London: Longmans, 1957).

18　David Richardson, 'Slavery and Bristol's "Golden Age"', *Slavery and Abolition*, 26/1 (2005), pp. 35–54. Regions of trade for slave voyages outfitted in Bristol are mapped in Eltis and Richardson, *Atlas of the Transatlantic Slave Trade*, p. 51.

19　Kenneth Morgan, 'Liverpool's Dominance in the British Atlantic Slave Trade, 1740–1807' and Stephen D. Behrendt, 'Human Capital in the British Slave Trade', in David Richardson, Suzanne Schwarz and Anthony Tibbles (eds), *Liverpool and Transatlantic Slavery* (Liverpool: Liverpool University Press, 2007), pp. 14–42, 66–97. Regions of trade for slave voyages outfitted in Liverpool are mapped in Eltis and Richardson, *Atlas of the Transatlantic Slave Trade*, p. 52.

20 Jay Coughtry, *The Notorious Triangle: Rhode Island and the African Slave Trade, 1700–1807* (Philadelphia: Temple University Press, 1981); David Richardson, 'Slavery, Trade and Economic Growth in Eighteenth-Century New England', in Barbara L. Solow (ed.), *Slavery and the Atlantic System* (Cambridge: Cambridge University Press, 1991), pp. 237–64. Regions of trade for slave voyages dispatched from Rhode Island are mapped in Eltis and Richardson, *Atlas of the Transatlantic Slave Trade*, p. 71.

21 The most recent overview of this traffic is David Eltis, 'The U.S. Transatlantic Slave Trade, 1644–1867: An Assessment', *Civil War History*, 54/4 (2008), pp. 347–78, which revises the double counting of data on US slave imports found throughout James A. McMillin, *The Final Victims: Foreign Slave Trade to North America, 1783–1810* (Columbia, SC: University of South Carolina Press, 2005).

22 The flows of the French slave trade are outlined in Robert Louis Stein, *The French Slave Trade in the Eighteenth Century: An Old Regime Business* (Madison, WI: University of Wisconsin Press, 1979) and David Geggus, 'The French Slave Trade: An Overview', *William and Mary Quarterly*, 3rd series, LVIII/1 (2001), pp. 119–38. See also David Todd, *Free Trade and its Enemies in France, 1814–1851* (Cambridge: Cambridge University Press, 2015), p. 41.

23 Geggus, 'The French Slave Trade,' p. 122.

24 Stein, *The French Slave Trade*, p. 133.

25 Eltis and Richardson, *An Atlas of the Transatlantic Slave Trade*, p. 75.

26 The best overviews of the Dutch slave trade are by Johannes Menna Postma: see *The Dutch in the Atlantic Slave Trade, 1600–1815* (Cambridge: Cambridge University Press, 1990) and 'A Reassessment of the Dutch Atlantic Slave Trade', in Johannes Postma and Victor Enthoven (eds), *Riches from Atlantic Commerce: Dutch Transatlantic Trade and Shipping, 1585–1817* (Leiden: Brill, 2003), pp. 115–38. See also Rik van Welie, 'Patterns of Slave Trading and Slavery in the Dutch Colonial World, 1596–1863', in Gert Oostindie (ed.), *Dutch Colonialism, Migration and Cultural Heritage* (Leiden: Brill, 2008), pp. 155–260.

27 Emmer, 'Slavery and the Slave Trade of the Minor Atlantic Powers', pp. 470–1.

28 Eltis and Richardson, 'A New Assessment of the Transatlantic Slave Trade', pp. 31, 34.

29 For the flows of the Danish slave trade, see Erik Gobel, 'Danish Trade to the West Indies and Guinea, 1671–1754', *Scandinavian Economic History Review*, 31/1 (1983), pp. 21–49, and Dan H. Anderson, 'Denmark-Norway, Africa, and the Caribbean, 1660–1917: Modernization financed by Slaves and Sugar?', in P. C. Emmer, O. Pétré-Grenouilleau and J. V. Roitman (eds), *A 'Deus ex Machina' Revisited. Atlantic Colonial Trade and European Economic Development* (Leiden: Brill, 2006), p. 298.

30 The designations are not without problems. Historically, Europeans

referred to an 'Upper Guinea' region that is represented in the table under three separate categories: Senegambia, Sierra Leone and the Windward Coast. See Paul E. Lovejoy, 'The Upper Guinea Coast and the Transatlantic Slave Trade Database', *African Economic History*, 38/1 (2009), pp. 1–27, and 'Extending the Frontiers of Transatlantic Slavery, Partially', *Journal of Interdisciplinary History*, XL/1 (2009), pp. 57–70.

31 Virginia Bever Platt, 'The East India Company and the Madagascar Slave Trade,' *William and Mary Quarterly*, 3rd series, XXVI/4 (1969), pp. 548–77.

32 Philip D. Morgan, 'Ending the Slave Trade: A Caribbean and Atlantic Context', in Derek R. Peterson (ed.), *Abolitionism and Imperialism in Britain, Africa, and the Atlantic* (Athens, OH: Ohio University Press, 2010), pp. 111–13.

33 James Walvin, *Atlas of Slavery* (Harlow: Pearson Longman, 2006), pp. 55–7; Candido, *An African Slaving Port and its Hinterland.*

34 Factors influencing the regional supply of slaves are discussed in Paul E. Lovejoy and Jan S. Hogendorn, 'Slave Marketing in West Africa', in Henry A. Gemery and Jan S. Hogendorn (eds), *The Uncommon Market: Essays in the Economic History of the Atlantic Slave Trade* (New York: Academic Press, 1979), pp. 213–35, and David Richardson, 'Cultures of Exchange: Atlantic Africa in the Era of the Slave Trade', *Transactions of the Royal Historical Society*, 6th series, 19 (2009), pp. 151–79.

35 Eltis and Richardson, *Atlas of the Transatlantic Slave Trade*, p. 90. For an older analysis of the dimensions of this trade, see Joseph C. Miller, 'The Number, Origins, and Destinations of Slaves in the Eighteenth-Century Angolan Slave Trade', in Joseph E. Inikori and Stanley L. Engerman (eds), *The Atlantic Slave Trade: Effects on Economies, Societies, and Peoples in Africa, the Americas, and Europe* (Durham, NC: Duke University Press, 1992), pp. 77–115.

36 Daniel B. Domingues da Silva, 'The Atlantic Slave Trade from Angola: A Port-by-Port Estimate of Slaves Embarked, 1701–1867', *International Journal of African Historical Studies*, 46/1 (2013), p. 111.

37 Miller, *Way of Death*, pp. 140–53, 234–41.

38 Paul E. Lovejoy, *Transformations in Slavery: A History of Slavery in Africa*, 2nd edn (Cambridge: Cambridge University Press, 2000), pp. 53–4; Joseph C. Miller, 'The Slave Trade in Congo and Angola', in Martin L. Kilson and Robert I. Rotberg (eds), *The African Diaspora: Interpretive Essays* (Cambridge, MA: Harvard University Press, 1976), pp. 75–113. See also Phyllis I. Martin, *The External Trade of the Loango Coast, 1576–1870* (Oxford: Oxford University Press, 1972).

39 Domingues da Silva, 'The Atlantic Slave Trade from Angola', pp. 116–18. The locations of slaves leaving West Central Africa and their destinations in the Americas are mapped in Eltis and Richardson, *Atlas of the Transatlantic Slave Trade*, pp. 138–9, 141–3, 145, 147–9, 151, 153.

40 Lovejoy, *Transformations in Slavery*, pp. 56–7; I. A. Akinjogbin,

Dahomey and its Neighbours, 1708–1818 (Cambridge: Cambridge University Press, 1967); Robin Law, *The Slave Coast of West Africa 1550–1750: The Impact of the Atlantic Slave Trade on an African Society* (Oxford: Clarendon Press, 1991).

41 Patrick Manning, 'The Slave Trade in the Bight of Benin, 1640–1890', in Gemery and Hogendorn (eds), *The Uncommon Market*, pp. 107–25.

42 David Eltis, 'The Volume and Structure of the Transatlantic Slave Trade: A Reassessment', *William and Mary Quarterly*, 58/1 (2001), p. 34; Robin Law, *Ouidah: The Social History of a West African Slaving Port, 1727–1892* (Athens, OH: Ohio University Press, 2005); Eltis and Richardson, *Atlas of the Transatlantic Slave Trade*, pp. 121–2.

43 David Eltis, 'The Diaspora of Yoruba Speakers, 1650–1865: Dimensions and Implications', in Toyin Falola and Matt D. Childs (eds), *The Yoruba Diaspora in the Atlantic World* (Bloomington, IN: Indiana University Press, 2004), pp. 23–4, 28–9.

44 The slave trade from the Bight of Biafra is mapped in Eltis and Richardson, *Atlas of the Transatlantic Slave Trade*, pp. 126–7, 129–32, 134–5.

45 G. Ugo Nwokeji, *The Slave Trade and Culture in the Bight of Biafra: An African Society in the Atlantic World* (Cambridge: Cambridge University Press, 2010).

46 Lovejoy, *Transformations in Slavery*, pp. 59–60; Paul E. Lovejoy and David Richardson, 'The Slave Ports of the Bight of Biafra in the Eighteenth Century', in Carolyn A. Brown and Paul E. Lovejoy (eds), *Repercussions of the Atlantic Slave Trade: The Interior of the Bight of Biafra and the African Diaspora* (Trenton, NJ: Africa World Press, 2011), pp. 19–56; Kenneth Morgan, 'The Slave Trade at the Bight of Biafra: An Overview', in Toyin Falola and Raphael C. Njoku (eds), *Igbo in the Atlantic World: African Origins and Diasporic Destinations* (Bloomington, IN: Indiana University Press, 2016).

47 Lovejoy, *Transformations in Slavery*, p. 57.

48 Walter Rodney, 'Gold and Slaves on the Gold Coast', *Transactions of the Historical Society of Ghana*, 10 (1969), pp. 13–28; David Eltis, *The Rise of African Slavery in the Americas* (Cambridge: Cambridge University Press, 2000), pp. 150–1.

49 Lovejoy, *Transformations in Slavery*, p. 58; Rebecca Shumway, *The Fante and the Transatlantic Slave Trade* (Rochester, NY: University of Rochester Press, 2011), pp. 57–8.

50 Kwame Yeboa Daaku, *Trade and Politics on the Gold Coast, 1600–1720* (Oxford: Oxford University Press, 1970); A. W. Lawrence, *Fortified Trade Posts: The English in West Africa, 1645–1822* (London: Jonathan Cape, 1969); Randy J. Sparks, *Where the Negroes are Masters: An African Port in the Era of the Slave Trade* (Cambridge: Cambridge University Press, MA, 2014).

51 See also Edward E. Reynolds, *Trade and Economic Change on the Gold Coast, 1807–1874* (London: Longman, 1974). Slave trade locations on the Gold Coast are mapped in Eltis and Richardson, *Atlas of the Transatlantic Slave Trade*, pp. 112, 114, 116, 118.

52 David Eltis, Paul E. Lovejoy and David Richardson, 'Slave-Trading Ports: Towards an Atlantic-Wide Perspective, 1672–1832', in Robin Law and Silke Strickrodt (eds), *Ports of the Slave Trade (Bights of Benin and Biafra)* (Stirling: University of Stirling, 1999), p. 18.

53 Lovejoy, *Transformations in Slavery*, pp. 60–1.

54 Kenneth Morgan, 'Liverpool Ascendant: British Merchants and the Slave Trade on the Upper Guinea Coast, 1701–1808', in Paul E. Lovejoy and Suzanne Schwarz (eds), *Slavery, Abolition and the Transition to Colonialism in Sierra Leone* (Trenton, NJ: Africa World Press, 2014), pp. 27–48.

55 Eltis, 'The Volume and Structure of the Transatlantic Slave Trade,' pp. 33–4. The slave trade from Upper Guinea is mapped in Eltis and Richardson, *Atlas of the Transatlantic Slave Trade*, pp. 96–7, 100, 102, 104–6, 108.

56 The slave trade from Southeast Africa is mapped in Eltis and Richardson, *Atlas of the Transatlantic Slave Trade*, pp. 155–6, 158.

57 Lovejoy, *Transformations in Slavery*, pp. 150–1.

58 For a good overview of the plantation sector, see Philip D. Curtin, *The Rise and Fall of the Plantation Complex: Essays in Atlantic History* (Cambridge: Cambridge University Press, 1990).

59 Michael Tadman, 'The Demographic cost of Sugar: Debates on Slave Societies and Natural Increase in the Americas', *American Historical Review*, 105/5 (2000), pp. 1534–75.

60 Borucki, Eltis and Wheat, 'Atlantic History and the Slave Trade to Spanish America', pp. 434, 440.

61 Stuart B. Schwartz, *Sugar Plantations in the Formation of Brazilian Society: Bahia, 1550–1835* (New York: Cambridge University Press, 1985), pp. 36, 39, 45.

62 Eltis and Richardson, *Atlas of the Transatlantic Slave Trade*, pp. 264–7.

63 Eltis, 'The Volume and Structure of the Transatlantic Slave Trade', pp. 30–1.

64 Daniel Barros Domingues da Silva and David Eltis, 'The Slave Trade to Pernambuco, 1561–1851', in Eltis and Richardson (eds), *Extending the Frontiers*, pp. 95, 104, 113.

65 Daniel Domingues da Silva, 'The Atlantic Slave Trade to Maranhão, 1680–1846: Volume, Routes and Organisation', *Slavery and Abolition*, 29 no. 4 (2008), pp. 471–501.

66 Curtin, *The Rise and Fall of the Plantation Complex*, pp. 190–1; Schwartz, *Sugar Plantations in the Formation of Brazilian Society*; Alexandre Vieira Ribeiro, 'The Transatlantic Slave Trade to Bahia, 1582–1851', in Eltis and Richardson (eds), *Extending the Frontiers*, pp. 133–4, 136–7, 145–6, 148–9.

67 Manolo Florentino, 'The Slave Trade, Colonial Markets, and Slave Families in Rio de Janeiro, Brazil, ca. 1790–ca. 1830', in Eltis and Richardson (eds), *Extending the Frontiers*, pp. 278, 281. The locations of slaves arriving in Brazil are mapped in Eltis and Richardson, *Atlas of the Transatlantic Slave Trade*, pp. 259, 261.

68 Alex Borucki, 'The "African Colonists" of Montevideo: New Light on

the Illegal Slave Trade to Rio de Janeiro and the Río de la Plata (1830–42)', *Slavery and Abolition*, 30/3 (2009), pp. 427–44.

69   Trevor Burnard and Kenneth Morgan, 'The Dynamics of the Slave Market and Slave Purchasing Patterns in Jamaica, 1655–1788', *William and Mary Quarterly*, LVIII/1 (2001), pp. 205–28.

70   Richardson, 'The British Empire and the Atlantic Slave Trade,' pp. 456–8; J. R. Ward, 'The British West Indies in the Age of Abolition, 1748–1815', in Marshall (ed.), *The Oxford History of the British Empire*, II, pp. 415–39. The African coastal origins of slaves imported into the British Caribbean are mapped in Eltis and Richardson, *Atlas of the Transatlantic Slave Trade*, pp. 232, 234–5, 237, 245–7, 249, 252–3, 255.

71   Captive flows of slaves between African and South American regions are mapped in Eltis and Richardson, *Atlas of the Transatlantic Slave Trade*, p. 257.

72   Borucki, Eltis and Wheat, 'Atlantic History and the Slave Trade to Spanish America', pp. 454–5; Nicholas P. Cushner, *Farm and Factory: The Jesuits and the Development of Agrarian Capitalism in Colonial Quito, 1600–1767* (Albany, NY: State University of New York Press, 1982) and idem, *Lords of the Land: Sugar, Wine and Jesuit Estates of Coastal Peru, 1600–1767* (Albany, NY: State University of New York Press, 1980).

73   For the flow of slaves from Africa to Cuba, see the map in Eltis and Richardson, *Atlas of the Transatlantic Slave Trade*, p. 230.

74   David R. Murray, *Odious Commerce: Britain, Spain and the Abolition of the Cuban Slave Trade* (Cambridge: Cambridge University Press, 1980); David Eltis, *Economic Growth and the Ending of the Transatlantic Slave Trade* (Oxford: Oxford University Press, 1987), pp. 56, 190–1.

75   Eltis and Richardson, *Atlas of the Transatlantic Slave Trade*, p. 269; Alex Borucki, 'The Slave Trade to the Río de la Plata, 1777–1812: Trans-Imperial Networks and Atlantic Warfare', *Colonial Latin American Review*, 20/1 (2011), pp. 81–107. For the ports receiving slaves in Río de la Plata, see Eltis and Richardson, *Atlas of the Transatlantic Slave Trade*, p. 262.

76   Linda A. Newson and Susie Minchin, *From Capture to Sale: The Portuguese Slave Trade to Spanish South America in the Early Seventeenth Century* (Leiden: Brill, 2007), pp. 136–7.

77   The flow of slaves to French colonies is illustrated in Eltis and Richardson, *Atlas of the Transatlantic Slave Trade*, pp. 238, 243, 248.

78   James Pritchard, David Eltis and David Richardson, 'The Significance of the French Slave Trade to the Evolution of the French Atlantic World before 1716', in Eltis and Richardson (eds), *Extending the Frontiers*, p. 215.

79   Stein, *The French Slave Trade*, pp. 20–40.

80   Geggus, 'The French Slave Trade', p. 126.

81   Johannes Postma, 'Surinam and its Atlantic Connections, 1667–1795', in Postma and Enthoven (eds), *Riches from Atlantic Commerce*, pp. 287–322; Karwan Fatah-Black, 'Paramibo as Dutch and Atlantic

Nodal Point, 1640–1795', in Gert Oostindie and Jessica V. Roitman (eds), *Dutch Atlantic Connections: Linking Empires, Bridging Borders* (Leiden: Brill, 2014), pp. 52–71. Maps depicting the flow of slaves from Africa to Dutch colonies are included in Eltis and Richardson, *Atlas of the Transatlantic Slave Trade*, pp. 239, 241.

82 Eltis, 'The Volume and Structure of the Transatlantic Slave Trade', p. 31.

83 Emmer, 'Slavery and the Slave Trade of the Minor Atlantic Powers', p. 469; B. W. Higman (ed.), Neville A. T. Hall, *Slave Society in the Danish West Indies: St Thomas, St John and St Croix* (Mona: University of the West Indies Press, 1992). For the flows of the slave trade to the Danish West Indies, see Eltis and Richardson, *Atlas of the Transatlantic Slave Trade*, p. 250.

84 Peter H. Wood, *Black Majority: Negroes in South Carolina from 1670 through the Stono Rebellion* (New York: W.W. Norton & Co., 1974).

85 Philip D. Morgan, *Slave Counterpoint: Black Culture in the Eighteenth-Century Chesapeake and Lowcountry* (Chapel Hill, NC: University of North Carolina Press, 1998), pp. 58–62, 134–45, 149–70.

86 Eltis, 'The U.S. Transatlantic Slave Trade.' Slaves arriving at North American ports are mapped in Eltis and Richardson, *Atlas of the Transatlantic Slave Trade*, pp. 207–8, 210.

87 Alex Borucki, 'Trans-Imperial History in the Making of the Slave Trade to Venezuela, 1526–1811', *Itinerario*, 36/2 (2012), pp. 29–54.

88 Rachel Sarah O'Toole, *Bound Lives: Africans, Indians, and the Making of Race in Colonial Peru* (Pittsburgh: University of Pittsburgh Press, 2012), p. 40.

89 Three studies by Gregory E. O'Malley have documented this trade: 'Beyond the Middle Passage: Slave Migration from the Caribbean to North America, 1619–1807', *William and Mary Quarterly*, 3rd series, LXVI/1 (2009), pp. 125–72; 'Slave Trading Entrepôts and their Hinterlands: Continued Forced Migrations after the Middle Passage to North America', in David T. Gleeson and Simon Lewis (eds), *Ambiguous Anniversary: The Bicentennial of the International Slave Trade Bans* (Columbia, SC: University of South Carolina Press, 2012), pp. 99–124; and *Final Passages: The Intercolonial Slave Trade of British America, 1619–1807* (Chapel Hill, NC: University of North Carolina Press, 2014). See also Nadine Hunt, 'Scattered Memories: The Intra-Caribbean Slave Trade to Spanish America', in Ana Lucia Araujo, Mariana P. Candido and Paul E. Lovejoy (eds), *Crossing Memories: Slavery and African Diaspora* (Trenton, NJ: Africa World Press, 2011), pp. 105–27.

90 O'Malley, 'Beyond the Middle Passage,' pp. 135–68.

91 David Eltis, 'The Traffic in Slaves between the British West Indian Colonies, 1807–1833', *Economic History Review*, 2nd series, 25/1 (1972), pp. 55–64; Higman, *Slave Populations of the British Caribbean*, pp. 79–85; Hilary McD. Beckles, '"An Unfeeling Traffic": The Intercolonial Movement of Slaves in the British Caribbean, 1807–1833', in Walter Johnson (ed.), *The Chattel Principle: Internal Slave Trades in the Americas* (New Haven, CT: Yale University Press, 2004), pp. 256–74.

92 Michael Tadman, *Speculators and Slaves: Masters, Traders, and Slaves in the Old South* (Madison, WI: University of Wisconsin Press, 1989); idem, 'Internal Slave Trades', in Robert L. Paquette and Mark M. Smith (eds), *The Oxford Handbook of Slavery in the Americas* (Oxford: Oxford University Press, 2010), pp. 625–42; and Robert W. Slenes, 'The Brazilian Internal Slave Trade, 1850–1888: Regional Economies, Slave Experience, and the Politics of a Peculiar Market', in Johnson (ed.), *The Chattel Principle*, pp. 325–70.

93 Steven Deyle, *Carry Me Back: The Domestic Slave Trade in American Life* (New York: Oxford University Press, 2005), pp. 4, 5, 153; Walter Johnson, *Soul by Soul: Life Inside the Antebellum Slave Market* (Cambridge, MA: Harvard University Press, 1999).

94 Slenes, 'The Brazilian Internal Slave Trade', pp. 329, 332; Herbert S. Klein, 'The Internal Slave Trade in Nineteenth-Century Brazil: A Study of Slave Importations into Rio de Janeiro in 1852', *Hispanic American Historical Review*, 51/4 (1971), pp. 567–85; Richard Graham, 'Another Middle Passage? The Internal Slave Trade in Brazil', in Johnson (ed.), *The Chattel Principle*, pp. 291–324.

Chapter 2: The Slaving Business

1 For a map of these winds and ocean currents, see David Eltis and David Richardson, *Atlas of the Transatlantic Slave Trade* (New Haven, CT: Yale University Press, 2010), p. 8.

2 Daniel Domingues da Silva, 'The Atlantic Slave Trade to Maranhão, 1680–1846: Volume, Routes and Organisation', *Slavery and Abolition*, 29 no. 4 (2008), pp. 485–6.

3 The model of a triangular trade is discussed in B. W. Higman, *Writing West Indian Histories* (London and Basingstoke: Macmillan Education, 1999), pp. 188–91.

4 For the history of these companies, see P. C. Emmer, 'The West India Company, 1621–1791: Dutch or Atlantic?', in Leonard Blussé and Femme Gaastra (eds), *Companies and Trade: Essays on Overseas Trading companies during the Ancien Regime* (The Hague: Springer, 1981), pp. 71–96; Abdoulaye Ly, *La compagnie du Sénégal* (Dakar: Ifan Ch. A Diop, 1958); J. W. Blake, 'The English Guinea Company, 1618–1660: An Early Example of the Chartered Company in Colonial Development', *Proceedings of the Belfast Natural History and Philosophical Society*, 3 (1945–6), pp. 14–27; George Frederick Zook, *The Company of Royal Adventurers Trading into Africa* (Lancaster, PA: BiblioLife, 1919); K. G. Davies, *The Royal African Company* (London: Longmans, 1957).

5 Adam Jones, *Brandenburg Sources for West African History 1680–1700* (Stuttgart: Steiner, 1985).

6 Davies, *The Royal African Company*, pp. 153–7.

7 Johannes Menne Postma, *The Dutch in the Atlantic Slave Trade 1600–1815* (Cambridge: Cambridge University Press, 1990), pp. 61–2, 126–7.

8 Kwesi J. Anquandah, *Castles and Forts of Ghana* (Accra: Sedco Publishing, 1999); Rebecca Shumway, 'Castle Slaves of the Eighteenth-Century Gold Coast (Ghana)', *Slavery and Abolition*, 35/1 (2014), pp. 84–98; Per O. Hernaes, '"Fort Slavery" at Christiansborg on the Gold Coast: Wage Slavery in the Making?', in Per O. Hernaes and Tore Iversen (eds), *Slavery across Time and Space* (Trondheim: Department of History, University of Trondheim, 2002), pp. 197–229.

9 K. G. Davies, 'The Living and the Dead: White Mortality in West Africa, 1684–1732', in Stanley L. Engerman and Eugene D. Genovese (eds), *Race and Slavery in the Western Hemisphere: Quantitative Studies* (Princeton, NJ: Princeton University Press, 1975), p. 93.

10 Davies, *The Royal African Company*, pp. 241, 251; William St Clair, *The Grand Slave Emporium: Cape Coast Castle and the British Slave Trade* (London: Profile Books, 2006).

11 Eltis and Richardson, *Atlas of the Transatlantic Slave Trade*, pp. 116, 118, 123. On these forts see A. W. Lawrence, *Fortified Trade-Posts: The English in West Africa 1645–1822* (London: Jonathan Cape, 1969); Albert Van Dantzig, *Forts and Castles of Ghana* (Accra: Sedco Publishing, 1980); Edmund Abaka, *House of Slaves and 'Door of No Return': Gold Coast/Ghana Slave Forts, Castles & Dungeons and the Atlantic Slave Trade* (Trenton, NJ: Africa World Press, 2012). Changes in the ownership of these forts are explained in Kenneth Morgan (ed.), *The British Transatlantic Slave Trade. Volume 2. The Royal African Company* (London: Pickering & Chatto, 2003), pp. 330–45.

12 Davies, *The Royal African Company*; pp. 74, 87, 205; William Robert Scott, *The Constitution and Finance of English, Scottish and Irish Joint-Stock Companies to 1720*, 3 vols (Cambridge: Cambridge University Press, 1910–12), II, pp. 20–35.

13 James Pritchard, *In Search of Empire: The French in the Americas, 1670–1730* (Cambridge: Cambridge University Press, 2004), p. 218.

14 António de Almeida Mendes, 'The Foundations of the System: A Reassessment of the Slave Trade to the Spanish Americas in the Sixteenth and Seventeenth Centuries', in David Eltis and David Richardson (eds), *Extending the Frontiers: Essays on the New Transatlantic Slave Trade Database* (New Haven, CT: Yale University Press, 2008), p. 70.

15 Ibid., p. 75; Linda A. Newson and Susie Minchin, *From Capture to Sale: The Portuguese Slave Trade to Spanish South America in the Early Seventeenth Century* (Leiden: Brill, 2007), pp. 9, 19.

16 Mendes, 'The Foundations of the System', p. 82.

17 Elizabeth Donnan, 'The Early Days of the South Sea Company, 1711–1718', *Journal of Economic and Business History*, 2 (1930), pp. 419–50; Colin A. Palmer, *Human Cargoes: The British Slave Trade to Spanish America, 1700–1739* (Champaign-Urbana, IL: University of Illinois Press, 1981).

18 Josep M. Delgado Ribas, 'The Slave Trade in the Spanish Empire (1501–1808): The Shift from Periphery to Center', in Josep M. Fradera and Christopher Schmidt-Nowara (eds), *Slavery & Antislavery in Spain's Atlantic Empire* (New York: Berghahn Books, 2013), p. 34.

19 Alex Borucki, David Eltis and David Wheat, 'Atlantic History and the Slave Trade to Spanish America', *American Historical Review*, 120/2 (2015), p. 443.

20 William A. Pettigrew, *Freedom's Debt: The Royal African Company and the Politics of the Atlantic Slave Trade, 1672–1752* (Chapel Hill, NC: University of North Carolina Press, 2013), pp. 20–1.

21 David Richardson, 'Profits in the Liverpool Slave Trade: The Accounts of William Davenport, 1757–1784', in Roger Anstey and P. E. H. Hair (eds), *Liverpool, the African Slave Trade, and Abolition*, enlarged edn (Liverpool: Liverpool University Press, 1989), p. 67; Robert Louis Stein, *The French Slave Trade in the Eighteenth Century: An Old Regime Business* (Madison, WI: University of Wisconsin Press, 1979), pp. 151–6.

22 Stephen D. Behrendt, 'The Captains in the British Slave Trade from 1785 to 1807', *Transactions of the Historic Society of Lancashire and Cheshire*, 140 (1991), pp. 40–5. For the situation in France see Stein, *The French Slave Trade*, p. 159.

23 For an example of a pool of maritime traders and workers at a major slave port, see Stephen D. Behrendt, 'Human Capital in the British Slave Trade', in David Richardson, Suzanne Schwarz and Anthony Tibbles (eds), *Liverpool and Transatlantic Slavery* (Liverpool: Liverpool University Press, 2007), pp. 66–97.

24 David Richardson, 'West African Consumption Patterns and their Influence on the Eighteenth-Century English Slave Trade', in Henry A. Gemery and Jan S. Hogendorn (eds), *The Uncommon Market: Essays in the Economic History of the Atlantic Slave Trade* (New York: Academic Press, 1979), pp. 303–30; Stanley Alpern, 'What Africans got for their Slaves: A Master List of European Trade Goods', *History in Africa*, 22 (1995), pp. 5–43.

25 Stephen D. Behrendt, A. J. H. Latham and David Northrup (eds), *The Diary of Antera Duke, an Eighteenth-Century African Slave Trader* (Oxford: Oxford University Press, 2010).

26 Marion Johnson, ed. J. T. Lindblad and Robert Ross, *Anglo-African Trade in the Eighteenth Century* (Leiden: Brill, 1990).

27 Richardson, 'West African Consumption Patterns', pp. 312–14.

28 Marion Johnson, 'Technology, Competition, and African Crafts', in Clive Dewey and A. G. Hopkins (eds), *The Imperial Impact: Studies in the Economic History of Africa and India* (London: Athlone Press, 1978), p. 268.

29 W. A. Richards, 'The Import of Firearms into West Africa in the Eighteenth Century', *Journal of African History*, 21/1 (1980), pp. 43–59.

30 L. M. Pole, 'Decline or Survival? Iron Production in West Africa from the Seventeenth to the Twentieth Centuries', *Journal of African History*, 23/4 (1982), pp. 503–13.

31 José Curto, *Enslaving Spirits: The Portuguese-Brazilian Alcohol Trade at Luanda and its Hinterland, c. 1550–1830* (Leiden: Brill, 2004).

32 Coughtry, *The Notorious Triangle*, pp. 80–6, 106–18.

33 For an example of a letter to the captain of a slave ship, see Bruce L. Mouser, '"Keep hur Bottom Well Paid with Stuff": A Letter of Instruction for a Slaving Venture to the Upper Guinea Coast in 1760', in Paul E. Lovejoy and Suzanne Schwarz (eds), *Slavery, Abolition and the Transition to Colonialism in Sierra Leone* (Trenton, NJ: Africa World Press, 2014), pp. 51–67.

34 Behrendt, 'Human Capital in the British Slave Trade', p. 70.

35 Plenty of evidence to support this generalization can be found among the individual slaving voyages listed at www.slavevoyages.org

36 Ty Reese, 'Facilitating the Slave Trade: Company Slaves at Cape Coast Castle, 1750–1807', *Slavery and Abolition*, 31/3 (2010), pp. 363–77.

37 Simon P. Newman, *A New World of Labor: The Development of Plantation Slavery in the British Atlantic* (Philadelphia: University of Pennsylvania Press, 2013), pp. 108–36.

38 Behrendt, 'Human Capital in the British Slave Trade', pp. 67–9.

39 Postma, *The Dutch in the Atlantic Slave Trade*, p. 136.

40 Randy J. Sparks, *Where the Negroes are Masters: An African Port in the Era of the Slave Trade* (Cambridge, MA: Harvard University Press, 2014), pp. 20–1.

41 Newson and Minchin, *From Capture to Sale*, pp. 9, 33, 57.

42 See Paul E. Lovejoy and David Richardson, 'Letters of the Old Calabar Slave Trade, 1760–1789', in Vincent Carretta and Philip Gould (eds), *Genius in Bondage: Literature of the Early Black Atlantic* (Lexington, KY: University of Kentucky Press, 2001), pp. 89–115.

43 Kenneth Morgan, 'Liverpool Ascendant: British Merchants and the Slave Trade on the Upper Guinea Coast, 1701–1808', in Lovejoy and Schwarz (eds), *Slavery, Abolition and the Transition to Colonialism*, pp. 27–48.

44 Jan Hogendorn and Marion Johnson, *The Shell Money of the Slave Trade* (Cambridge: Cambridge University Press, 1986).

45 Lars Sundström, *The Exchange Economy of Pre-Colonial Tropical Africa* (London: C. Hurst & Co. Publishers Ltd, 1974); Marion Johnson, 'The Ounce Trade in Eighteenth Century West Africa', *Journal of African History*, 7/2 (1966), pp. 197–214.

46 Paul E. Lovejoy and David Richardson, 'The Business of Slaving: Pawnship in Western Africa, c. 1600–1810', *Journal of African History*, 42/1 (2001), pp. 67–89; Toyin Falola and Paul E. Lovejoy (eds), *Pawnship, Slavery, and Colonialism in Africa* (Trenton, NJ: Africa World Press, 2003).

47 Randy J. Sparks, 'The Two Princes of Calabar: An Atlantic Odyssey from Slavery to Freedom,' *William and Mary Quarterly*, 3rd series, LIX/1 (2002), pp. 560, 562.

48 Lovejoy, *Transformations in Slavery*, pp. 96, 98.

49 Quoted in Sparks, *Where the Negroes are Masters*, p. 135.

50 Dane Kennedy, *The Last Blank Spaces: Exploring Africa and Australia* (Cambridge, MA: Harvard University Press, 2013).

51 David Northrup, 'West Africans and the Atlantic, 1550–1800', in

Philip D. Morgan and Sean Hawkins (eds), *The Oxford History of the British Empire Companion Series: Black Experience and the Empire* (Oxford: Oxford University Press, 2004), pp. 38–9; Robin Hallett, *The Penetration of Africa: European Exploration in North and West Africa to 1815* (New York: Frederick A. Praeger, 1965).

52 David Eltis, 'African and European Relations in the Last Century of the Transatlantic Slave Trade', in Olivier Pétré-Grenouilleau (ed.), *From Slave Trade to Empire: Europe and the Colonisation of Black Africa 1780s–1880s* (London: Routledge, 2004), p. 36.

53 Candido, *An African Slaving Port and the Atlantic World*, p. 147.

54 Arlino Manuel Caldeira, 'Angola and Seventeenth-Century South Atlantic Trade' and Mariana P. Candido, 'Trade Networks in Benguela, 1700–1850', in David Richardson and Filipa Ribeiro da Silva (eds), *Networks and Trans-Cultural Exchange: Slave Trading in the South Atlantic, 1590–1867* (Leiden: Brill, 2014), pp. 116, 152–3.

55 Candido, *An African Slaving Port and the Atlantic World*, pp. 91, 99, 147, 162, 165–6, 176, 179, 181, 187–9, 214–34.

56 Sparks, *Where the Negroes are Masters*, p. 135.

57 Philip D. Morgan, 'African Migration', in Mary K. Cayton, Elliot J. Gorn and Peter W. Williams (eds), *Encyclopedia of American Social History*, 3 vols (New York: Charles Scribner, 1993), II, p. 799.

58 Philip Misevich, 'The Origins of Slaves Leaving the Upper Guinea Coast in the Nineteenth Century', in Eltis and Richardson (eds), *Extending the Frontiers*, pp. 169–70.

59 G. Ugo Nwokeji and David Eltis, 'Characteristics of Captives Leaving the Cameroons for the Americas, 1822–37', *Journal of African History*, 43/2 (2002), pp. 191–210.

60 For illustrations of these implements of physical coercion, see *Captive Passage: The Transatlantic Slave Trade and the Making of the Americas* (Washington DC: Smithsonian Institution Press, 2002), pp. 52, 66.

61 There are good summary descriptions of these trades in Lovejoy, *Transformations in Slavery*, pp. 9–18, 24–45, 112–33, 152–8, 191–251.

62 James F. Searing, *West African Slavery and Atlantic Commerce: The Senegal River Valley, 1700–1860* (Cambridge: Cambridge University Press, 1993), pp. 34–5; Sean Kelley, 'The Dirty Business of Panyarring and Palaver: Slave Trading on the Upper Guinea Coast in the Eighteenth Century', in Lovejoy and Schwarz (eds), *Slavery, Abolition and the Transition to Colonialism*, pp. 89–107.

63 David Richardson and Filipa Ribeiro da Silva, 'The South Atlantic Slave Trade in Historical Perspective', in Richardson and Ribeiro da Silva (eds), *Networks and Trans-Cultural Exchange*, p. 25.

64 David Northrup, *Trade Without Rulers: Pre-Colonial Economic Development in South-Eastern Nigeria* (Oxford: Oxford University Press, 1978), pp. 105, 151.

65 David Eltis and Stanley L. Engerman, 'Fluctuations in Age and Sex Ratios in the Transatlantic Slave Trade, 1663–1864', *Economic History*

Review, new series, 46/2 (1993), pp. 308–23; David Eltis and Stanley L. Engerman, 'Was the Slave Trade Dominated by Men?', *Journal of Interdisciplinary History*, 23/2 (1992), pp. 237–57.

66 P. E. H. Hair, *The Atlantic Slave Trade and Black Africa* (London: The Historical Association, 1978), p. 27.

67 Paul E. Lovejoy, 'The Children of Slavery – The Transatlantic Phase', *Slavery and Abolition*, 27/2 (2006), pp. 197–217; Audra A. Diptee, 'African Children in the British Slave Trade during the late Eighteenth Century', *ibid.*, 27/2 (2006), pp. 183–96.

68 Stephen D. Behrendt, 'Ecology, Seasonality, and the Transatlantic Slave Trade', in Bernard Bailyn and Patricia L. Denault (eds), *Soundings in Atlantic History: Latent Structures and Intellectual Currents, 1500–1830* (Cambridge, MA: Harvard University Press, 2009), pp. 44–85, 461–85.

69 Marcus Wood, *Blind Memory: Visual Representations of Slavery in England and America, 1780–1865* (Manchester: Manchester University Press, 2000), pp. 25–9.

70 Marcus Rediker, *The Slave Ship: A Human History* (New York: Penguin Books, 2007), pp. 204–5, 251.

71 Colin A. Palmer, 'The Middle Passage', in *Captive Passage*, p. 60.

72 For insight into the captives' experience of the Atlantic crossing, see Stephanie E. Smallwood, *Saltwater Slavery: A Middle Passage from Africa to American Diaspora* (Cambridge, MA: Harvard University Press, 2007), pp. 122–52.

73 J. Cuvelier, *Relations sur le Congo du Père Laurent de Lucques 1700–1707* (Brussels: Institut Royal Colonial Belge, 1953), p. 283.

74 'A Curious and Exact Account of a Voyage to Congo in the Years 1666 and 1667', in A. Churchill (ed.), *A Collection of Voyages and Travels*, 8 vols (London: assignment from Messieurs Churchill, 1752), I, p. 507.

75 Olaudah Equiano, *The Life of Olaudah Equiano, or Gustavus Vassa, the African* (Leeds, 1814; repr. Mineola, NY: Project Gutenburg, 1999), p. 232.

76 Calculated from www.slavevoyages.org (accessed 18 March 2015).

77 Herbert S. Klein and Stanley L. Engerman, 'Slave Mortality in the British Slave Trade 1791–1797', in Anstey and Hair (eds), *Liverpool, the African Slave Trade, and Abolition*, pp. 113–22; Herbert S. Klein, Stanley L. Engerman, Robin Haines and Ralph Shlomowitz, 'Transoceanic Mortality: The Slave Trade in Comparative Perspective', *William and Mary Quarterly*, 3rd series, LVIII/1 (2001), pp. 93–118.

78 Joseph C. Miller, 'The Significance of Drought, Disease and Famine in the Agriculturally Marginal Zones of West-Central Africa', *Journal of African History*, 23/1 (1982), pp. 28–30.

79 Robert L. Stein, 'Mortality in the Eighteenth-Century French Slave Trade', *Journal of African History*, 21/1 (1980), pp. 38–9.

80 Richard A. Steckel and Richard A. Jensen, 'New Evidence on the Causes of Slave and Crew Mortality in the Atlantic Slave Trade', *Journal of Economic History*, 46/1 (1986), pp. 57–77.

81 Kenneth F. Kiple and Brian T. Higgins, 'Mortality Caused by Dehydration During the Middle Passage', in Joseph E. Inikori and Stanley L. Engerman

(eds), *The Atlantic Slave Trade: Effects on Economies, Societies, and Peoples in Africa, the Americas, and Europe* (Durham, NC: Duke University Press, 1992), pp. 321–38.

82 James Walvin, *The Zong: A Massacre, the Law and the End of Slavery* (New Haven, CT: Yale University Press, 2011).

83 Patrick Richardson, *Empire and Slavery* (London: Prentice Hall Press, 1968), p. 18.

84 Stephen D. Behrendt, 'Crew Mortality in the Transatlantic Slave Trade in the Eighteenth Century', *Slavery and Abolition*, 18/1 (1997), pp. 49–71.

85 David Richardson, 'Shipboard Revolts, African Authority, and the Atlantic Slave Trade', *William and Mary Quarterly*, 3rd series, LVIII/1 (2001), pp. 69–92; Eric Taylor, *If We Must Die: Shipboard Insurrections in the Era of the Atlantic Slave Trade* (Baton Rouge, LA: Louisiana State University Press, 2009).

86 Rediker, *The Slave Ship*, pp. 204–6.

87 Selwyn H. H. Carrington, *The Sugar Industry and the Abolition of the Slave Trade, 1775–1810* (Gainesville, FL: University Press of Florida, 2002), pp. 192–4.

88 For a case study of these factors, see Nicholas Radburn, 'Guinea Factors, Slave Sales, and the Profits of the Transatlantic Slave Trade in Late Eighteenth-Century Jamaica: The Case of John Tailyour', *William and Mary Quarterly*, 3rd series, LXXII/2 (2015), pp. 243–86.

89 For an example of the detailed instructions to captains of slave ships, see Henry Bright et al. to Captain James McTaggart, 5 March 1759, in Kenneth Morgan (ed.), *The Bright-Meyler Papers: A Bristol-West India Connection, 1732–1837* (Oxford: Oxford University Press, 2007), pp. 348–9.

90 Quoted in Richard Pares, *A West-India Fortune* (London: Longmans, 1950), p. 121. Pares does not provide a date for this quotation.

91 Christopher Fyfe (ed.), *Anna Maria Falconbridge, Narrative of Two Voyages to the River Sierra Leone during the years 1791–1792–1793 and the Journal of Isaac DuBois with Alexander Falconbridge: An Account of the Slave Trade on the Coast of Africa* (Liverpool: Liverpool University Press, 2000), pp. 216–17. For 'scrambles' in another location, see Sean Kelley, 'Scrambling for Slaves: Captive Sales in Colonial South Carolina', *Slavery and Abolition*, 34/1 (2013), pp. 1–21.

92 Kenneth Morgan, 'Slave Sales in Colonial Charleston', *English Historical Review*, 113/453 (1998), p. 913.

93 David W. Galenson, *Traders, Planters and Slaves: Market Behavior in Early English America* (Cambridge: Cambridge University Press, 1986); Trevor Burnard and Kenneth Morgan, 'The Dynamics of the Slave Market and Slave Purchasing Patterns in Jamaica, 1655–1788', *William and Mary Quarterly*, 3rd series, LVIII/1 (2001), pp. 205–28.

94 Darold D. Wax, 'Preferences for Slaves in Colonial America', *Journal of Negro History*, 58/4 (1973), pp. 371–401; Daniel C. Littlefield, *Rice and Slaves: Ethnicity and the Slave Trade in Colonial South Carolina* (Baton Rouge, LA: Louisiana State University Press, 1981), pp. 9–10;

Trevor Burnard, 'The Atlantic Slave Trade and African Ethnicities in Seventeenth-Century Jamaica', in Richardson et al. (eds), *Liverpool and Transatlantic Slavery*, pp. 144–5; David Geggus, 'The French Slave Trade: An Overview', *William and Mary Quarterly*, 3rd series, LVIII/1 (2001), pp. 127–8.

95 Gwendolyn Midlo Hall, *Slavery and African Ethnicities in the Americas: Restoring the Links* (Chapel Hill, NC: University of North Carolina Press, 2005).

96 Joseph C. Miller, 'Retention, Reinvention, and Remembering: Restoring Identities through Enslavement in Africa and under Slavery in Brazil', in José C. Curto and Paul E. Lovejoy (eds), *Enslaving Connections: Changing Cultures of Africa and Brazil during the Era of Slavery* (Amherst, NY: Prometheus Books, 2004), pp. 81–121.

97 Rediker, *The Slave Ship*, pp. 251–2.

98 Jacob M. Price, 'Credit in the Slave Trade and Plantation Economies', in Barbara L. Solow (ed.), *Slavery and the Rise of the Atlantic System* (Cambridge: Cambridge University Press, 1991), pp. 305–23; Kenneth Morgan, 'Remittance Procedures in the Eighteenth-Century British Slave Trade', *Business History Review*, 79/4 (2005), pp. 715–49; Kenneth Morgan, 'Merchant Networks, the Guarantee System, and the Slave Trade to Jamaica in the 1790s', *Slavery and Abolition*, 37 (2016).

99 David Richardson (ed.), *Bristol, Africa and the Eighteenth Century Slave Trade to America*, 4 vols (Bristol: Bristol Record Society, 1986–96), I, p. xviii, IV, p. xviii; David Richardson, 'Liverpool and the English Slave Trade', in Anthony Tibbles (ed.), *Transatlantic Slavery: Against Human Dignity* (London: Stationary Office Books, 1994), p. 75.

100 Trevor Burnard, 'Kingston, Jamaica: Crucible of Modernity', in Jorge Cañizares-Esguerra, Matt D. Childs and James Sidbury (eds), *The Black Urban Atlantic in the Age of the Slave Trade* (Philadelphia: University of Pennsylvania Press, 2013), pp. 126–7.

101 Guillaume Daudin, 'Profitability of Slave and Long-Distance Trading in Context: The Case of 18th-century France', *Journal of Economic History*, 64/1 (2004), pp. 144–71.

102 Eric Williams, *Capitalism and Slavery* (Chapel Hill, NC: University of North Carolina Press, 1944), p. 36.

103 Richardson, 'Profits in the Liverpool Slave Trade', pp. 60–90.

104 T. S. Ashton, *Economic Fluctuations in England 1700–1800* (Oxford: Oxford University Press, 1959), p. 187.

105 Williams, *Capitalism and Slavery*, p. 105.

106 An assessment of the relevant historiography on supply-side and demand-led explanations of British industrialization is found in Joseph E. Inikori, *Africans and the Industrial Revolution: A Study in International Trade and Economic Development* (Cambridge: Cambridge University Press, 2002), pp. 89–155.

107 David Richardson, 'The Slave Trade, Sugar and British Economic Growth, 1748–1776', *Journal of Interdisciplinary History*, 17/4 (1987), pp. 739–69.

108 David Eltis and Stanley L. Engerman, 'The Importance of Slavery and the Slave Trade to Industrializing Britain', *Journal of Economic History*, 60/1 (2000), pp. 123–44.

109 Kenneth Morgan, *Slavery, Atlantic Trade and the British Economy, 1660–1800* (Cambridge: Cambridge University Press, 2000), pp. 97–8.

110 Eltis and Engerman, 'The Importance of Slavery and the Slave Trade to Industrializing Britain', pp. 123–44; Stanley L. Engerman, 'The Atlantic Economy of the Eighteenth Century: Some Speculations on Economic Development in Britain, America, Africa and Elsewhere', *Journal of European Economic History*, 24/1 (1995), pp. 145–75; Pieter C. Emmer, 'The Rise and Decline of the Dutch Atlantic, 1600–1800', in Oostindie and Roitman (eds), *Dutch Atlantic Connections*, p. 349.

111 Karwan Fatah-Black and Matthias van Rossum, 'Beyond Profitability: The Dutch Transatlantic Slave Trade and its Economic Impact', *Slavery and Abolition*, 36/1 (2015), pp. 63–83.

Chapter 3: Plantation Slavery

1 For detailed case studies of these types of slavery, see Verene A. Shepherd, *Livestock, Sugar and Slavery: Contested Terrain in Colonial Jamaica* (Kingston: Ian Randle Publishers, 2009) and David M. Stark, *Slave Families and the Hato Economy in Puerto Rico* (Gainesville, FL: University Press of Florida, 2015).

2 David Wheat, *Atlantic Africa and the Spanish Caribbean, 1570–1640* (Chapel Hill, NC: University of North Carolina Press, 2015); Alex Borucki, David Eltis and David Wheat, 'Atlantic History and the Slave Trade to Spanish America', *American Historical Review*, 120/2 (2015), pp. 454–5; George Reid Andrews, *Afro-Latin America 1800–2000* (Oxford: Oxford University Press, 2004), pp. 14–15.

3 Overviews of staple crop plantation production include J. H. Galloway, *The Sugar Cane Industry: An Historical Geography from its Origins to 1914* (Cambridge: Cambridge University Press, 1989) and Philip D. Morgan, *Slave Counterpoint: Black Culture in the Eighteenth-Century Chesapeake and Lowcountry* (Chapel Hill, NC: University of North Carolina Press, 1998).

4 Carole Shammas, 'The Revolutionary Impact of European Demand for Tropical Goods', in John J. McCusker and Kenneth Morgan (eds), *The Early Modern Atlantic Economy* (Cambridge: Cambridge University Press, 2000), pp. 163–85; James Walvin, *Fruits of Empire: Exotic Produce and British Taste, 1660–1800* (New York: Macmillan Press, 1997).

5 This paragraph largely follows Philip D Curtin, *The Rise and Fall of the Plantation Complex: Essays in Atlantic History* (Cambridge: Cambridge University Press, 1990), pp. 11–13.

6 Orlando Patterson, *Slavery and Social Death: A Comparative Study* (Cambridge, MA: Harvard University Press, 1985).

7   Vincent Brown, 'Social Death and Political Life in Some Recent Histories of Slavery', *American Historical Review*, 114/5 (2009), pp. 1231–49.

8   Richard Price, 'The Concept of Creolization', in David Eltis and Stanley L. Engerman (eds), *The Cambridge World History of Slavery. Volume 3. AD 1420–AD 1804* (Cambridge: Cambridge University Press, 2011), pp. 513–37. For retention and reshaping of African ethnicities, see Michael A. Gomez, *Exchanging Our Country Marks: The Transformation of African Identities in the Colonial and Antebellum South* (Chapel Hill, NC: University of North Carolina Press, 1998) and Gwendolyn Midlo Hall, *Slavery and African Ethnicities in the Americas: Restoring the Links* (Chapel Hill, NC: University of North Carolina Press, 2005).

9   These ideas are illustrated and analysed at length in studies such as Winthrop D. Jordan, *White over Black: English and American Attitudes toward the Negro, 1550–1812* (Chapel Hill, NC: University of North Carolina Press, 1968); Anthony J. Barker, *The African Link: British Attitudes to the Negro in the Era of the Atlantic Slave Trade, 1550–1807* (London: Frank Cass Publishers, 1978); William B. Cohen, *The French Encounter with Africans: White Response to Blacks, 1530–1880* (Bloomington, IN: Indiana University Press, 1980).

10 These ideas were common over many centuries: see David M. Goldenberg, *The Curse of Ham: Race and Slavery in Early Judaism, Christianity, and Islam* (Princeton, NJ: Princeton University Press, 2003).

11 Davis, *Inhuman Bondage*, pp. 48–76.

12 David Eltis, *The Rise of African Slavery in the Americas* (Cambridge: Cambridge University Press, 2000), pp. 1–84.

13 David Brion Davis, *The Problem of Slavery in Western Culture* (Ithaca, NY: Cornell University Press, 1966), pp. 114–16.

14 Ibid., pp. 118–20; James Farr, '"So Vile and Miserable an Estate": The Problem of Slavery in Locke's Political Thought', *Political Theory*, 14/2 (1986), pp. 263–89; Wayne Glausser, 'Three Approaches to Locke and the Slave Trade', *Journal of the History of Ideas*, 51/2 (1990), pp. 199–216.

15 For the involvement of Africans in slavery and the slave trade before the era of transatlantic slavery, see John Thornton, *Africa and Africans in the Making of the Atlantic World, 1400–1800*, 2nd edn (New York: Cambridge University Press, 1998), pp. 72–125.

16 Kenneth Morgan, *Slavery and the British Empire: From Africa to America* (Oxford: Oxford University Press, 2007), p. 24.

17 Eltis, *The Rise of African Slavery in the Americas*, pp. 1–84.

18 David Eltis and Stanley L. Engerman, 'Dependence, Servility, and Coerced Labor in Time and Space', in Eltis and Engerman (eds), *The Cambridge World History of Slavery*, III, pp. 14–15.

19 Kris Lane, 'Africans and Natives in the Mines of Spanish America', in Matthew Restall (ed.), *Beyond Black and Red: African-Native Relations in Colonial Latin America* (Albuquerque, NM: University of New Mexico Press, 2005), pp. 159–84.

20 John M. Murrin, 'Beneficiaries of Catastrophe: The English Colonies in America', in Eric Foner (ed.), *The New American History*, rev. edn (Philadelphia: Temple University Press, 1997), p. 8.

21 B. W. Higman, *A Concise History of the Caribbean* (Cambridge: Cambridge University Press, 2011), p. 76.

22 Morgan, *Slavery and the British Empire*, pp. 19–20.

23 This argument has been made for the Chesapeake: see James Axtell, 'Colonial America without the Indians', in *After Columbus: Essays in the Ethnohistory of Colonial North America* (New York: Oxford University Press, 1988), pp. 222–43.

24 Burucki, Eltis and Wheat, 'Atlantic History and the Slave Trade to Spanish America', p. 457.

25 Morgan, *Slavery and the British Empire*, pp. 11, 27, 29. See also John J. McCusker and Russell R. Menard, 'The Origins of Slavery in the Americas', in Mark M. Smith and Robert L. Paquette (eds), *The Oxford Handbook of Slavery in the Americas* (New York: Oxford University Press, 2010), pp. 275–92.

26 David Eltis and Stanley L. Engerman, 'Fluctuations in Sex and Age Ratios in the Transatlantic Slave Trade, 1663–1864', *Economic History Review*, 2nd series, 46/2 (1993), pp. 308–23; Paul E. Lovejoy, 'The Children of Slavery – The Transatlantic Phase', *Slavery and Abolition*, 27/2 (2006), pp. 197–217; B. W. Higman, 'Demography and Family Structures', in Eltis and Engerman (eds), *The Cambridge World History of Slavery*, III, p. 490.

27 Philip D. Curtin, 'Epidemiology and the Slave Trade', *Political Science Quarterly*, 83/2 (1968), pp. 190–216; Morgan, *Slave Counterpoint*, pp. 80–95.

28 Borucki, Eltis and Wheat, 'Atlantic History and the Slave Trade to Spanish America', p. 458.

29 Laird W. Bergad, *The Comparative Histories of Slavery in Brazil, Cuba, and the United States* (Cambridge: Cambridge University Press, 2007), pp. 96–7.

30 This is a central theme in Lorena S. Walsh, 'The African American Population of the Colonial United States', and Richard H. Steckel, 'The African American Population of the United States, 1790–1920', in Michael R. Haines and Richard H. Steckel (eds), *A Population History of North America* (Cambridge: Cambridge University Press, 2000), pp. 191–240, 433–82.

31 Morgan, *Slavery and the British Empire*, p. 85.

32 Andrews, *Afro-Latin America*, pp. 17–18.

33 Bergad, *The Comparative Histories of Slavery*, p. 98.

34 Herbert S. Klein and Stanley L. Engerman, 'Fertility Differentials between Slaves in the United States and the British West Indies: A Note on Lactation Practices and their Possible Implications', *William and Mary Quarterly*, 3rd series, XXXV/2 (1978), pp. 357–74. This is supported by evidence from Barbados: see Jerome S. Handler and Robert S. Corruccini, 'Weaning among West Indian Slaves: Historical and Bioanthropological Evidence from Barbados', ibid., XLIII/1 (1986), pp. 111–17.

35 Morgan, *Slave Counterpoint*, p. 87.
36 Ibid., pp. 134–45.
37 Bergad, *The Comparative Histories of Slavery*, p. 99; Robert W. Fogel and Stanley L. Engerman, *Time on the Cross: The Economics of American Negro Slavery* (Boston and Toronto: Little Brown & Co., 1974), pp. 109–17; B. W. Higman, *Slave Populations of the British Caribbean, 1807–1834* (Baltimore, MD: Johns Hopkins University Press, 1984), p. 292; David Eltis, 'Nutritional Trends in Africa and the Americas: The Height of Africans, 1819–1839', *Journal of Interdisciplinary History*, 12/3 (1982), pp. 453–75.
38 Arguments for and against this contention are presented in Fogel and Engerman, *Time on the Cross*, pp. 78–86, and Richard Sutch, 'The Breeding of Slaves for Sale and the Westward Expansion of Slavery, 1850–1860', in Stanley L. Engerman and Eugene D. Genovese (eds), *Race and Slavery in the Western Hemisphere: Quantitative Studies* (Princeton, NJ: Princeton University Press, 1975), pp. 173–210.
39 Higman, *Slave Populations of the British Caribbean*, p. 325.
40 A. Meredith John, *The Plantation Slaves of Trinidad: A Mathematical and Demographic Enquiry, 1783–1816* (Cambridge: Cambridge University Press, 1988), pp. 116, 162.
41 Russell R. Menard and Stuart B. Schwartz, 'Was there a Plantation Demographic Regime in the Americas?', in *The Peopling of the Americas*, 4 vols. (Liege: International Union for the Scientific Study of Population, 1992), I, pp. 51–66; Michael Tadman, 'The Demographic Cost of Sugar: Debates on Slave Societies and Natural Increase in the Americas', *American Historical Review*, 105/5 (2000), pp. 1534–75.
42 Kenneth Morgan, 'Slave Women and Reproduction in Jamaica, ca. 1776–1834', in Gwyn Campbell, Suzanne Miers and Joseph C. Miller (eds), *Women and Slavery. Volume Two. The Modern Atlantic* (Athens, OH: Ohio University Press, 2008), p. 31. For a similar situation on Louisiana sugar plantations, see Richard Follett, 'Gloomy Melancholy: Sexual Reproduction Among Louisiana Slave Women, 1840–60', ibid., p. 61.
43 Morgan, 'Slave Women and Reproduction', p. 33.
44 Ibid., p. 45; Follett, 'Gloomy Melancholy', p. 69.
45 Kenneth Morgan, 'The Struggle for Survival: Slave Infant Mortality in the British Caribbean in the late Eighteenth and Nineteenth Centuries', in Gwyn Campbell, Suzanne Miers and Joseph C. Miller (eds), *Children in Slavery Through the Ages* (Athens, OH: Ohio University Press, 2009), pp. 187–203.
46 Richard B. Sheridan, *Doctors and Slaves: A Medical and Demographic History of Slaves in the British West Indies, 1680–1834* (Cambridge: Cambridge University Press, 1985), pp. 216–19, 236–7.
47 Higman, *Slave Populations of the British Caribbean*, pp. 278–9; Kenneth F. Kiple, *The Caribbean Slave: A Biological History* (Cambridge: Cambridge University Press, 1984).
48 On miscegenation and racial mixture in slave societies see Richard H.

Steckel, 'Miscegenation and the American Slave Schedules', *Journal of Interdisciplinary History*, 11/2 (1980), pp. 251–63, and Gary B. Nash, 'The Hidden History of Mestizo America', *Journal of American History*, 82/3 (1995), pp. 941–64.

49 B. W. Higman, 'The Slave Family and Household in the British West Indies, 1800–1834', *Journal of Interdisciplinary History*, 6/2 (1975), pp. 261–87; Higman, *Slave Populations of the British Caribbean*, pp. 364–73.

50 Morgan, *Slave Counterpoint*, pp. 508–9.

51 Ibid., p. 500.

52 Emily West, *Chains of Love: Slave Couples in Antebellum South Carolina* (Urbana, IL: University of Illinois Press, 2004), pp. 150, 157–8.

53 Bergad, *The Comparative Histories of Slavery*, p. 169; Herbert G. Gutman, *The Black Family in Slavery and Freedom, 1750–1925* (New York: Vintage, 1976); John W. Blassingame, *The Slave Community: Plantation Life in the Antebellum South* (New York: Oxford University Press, 1972).

54 See two studies by Alida C. Metcalf: 'Searching for the Slave Family in Colonial Brazil: A Reconstruction from São Paulo', *Journal of Family History*, 16/3 (1991), pp. 283–97, and *Family and Frontier in Colonial Brazil: Santana de Parnaibá, 1580–1822* (Berkeley and Los Angeles, CA: University of California Press, 1992).

55 Stuart B. Schwartz, *Sugar Plantations in the Formation of Brazilian Society: Bahia 1550–1835* (Cambridge: Cambridge University Press, 1986), pp. 395–9; Herbert S. Klein and Francisco Vidal Luna, *Slavery in Brazil* (Cambridge: Cambridge University Press, 2010), p. 228.

56 Richard Graham, 'Slave Families on a Rural Estate in Colonial Brazil', *Journal of Social History*, 9/3 (1976), pp. 382–402.

57 Mary C. Karasch, *Slave Life in Rio de Janeiro, 1808–1850* (Princeton, NJ: Princeton University Press, 1987), pp. 287–98.

58 Bergad, *The Comparative Histories of Slavery*, pp. 175–6.

59 Karen Y. Morrison, *Cuba's Racial Crucible: The Sexual Economy of Social Identities, 1750–2000* (Bloomington, IN: Indiana University Press, 2015), p. 159.

60 The complexity of the occupational allocation of slaves in urban and rural areas is documented in Higman, *Slave Populations of the British Caribbean*, pp. 188–99, 247–50.

61 Morgan, *Slavery and the British Empire*, p. 104. The deployment of gang labour in Virginia, Barbados and Jamaica is examined in Justin Roberts, *Slavery and the Enlightenment in the British Atlantic, 1750–1807* (New York: Cambridge University Press, 2013), pp. 131–60.

62 Charles Joyner, *Down by the Riverside: A South Carolina Slave Community* (Urbana, IL: University of Illinois Press, 1984), p. 43.

63 Morgan, *Slave Counterpoint*, pp. 105–6, 179–203; William Dusinberre, *Them Dark Days: Slavery in the American Rice Swamps* (New York: Oxford University Press, 1996), p. 32.

64 Kenneth M. Stampp, *The Peculiar Institution: Slavery in the Ante-Bellum South* (New York: Easton Press, 1956), pp. 45–6, 55.

65 Morgan, *Slavery and the British Empire*, pp. 108–9; Roberts, *Slavery and the Enlightenment*, pp. 120–7.

66 Sue Peabody, 'Slavery, Freedom and the Law in the Atlantic World, 1492–1807', in Eltis and Engerman (eds), *The Cambridge World History of Slavery*, III, pp. 600–1; Elsa V. Goveia, 'The West Indian Slave Laws of the Eighteenth Century', *Revista de Ciencias Sociales*, IV/1 (1960), pp. 75–105.

67 Sue Peabody and Keila Grinberg, *Slavery, Freedom, and the Law in the Atlantic World: A Brief History with Documents* (Boston: Palgrave Macmillan, 2007), p. 21.

68 Peabody and Grinberg, *Slavery, Freedom and the Law in the Atlantic World*, pp. 594–628; C. R. Boxer, *The Golden Age of Brazil, 1695–1750: Growing Pains of a Colonial Society* (Berkeley, CA: Sociedade de Estudos Historicos Dom Pedro Secundo, Rio de Janeiro/California University Press, 1962), pp. 138–40.

69 Bernard Moitt, *Women and Slavery in the French Antilles, 1635–1848* (Bloomington, IN: Indiana University Press, 2001), pp. 38, 82, 104, 137.

70 C. Duncan Rice, *The Rise and Fall of Black Slavery* (Baton Rouge, LA: Louisiana State University Press, 1975), p. 75.

71 William M. Wiecek, 'The Statutory Law of Slavery and Race in the Thirteen Mainland Colonies of British America', *William and Mary Quarterly*, XXXIV/2 (1977), pp. 258–80; Thomas D. Morris, *Southern Slavery and the Law, 1619–1860* (Chapel Hill, NC: University of North Carolina Press, 1996).

72 Edward B. Rugemer, 'The Development of Mastery and Race in the Comprehensive Slave Codes of the Greater Caribbean during the Seventeenth Century', *William and Mary Quarterly*, LXX/3 (2013), pp. 429–58.

73 Goveia, 'The West Indian Slave Laws', pp. 75–105; D. Barry Gaspar, '"Rigid and Inclement": Origins of the Jamaica Slave Laws of the Seventeenth Century', in Christopher L. Tomlins and Bruce H. Mann (eds), *The Many Legalities of Early America* (Chapel Hill, NC: University of North Carolina Press, 2001), pp. 78–96.

74 D. Barry Gaspar, 'Ameliorating Slavery: The Leeward Islands Slave Act of 1798', in Robert L. Paquette and Stanley L. Engerman (eds), *The Lesser Antilles in the Age of European Expansion* (Gainesville, FL: University Press of Florida, 1997), pp. 241–58.

75 David Waldstreicher, *Slavery's Constitution: From Revolution to Ratification* (New York: Oxford University Press, 2009); Kenneth Morgan, 'Slavery and the Debate over Ratification of the United States Constitution', *Slavery and Abolition*, 22/3 (2001), pp. 40–65.

76 Morris, *Southern Slavery and the Law*.

77 Gary B. Nash and Jean Soderlund, *Freedom by Degrees: Emancipation in Pennsylvania and Its Aftermath: Emancipation in Eighteenth-century Pennsylvania and its Aftermath* (New York: Oxford University Press, 1991); David N. Gellman, *Emancipating New York: The Politics of Slavery and Freedom, 1777–1827* (Baton Rouge, LA: Louisiana State

University Press, 2006); James J. Gigantino II, *The Ragged Road to Abolition: Slavery and Freedom in New Jersey, 1775–1865* (Philadelphia: University of Pennsylvania Press, 2014).

78   Don E. Fehrenbacher, ed. Ward M. McAfee, *The Slaveholding Republic: An Account of the United States Government's Relations to Slavery* (New York: Oxford University Press, 2001).

79   Lawrence W. Levine, *Black Culture and Black Consciousness: Afro-American Folk Thought from Slavery to Freedom* (New York: Oxford University Press, 1977), pp. 132–3.

80   Roger D. Abrahams and John F. Szwed (eds), *After Africa: Extracts from British Travel Accounts and Journals of the Seventeenth, Eighteenth, and Nineteenth Centuries concerning the Slaves, their Manners, and Customs in the British West Indies* (New Haven, CT: Yale University Press, 1983), pp. 384–5.

81   Mary Turner, 'Religious Beliefs', in Franklin W. Knight (ed.), *General History of the Caribbean. Volume III. The Slave Societies of the Caribbean* (London: Unesco Publishing/Macmillan Education, 1997), p. 289.

82   Thornton, *Africa and Africans in the Making of the Atlantic World*, pp. 235–71. See also Mechal Sobel, *Trabelin' On: The Slave Journey to an Afro-Baptist Faith* (Princeton, NJ: Princeton University Press, 1988).

83   Sylvia R. Frey, 'Remembered Pasts: African Atlantic Religions', in Gad Heuman and Trevor Burnard (eds), *The Routledge History of Slavery* (Abingdon: Routledge, 2011), pp. 153–5; Linda M. Heywood and John K. Thornton, *Central Africans, Atlantic Creoles, and the Foundation of the Americas, 1585–1660* (Cambridge: Cambridge University Press, 2007), pp. 170–96.

84   James H. Sweet, *Recreating Africa: Culture, Kinship, and Religion in the African-Portuguese World, 1441–1770* (Chapel Hill, NC: University of North Carolina Press, 2003), pp. 191–215.

85   Jenny Shaw, *Everyday Life in the Early Caribbean: Irish, Africans and the Construction of Difference* (Athens, GA: University of Georgia Press, 2013), p. 123.

86   Diana Paton, *The Cultural Politics of Obeah: Religion, Colonialism and Modernity in the Caribbean World* (Cambridge: Cambridge University Press, 2015).

87   Vincent Brown, *The Reaper's Garden: Death and Power in the World of Atlantic Slavery* (Cambridge, MA: Harvard University Press, 2008); Diana Paton and Maarit Forde (eds), *Obeah and Other Powers: The Politics of Caribbean Religion and Healing* (Durham, NC: Duke University Press, 2012).

88   On baptism see Stephen Gudeman and Stuart B. Schwartz, '"Cleansing Original Sin": Godparenthood and the Baptism of Slaves in Eighteenth-Century Bahia', in Raymond T. Smith (ed.), *Kinship Ideology and Practice in Latin America* (Chapel Hill, NC: University of North Carolina Press, 1984), pp. 35–58.

89   Levine, *Black Culture and Black Consciousness*; Brown, *The Reaper's Garden*, pp. 64, 66, 68, 212–16, 218.

90 Sweet, *Recreating Africa*, p. 176.

91 Turner, 'Religious Beliefs', p. 298.

92 Albert J. Raboteau, *Slave Religion: the 'Invisible Institution' in the Antebellum South* (New York: Oxford University Press, 1978), p. 230.

93 Frank Tannenbaum, *Slave and Citizen: The Negro in the Americas* (New York: Vintage, 1947).

94 Colin A. Palmer, 'Religion and Magic in Mexican Slave Society, 1570–1650', in Engerman and Genovese (eds), *Race and Slavery in the Western Hemisphere*, pp. 312–13.

95 Herbert S. Klein, *Slavery in the Americas: A Comparative Study of Virginia and Cuba* (Chicago: Quadrangle Books, 1967), pp. 87–104; Margaret M. Olsen, *Slavery and Salvation in Colonial Cartagena de Indias* (Gainesville, FL: University Press of Florida, 2004), p. 61.

96 Gwendolyn Midlo Hall, *Social Control in Slave Plantation Societies: A Comparison of St Domingue and Cuba* (Baton Rouge, LA: Louisiana State University Press, 1971), pp. 102–3.

97 Rachel Sarah O'Toole, *Bound Lives: Africans, Indians, and the Making of Race in Colonial Peru* (Pittsburgh: University of Pittsburgh Press, 2012), pp. 32, 34.

98 Christine Hünefeldt, *Paying the Price of Freedom: Family and Labor among Lima's Slaves 1800–1854* (Berkeley and Los Angeles, CA: University of California Press, 1994), pp. 149–50.

99 Andrews, *Afro-Latin America*, p. 28.

100 Stuart B. Schwartz, *Slaves, Peasants, and Rebels: Reconsidering Brazilian Slavery* (Urbana and Chicago, IL: University of Illinois Press, 1992), p. 140.

101 Kathleen J. Higgins, *'Licentious Liberty' in a Brazilian Gold-Mining Region: Slavery, Gender, and Social Control in Eighteenth-Century Sabará, Minas Gerais* (University Park, PA: Pennsylvania State University Press, 1999), pp. 123–4.

102 Frank Lambert, *Pedlar in Divinity: George Whitefield and the Transatlantic Revivals, 1737–1770* (Princeton, NJ: Princeton University Press, 1994), pp. 153–4, 204–5.

103 Sylvia R. Frey and Betty Wood, *Come Shouting to Zion: African American Protestantism in the American South and British Caribbean to 1830* (Chapel Hill, NC: University of North Carolina Press, 1998); Albert J. Raboteau, 'The Slave Church in the Era of the American Revolution', in Ira Berlin and Ronald Hoffman (eds), *Slavery and Freedom in the Age of the American Revolution* (Urbana and Chicago, IL: University of Illinois Press, 1986), pp. 193–213.

104 Frey and Wood, *Come Shouting to Zion*, pp. 143, 145, 147.

105 J. Harry Bennett, Jr, *Bondsmen and Bishops: Slavery and Apprenticeship on the Codrington Plantations of Barbados, 1710–1838* (Berkeley, CA: University of California Press, 1958). See also Travis Glasson, *Mastering Christianity: Missionary Anglicanism and Slavery in the Atlantic World* (New York: Oxford University Press, 2012).

106 Richard S. Dunn, *A Tale of Two Plantations: Slave Life and Labor*

in Jamaica and Virginia (Cambridge, MA: Harvard University Press, 2014), pp. 224–31, 268–70; Sue Thomas, *Telling West Indian Lives: Life Narrative and the Reform of Plantation Slavery Cultures, 1804–1834* (New York: Oxford University Press, 2014), pp. 124–5.

107 Mary Turner, *Slaves and Missionaries: The Disintegration of Jamaican Slave Society, 1787–1834* (Urbana, IL: University of Illinois Press, 1998).

108 George Brandon, *Santeria from Africa to the New World: The Dead Sell Memories* (Bloomington, IN: Indiana University Press, 1993).

109 Bergad, *The Comparative Histories of Slavery*, p. 182.

110 Stuart B. Schwartz, *All Can be Saved: Religious Tolerance and Salvation in the Iberian Atlantic World* (New Haven, CT: Yale University Press, 2008), p. 199.

111 Frey, 'Remembered Pasts', p. 164.

112 Luis Nicolau Parés, *The Formation of Candomblé: Vodun History and Ritual in Brazil* (Chapel Hill, NC: University of North Carolina Press, 2013), pp. 89, 95.

113 Kate Ramsey, *The Spirits and the Law: Vodou and Power in Haiti* (Chicago: University of Chicago Press, 2011).

114 George Reid Andrews, *Blackness in the White Nation: A History of Afro-Uruguay* (Chapel Hill, NC: University of North Carolina Press, 2010), pp. 24, 26–7.

Chapter 4: Slave Resistance

1 Richard D. E. Burton, *Afro-Creole: Power, Opposition, and Play in the Caribbean* (Ithaca, NY: Cornell University Press, 1997), pp. 48–9.

2 David Barry Gaspar, 'Slavery, Amelioration, and Sunday Markets in Antigua, 1823–1831', *Slavery and Abolition*, 9/1 (1988), pp. 1–28.

3 Kenneth M. Stampp, *The Peculiar Institution: Slavery in the Ante-Bellum South* (New York: Easton Press, 1956), pp. 127–8.

4 Peter H. Wood, *Black Majority: Negroes in Colonial South Carolina from 1670 through the Stono Rebellion* (New York: W.W. Norton & Co., 1974), pp. 308–26.

5 Peter Charles Hoffer, *The Great New York Conspiracy of 1741: Slavery, Crime and Colonial Law* (Lawrence, KS: University Press of Kansas, 2003), pp. 72, 98–9, 102–3.

6 Michael Craton, *Testing the Chains: Resistance to Slavery in the British West Indies* (Ithaca, NY: Cornell University Press, 1982), pp. 303–4, 310, 312.

7 Manuel Barcia, *Seeds of Insurrection: Domination and Resistance on Western Cuban Plantations, 1808–1848* (Baton Rouge, LA: Louisiana State University Press, 2008), p. 108.

8 Michael Mullin, *Africa in America: Slave Acculturation and Resistance in the American South and the British Caribbean, 1736–1831* (Urbana, IL: University of Illinois Press, 1992), p. 255.

9   Pieter C. Emmer, 'Who Abolished Slavery in the Dutch Caribbean?', in Seymour Drescher and Pieter C. Emmer (eds), *Who Abolished Slavery? Slave Revolts and Abolitionism: A Debate with João Pedro Marques* (New York: Berghahn Books, 2010), p. 109.

10 Justin Roberts, 'The "Better Sort" and the "Poorer Sort": Wealth Inequality, Family Formation and the Economy of Energy on British Caribbean Sugar Plantations, 1750–1850', *Slavery and Abolition*, 35/3 (2014), pp. 458–73.

11 Justin Roberts, *Slavery and the Enlightenment in the British Atlantic, 1750–1807* (Cambridge: Cambridge University Press, 2013), pp. 274–5.

12 Philip J. Schwarz, *Twice Condemned: Slaves and the Criminal Laws of Virginia, 1705–1865* (Baton Rouge, LA: Louisiana State University Press, 1988), p. 95.

13 Emilia Viotti da Costa, *Crowns of Glory, Tears of Blood: The Demerara Slave Rebellion of 1823* (New York: Oxford University Press, 1994), p. 82.

14 Trevor Burnard, *Mastery, Tyranny, and Desire: Thomas Thistlewood and his Slaves in the Anglo-Jamaican World* (Chapel Hill, NC: University of North Carolina Press, 2004).

15 Stephanie M. H. Camp, *Closer to Freedom: Enslaved Women and Everyday Resistance in the Plantation South* (Chapel Hill, NC: University of North Carolina Press, 2004), pp. 15, 25.

16 Stuart B. Schwartz, *Slaves, Peasants, and Rebels: Reconsidering Brazilian Slavery* (Urbana and Chicago, IL: University of Illinois Press, 1992), pp. 105–8.

17 Manolo Florentino and Márcia Amantino, 'Runaways and *Quilombolas* in the Americas', in David Eltis and Stanley L. Engerman (eds), *The Cambridge World History of Slavery. Volume 3. AD 1420–AD 1804* (Cambridge: Cambridge University Press, 2011), p. 710.

18 John Ferdinand Dalziel Smyth, *A Tour of the United States of America*, 2 vols (Dublin: Arno Press, 1784), ii, p. 102.

19 For examples of slave runaway advertisements, see John Hope Franklin and Loren Schweninger, *Runaway Slaves: Rebels on the Plantation* (New York: Oxford University Press, 1999); Alvin O. Thompson, *Flight to Freedom: African Runaways and Maroons in the Americas* (Mona: University of the West Indies Press, 2006); Billy G. Smith and Richard Wojtowicz (eds), *Blacks who Stole Themselves: Advertisements for Runaways in the Pennsylvania Gazette, 1728–1790* (Philadelphia: University of Pennsylvania Press, 1989).

20 For a recent article that explores these issues, see Roberts, 'The "Better Sort" and the "Poorer Sort"', pp. 458–73.

21 Gerald W. Mullin, *Flight and Rebellion: Slave Resistance in Eighteenth-Century Virginia* (New York: Oxford University Press, 1972), pp. 35–7, 46, 92.

22 James Sidbury, 'Resistance to Slavery', in Gad Heuman and Trevor Burnard (eds), *The Routledge History of Slavery* (London: Routledge, 2011), p. 210.

23 B. W. Higman, *Slave Population and Economy in Jamaica, 1807–1834* (Cambridge: Cambridge University Press, 1976), p. 180.

24 N. A. T. Hall, 'Maritime Maroons: Grand Marronage from the Danish West Indies', *William and Mary Quarterly*, 3rd series, XLII/4 (1985), pp. 476–98.

25 Kenneth Morgan, *Slavery and Servitude in Colonial North America: A Short History* (New York: New York University Press, 2000), p. 99; Florentino and Amantino, 'Runaways and *Quilombolas* in the Americas', p. 716; David Geggus, 'On the Eve of the Haitian Revolution: Slave Runaways in Saint Domingue in the year 1790', *Slavery and Abolition*, 6/3 (1985), p. 117.

26 Marvin L. Michael Kay and Lorin Lee Cary, *Slavery in North Carolina 1748–1775* (Chapel Hill, NC: University of North Carolina Press, 1995), pp. 134, 268.

27 Mullin, *Flight and Rebellion*, p. 192; Philip D. Morgan, *Slave Counterpoint: Black Culture in the Eighteenth-Century Chesapeake and Lowcountry* (Chapel Hill, NC: University of North Carolina Press, 1998), p. 152.

28 Gad Heuman, 'Runaway Slaves in Nineteenth-Century Barbados', *Slavery and Abolition*, 6/3 (1985), pp. 102–3.

29 Philip D. Morgan and Andrew Jackson O'Shaughnessy, 'Arming Slaves in the American Revolution', in Christopher Leslie Brown and Philip D. Morgan (eds), *Arming Slaves: From Classical Times to the Modern Age* (New Haven, CT: Yale University Press, 2006), pp. 180–208.

30 Sylvia R. Frey, *Water from the Rock: Black Resistance in a Revolutionary Age* (Princeton, NJ: Princeton University Press, 1991); John N. Grant, 'Black Immigrants into Nova Scotia, 1776–1815', *Journal of Negro History*, 58/3 (1973), pp. 253–70. For an interesting evaluation of the numbers, see Cassandra Pybus, 'Jefferson's Faulty Math: The Question of Slave Defections in the American Revolution', *William and Mary Quarterly*, 3rd series, XLII/2 (2005), pp. 243–64.

31 Roger N. Buckley, *Slaves in Red Coats: The British West India Regiments, 1795–1815* (New Haven, CT: Yale University Press, 1979); idem, *The British in the West Indies: Society and the Military in the Revolutionary Age* (Gainesville, FL: University Press of Florida, 1998).

32 Joseph P. Reidy, 'Armed Slaves and the Struggles for Republican Liberty in the U.S. Civil War', in Brown and Morgan (eds), *Arming Slaves*, p. 275.

33 David Brion Davis, *The Problem of Slavery in the Age of Emancipation* (New York: Oxford University Press, 2014), p. 255; Steven Hahn, *The Political Worlds of Slavery and Freedom* (Cambridge, MA: Harvard University Press, 2009), pp. 13, 24, 27–38, 55–8.

34 For a case study see Paul Lokken, 'A Maroon Moment: Rebel Slaves in Early Seventeenth-Century Guatemala', *Slavery and Abolition*, 25/3 (2004), pp. 44–58.

35 Richard Price, 'Maroons and their Communities', in Richard Price (ed.), *Maroon Societies: Rebel Slave Communities in the Americas*, 3rd edn (Baltimore: John Hopkins University Press, 1996), pp. 1–30.

36 João Pedro Marques, 'Slave Revolts and the Abolition of Slavery: An Overinterpretation', in Drescher and Emmer (eds), *Who Abolished Slavery?*, p. 9.

37 Frederick P. Bowser, *The African Slave in Colonial Peru, 1524–1650* (Stanford, CA: Stanford University Press, 1974), pp. 187–8.

38 Arcaya M. Pedro, *Insurreción de los negros de la Serranía de Coro* (Caracas: Pan American Institute, 1930), pp. 23–49.

39 Barcia, *Seeds of Insurrection*, p. 49.

40 Aquiles Escalante, 'Palenques in Colombia', in Price (ed.), *Maroon Societies*, pp. 74, 76.

41 Florentino and Amantino, 'Runaways and *Quilombolas* in the Americas', p. 715.

42 Anthony McFarlane, 'Cimarrones and Palenques: Runaways and Resistance in Colonial Colombia', *Slavery and Abolition*, 6/3 (1985), p. 134.

43 Francisco Pérez de la Riva, 'Cuban Palenques', in Price (ed.), *Maroon Societies*, pp. 49–54, 57; Gabino La Rosa Corzo, *Runaway Slave Settlements in Cuba: Resistance and Repression* (Chapel Hill, NC: University of North Carolina Press, 2003).

44 Patrick J. Carroll, 'Mandinga: The Evolution of a Mexican Runaway Slave Community, 1735–1827', *Comparative Studies in Society and History*, 19/4 (1977), pp. 488–504.

45 George Reid Andrews, *Afro-Latin America 1800–2000* (New York: Oxford University Press, 2004), p. 38; R. Anderson, 'The Quilombo of Palmares: A New Overview of a Maroon State in Seventeenth-Century Brazil', *Journal of Latin American Studies*, 28/3 (1996), pp. 545–66.

46 Price, 'Maroons and their Communities', pp. 10–13.

47 Andrews, *Afro-Latin America*, p. 75.

48 Mavis Campbell, *The Maroons of Jamaica, 1655–1796: A History of Resistance, Collaboration and Betrayal* (Granby, MA: Bergin and Garvey, 1988), pp. 126–42.

49 Douglas Hall, *In Miserable Slavery: Thomas Thistlewood in Jamaica, 1750–1786* (Mona: University of the West Indies Press, 1989), pp. 96, 110.

50 Campbell, *The Maroons of Jamaica*, pp. 209–49.

51 Roquinaldo Ferreira, 'Slaving and Resistance to Slaving in West Central Africa', in Eltis and Engerman (eds), *The Cambridge World History of Slavery*, III, pp. 123–30.

52 James F. Searing, *West African Slavery and Atlantic Commerce: The Senegal River Valley, 1700–1860* (Cambridge: Cambridge University Press, 1993), p. 109.

53 Eric Robert Taylor, *If We Must Die: Shipboard Insurrections in the Era of the Atlantic Slave Trade* (Baton Rouge, LA: Louisiana State University Press, 2006). See also David Richardson, 'Shipboard Revolts, African Authority and the Atlantic Slave Trade', *William and Mary Quarterly*, 3rd series, LVIII/1 (2001), pp. 69–92.

54 Marcus Rediker, *The Amistad Rebellion: An Atlantic Odyssey of Slavery and Freedom* (New York: Penguin Books, 2012).

55 Lynne Guitar, 'Boiling it Down: Slavery on the First Commercial Sugarcane Ingenios in the Americas', in Jane G. Landers and Barry M. Robinson (eds), *Slaves, Subjects and Subversives: Blacks in Colonial Latin America* (Albuquerque, NM: University of New Mexico Press, 2006), pp. 49–52.

56 Eugene D. Genovese, *From Rebellion to Revolution: Afro-American Slave Revolts in the Making of the New World* (Baton Rouge, LA: Louisiana State University, 1979), pp. 12–15.

57 Ray A. Kea, '"When I die, I shall return to my own land": an "Amina" Slave Rebellion in the Danish West Indies, 1733–1734', in John Hunwick and Nancy Lawler (eds), *The Cloth of Many Colored Silks: Papers on History and Society Ghanian and Islamic in Honor of Ivor Wilks* (Evanston, IL: Northwestern University Press, 1996), pp. 159–93.

58 Genovese, *From Rebellion to Revolution*, pp. 12–15.

59 Ibid., pp. 16–17.

60 For an example of the brutal suppression of a slave revolt, see Wood, *Black Majority*, pp. 318–20.

61 James D. Rice, *Tales from a Revolution: Bacon's Rebellion and the Transformation of Early America* (Oxford: Oxford University Press, 2012).

62 Ibid.; Edmund S. Morgan, *American Slavery, American Freedom: The Ordeal of Colonial Virginia* (New York: Oxford University Press, 1975), pp. 250–70.

63 Peter C. Hoffer, *Cry Liberty: The Great Stono River Slave Rebellion of 1739* (New York: Oxford University Press, 2012), pp. 67–8, 77–121.

64 John K. Thornton, 'African Dimensions of the Stono Rebellion', *American Historical Review*, 96/4 (1991), pp. 1101–13.

65 Hoffer, *Cry Liberty*, pp. 127–31.

66 Douglas R. Egerton, *Gabriel's Rebellion: The Virginia Slave Conspiracies of 1800 and 1802* (Chapel Hill, NC: University of North Carolina Press, 1993); James Sidbury, *Ploughshares into Swords: Race, Rebellion, and Identity in Gabriel's Virginia, 1730–1810* (Cambridge: Cambridge University Press, 1997).

67 Sidbury, *Ploughshares into Swords*, pp. 95, 120–8; Egerton, *Gabriel's Rebellion*, pp. 119–46.

68 Stephen B. Oates, *The Fires of Jubilee: Nat Turner's Fierce Rebellion* (New York: HarperPerennials, 1990).

69 Eva Sheppard Wolf, *Race and Liberty in the New Nation: Emancipation in Virginia from the Revolution to Nat Turner's Rebellion* (Baton Rouge, LA: Louisiana State University Press, 2006), pp. 196–7, 199, 213, 217, 231, 235.

70 Trevor Burnard, 'Powerless Masters: The Curious Decline of Jamaican Sugar Planters in the Foundational Period of British Abolitionism', *Slavery and Abolition*, 32/2 (2011), p. 193.

71 Vincent Brown, *The Coromantee Wars: An Archipelago of Insurrection* (Cambridge, MA: Harvard University Press, 2015).

72 Trevor Burnard, 'Slavery and the Causes of the American Revolution in

Plantation British America', in Andrew Shankman (ed.), *The World of the Revolutionary American Republic: Land, Labor, and the Conflict for a Continent* (New York: Routledge, 2014), pp. 58–9, 62; Diana Paton, *The Cultural Politics of Obeah: Religion, Colonialism and Modernity* (Cambridge: Cambridge University Press, 2015), p. 41.

73 Claudius K. Fergus, *Revolutionary Emancipation: Slavery and Abolitionism in the British West Indies* (Baton Rouge, LA: Louisiana State University Press, 2013), pp. xii, 38–9.

74 Davis, *The Problem of Slavery in the Age of Emancipation*, p. 47.

75 Stanley L. Engerman, 'France, Britain and the Economic Growth of Colonial North America', in John J. McCusker and Kenneth Morgan (eds), *The Early Modern Atlantic Economy* (Cambridge: Cambridge University Press, 2000), p. 237.

76 Fergus, *Revolutionary Emancipation*, p. 79.

77 Carolyn E. Fick, *The Making of Haiti: The Saint Domingue Revolution from Below* (Knoxville, TN: University of Tennessee Press, 1990), pp. 240–1.

78 David Geggus, *Slavery, War, and Revolution: The British Occupation of Saint Domingue, 1793–1798* (Oxford: Clarendon Press, 1982), pp. 212, 383; Bernard Moitt, *Women and Slavery in the French Antilles, 1635–1848* (Bloomington, IN: Indiana University Press, 2001), pp. 136–7.

79 John Thornton, 'African Soldiers in the Haitian Revolution', *Journal of Caribbean History*, 25/1–2 (1992), pp. 58–81.

80 David Geggus, 'Toussaint Louverture and the Haitian Revolution', in R. William Weisberger (ed.), *Profiles of Revolutionaries in Atlantic History, 1750–1850* (New York: Columbia University Press, 2007), pp. 115–35.

81 Alfred N. Hunt, *Haiti's Influence on Antebellum America: Slumbering Volcano in the Caribbean* (Baton Rouge, LA: Louisiana State University Press, 1988), p. 23.

82 Ibid., p. 24.

83 Laurent Dubois, *Avengers of the New World: The Story of the Haitian Revolution* (Cambridge, MA: Harvard University Press, 2005).

84 Jeremy D. Popkin, *You are all Free: The Haitian Revolution and the Abolition of Slavery* (Cambridge: Cambridge University Press, 2010), pp. 379–80.

85 C. L. R. James, *The Black Jacobins: Toussaint L'Ouverture and the San Domingo Revolution* (New York: Penguin, 1963), p. 136.

86 Moitt, *Women and Slavery in the French Antilles*, pp. 127–30; Laurent Dubois, 'The Promise of Revolution: Saint-Domingue and the Struggle for Autonomy in Guadeloupe, 1797–1802', in David P. Geggus (ed.), *The Impact of the Haitian Revolution in the Atlantic World* (Columbia, SC: University of South Carolina Press, 2001), pp. 112–34.

87 Bernard Moitt, 'Slave Resistance in Guadeloupe and Martinique, 1791–1848', *Journal of Caribbean History*, 25/1–2 (1991), pp. 136–59.

88 Moitt, *Women and Slavery in the French Antilles*, pp. 130–2; Rebecca Hartkopf Schloss, *Sweet Liberty: The Final Days of Liberty in Martinique* (Philadelphia: University of Pennsylvania Press, 2009).

89 David Geggus, 'The Enigma of Jamaica in the 1790s: New Light on the Causes of Slave Rebellions', *William and Mary Quarterly*, XLIV/2 (1987), pp. 274–99.

90 Craton, *Testing the Chains*, pp. 183–90.

91 Matt D. Childs, *The 1812 Aponte Rebellion in Cuba and the Struggle against Atlantic Slavery* (Chapel Hill, NC: University of North Carolina Press, 2006), pp. 120, 128, 147, 154.

92 Johannes Postma, *Slave Revolts* (Westport, CT: Greenwood Press, 2008), p. 66.

93 Karen Robert, 'Slavery and Freedom in the Ten Years' War: Cuba, 1868–1878', *Slavery and Abolition*, 13/3 (1992), pp. 181–200; Robert L. Paquette, *Sugar is Made with Blood: The Conspiracy of La Escalera and the Conflict between Empires over Slavery in Cuba* (Middletown, CT: Wesleyan University Press, 1988), pp. 4, 71–2, 209–13, 219–22, 229, 233, 235, 264.

94 Craton, *Testing the Chains*, pp. 257, 259, 269, 294; Michael Craton, 'Proto-Peasant Revolts? The Late Slave Rebellions in the British West Indies, 1816–1832', *Past and Present*, 85 (1979), pp. 99–125.

95 Hilary Beckles, *Black Rebellion in Barbados* (Bridgetown: Antilles Publications, 1984).

96 Craton, 'Proto-Peasant Revolts?', pp. 99–125.

97 Mary Turner, *Slaves and Missionaries: The Disintegration of Jamaican Slave Society, 1787–1834* (Urbana, IL: University of Illinois Press, 1982); Viotti da Costa, *Crowns of Glory, Tears of Blood*, pp. 9–15, 99–100.

98 Craton, *Testing the Chains*, pp. 295–7.

99 Ibid., p. 261.

100 Viotti da Costa, *Crowns of Glory, Tears of Blood*, p. 229.

101 Craton, *Testing the Chains*, p. 321.

102 Ibid., pp. 254–90.

103 Ibid., pp. 291–321; Gelien Matthews, *Caribbean Slave Revolts and the British Abolitionist Movement* (Baton Rouge, LA: Louisiana State University Press, 2006), p. 107.

104 Craton, 'Proto-Peasant Revolts?', pp. 99–125.

105 Genovese, *From Rebellion to Revolution*, p. 30; João José Reis, 'Slave Resistance in Brazil: Bahia, 1808–1835', *Luso-Brazilian Review*, 25/1 (1988), pp. 111–44.

106 Marques, 'Slave Revolts', p. 51.

107 Andrews, *Afro-Latin America*, pp. 75, 77; Dick Geary, '"Atlantic Revolution" or Local Difficulty: Aspects of Revolt in Brazil, 1780–1880', *Australian Journal of Politics and History*, 56/3 (2010), pp. 339–41, 346; Stuart B. Schwartz, 'Cantos and Quilombos', in Landers and Robinson (eds), *Slaves, Subjects and Subversives*, pp. 248–9.

108 João José Reis, *Slave Rebellion in Brazil: The Muslim Uprising of 1835 in Bahia* (Baltimore: John Hopkins University Press, 1993), pp. 40, 93,

Notes to Pages 114–117

96; R. K. Kent, 'African Revolt in Bahia: 24–25 January 1835', *Journal of Social History* 3/4 (1970), pp. 334–56.
109 Marques, 'Slave Revolts', p. 73.

Chapter 5: The Abolition of the Slave Trade

1 Richard Hellie, 'Russian Slavery and Serfdom, 1450–1804' and Ehud R. Toledano, 'Enslavement in the Ottoman Empire in the Early Modern Period', in David Eltis and Stanley L. Engerman (eds), *The Cambridge World History of Slavery. Volume 3. AD 1420–AD 1804* (Cambridge: Cambridge University Press, 2011), pp. 25–46, 275–95.

2 David Brion Davis, *The Problem of Slavery in Western Culture* (Ithaca, NY: Oxford University Press, 1966); *Inhuman Bondage: The Rise and Fall of Slavery in the New World* (New York: Oxford University Press, 2006).

3 Davis, *The Problem of Slavery in Western Culture*, pp. 116–17.

4 Christopher L. Brown, 'Slavery and Antislavery', in Nicholas Canny and Philip D. Morgan (eds), *Oxford Handbook on the Atlantic World, c. 1450–1820* (Oxford: Oxford University Press, 2011), pp. 602–17.

5 Andrew O'Shaughnessy, *An Empire Divided: The American Revolution and the British Caribbean* (Philadelphia: Temple University Press, 2000); David Beck Ryden, *West Indian Slavery and British Abolition, 1783–1807* (Cambridge: Cambridge University Press, 2009); B. W. Higman, 'The West India Interest in Parliament, 1807–1833', *Historical Studies*, 13/49 (1967), pp. 1–19.

6 Ryden, *West Indian Slavery and British Abolition*, pp. 21–4, 40–82.

7 Larry E. Tise, *Proslavery: A History of the Defense of Slavery in America, 1701–1840* (Athens, GA: University of Georgia Press, 1987), pp. 109, 115.

8 Davis, *The Problem of Slavery in Western Culture*, pp. 394–6, 402–8.

9 Roger Anstey, *The Atlantic Slave Trade and British Abolition 1760–1810* (London: Macmillan, 1975), pp. 98–106, 113–15.

10 Seymour Drescher, *The Mighty Experiment: Free Labor versus Slavery in British Emancipation* (New York: Oxford University Press, 2002), pp. 29–32.

11 Dee E. Andrews, *The Methodists and Revolutionary America, 1760–1800: the Shaping of an Evangelical Culture* (Princeton, NJ: Princeton University Press, 2000).

12 Jean R. Soderlund, *Quakers and Slavery: A Divided Spirit* (Princeton, NJ: Princeton University Press, 1985).

13 Anstey, *The Atlantic Slave Trade and British Abolition*, pp. 126, 130–3; Christopher L. Brown, 'Christianity and the Campaign against Slavery and the Slave Trade', in Stewart I. Brown and Timothy Tackett (eds), *The Cambridge History of Christianity. Volume 7. Enlightenment, Revolution, and Reawakening, 1660–1815* (Cambridge: Cambridge University Press, 2006), pp. 517–35.

14   Maurice Jackson, *Let This Voice be Heard: Anthony Benezet, Father of Atlantic Abolitionism* (Philadelphia: University of Pennsylvania Press, 2009); Geoffrey Plank, *John Woolman's Path to the Peaceable Kingdom: A Quaker in the British Empire* (Philadelphia, PA: University of Pennsylvania Press, 2012).

15   David Brion Davis, *The Problem of Slavery in the Age of Revolution, 1770–1823* (Ithaca, NY: Cornell University Press, 1975), pp. 213–54; Soderlund, *Quakers & Slavery*.

16   J. R. Oldfield, *Transatlantic Abolitionism in the Age of Revolution: An International History of Anti-Slavery, c. 1787–1820* (Cambridge: Cambridge University Press, 2013).

17   Christopher Leslie Brown, *Moral Capital: Foundations of British Abolitionism* (Chapel Hill, NC: University of North Carolina Press, 2006), pp. 391–433; Robin Blackburn, *The Overthrow of Colonial Slavery, 1776–1848* (London: Verso, 1988), pp. 133–44.

18   Seymour Drescher, 'The Shocking Birth of British Abolitionism', *Slavery and Abolition*, 33/4 (2012), pp. 571–93.

19   Stanley L. Engerman, 'Emancipations in Comparative Perspective: A Long and Wide View', in Gert Oostindie (ed.), *Fifty Years Later: Antislavery, Capitalism and Modernity in the Dutch Orbit* (Leiden: Brill, 1995), p. 227.

20   Svend E. Green-Pedersen, 'The Economic Considerations behind the Danish Abolition of the Negro Slave Trade', in Henry A. Gemery and Jan S. Hogendorn (eds), *The Uncommon Market: Essays in the Economic History of the Atlantic Slave Trade* (New York: Academic Press, 1979), pp. 402–17.

21   Daniel P. Hopkins, 'The Danish Ban on the Atlantic Slave Trade and Denmark's Colonial Ambitions, 1787–1807', *Itinerario*, 25/3–4 (2001), pp. 154–84; Pernille Røge, 'Why the Danes Got There First – A Trans-Imperial Study of the Abolition of the Danish Slave Trade in 1792', *Slavery and Abolition*, 35/4 (2014), pp. 576–92.

22   Erik Gøbel, 'The Danish Edict of 16th March 1792 to Abolish the Slave Trade', in Jan Parmentier and Sander Spanoghe (eds), *Orbis in Orbem: Liber amicorum John Everaert* (Ghent: Academia Press, 2001), pp. 252–62 (quotation on p. 262).

23   Hans Christian Johansen, 'The Reality behind the Demographic Arguments to Abolish the Danish Slave Trade', in David Eltis and James Walvin (eds), *The Abolition of the Atlantic Slave Trade: Origins and Effects in Europe, Africa, and the Americas* (Madison, WI: University of Wisconsin Press, 1981), pp. 224, 229.

24   The background to the two abolitions is explored in numerous books including Anstey, *The Atlantic Slave Trade and British Abolition*; Seymour Drescher, *Econocide: British Slavery in the Era of Abolition* (Pittsburgh: University of Pittsburgh Press, 1977); W. E. B. Du Bois, *The Suppression of the African Slave Trade to the United States of America 1638–1870* (Cambridge, MA: Harvard University Press, 1896); Don E. Fehrenbacher with Ward M. McAfee, *The Slaveholding Republic: An*

Account of the United States Government's Relations to Slavery (New York: Oxford University Press, 2001), pp. 135–50.

25 See the contemporary comments quoted in Matthew Mason, 'Keeping Up Appearances: The International Politics of Slave Trade Abolition in the Nineteenth-Century Atlantic World', *William and Mary Quarterly*, 3rd series, LXVI/4 (2009), pp. 809–10.

26 Data taken from www.slavevoyages.org (accessed 18 March 2015).

27 David Eltis, 'The U.S. Transatlantic Slave Trade, 1644–1867: An Assessment', *Civil War History*, 54/4 (2008), p. 370; David Eltis and David Richardson, 'A New Assessment of the Transatlantic Slave Trade', in David Eltis and David Richardson (eds), *Extending the Frontiers: Essays on the New Transatlantic Slave Trade Database* (New Haven, CT: Yale University Press, 2008), p. 48.

28 These different political traditions are well illustrated in relation to anti-slave trade politics in Dale H. Porter, *The Abolition of the Slave Trade in England, 1784–1807* (Hamden, CT: Archon Books, 1970) and Fehrenbacher with McAfee, *The Slaveholding Republic*. See also two studies by Paul Finkelman: 'Regulating the African Slave Trade', *Civil War History*, 54/4 (2008), pp. 379–405; 'The American Suppression of the African Slave Trade: Lessons on Legal Change, Social Policy, and Legislation', *Akron Law Review*, 433 (2009), pp. 458–61.

29 This was the phrase used by Edward Stanley, the Colonial Secretary, in 1833: see Drescher, *The Mighty Experiment*, p. 123.

30 The main contours of the vast scholarship on these issues can be found in Davis, *The Problem of Slavery in the Age of Revolution*; Blackburn, *The Overthrow of Colonial Slavery*; Seymour Drescher, *Abolition: A History of Slavery and Antislavery* (New York: Cambridge University Press, 2009).

31 J. R. Oldfield, *Popular Politics and British Anti-Slavery: The Mobilisation of Public Opinion against the Slave Trade, 1787–1807* (Manchester: University of Manchester Press, 1995); Kenneth Morgan, 'Proscription by Degrees: The Ending of the African Slave Trade to the United States', in David T. Gleeson and Simon Lewis (eds), *Ambiguous Anniversary: The Bicentennial of the International Slave Trade Bans* (Columbia, SC: University of South Carolina Press, 2012), pp. 1–34.

32 On these themes see Anstey, *The Atlantic Slave Trade and British Abolition*, pp. 264–73; James Walvin, *Black Ivory: A History of British Slavery* (London: HarperCollins, 1992), pp. 46–8; James Walvin, *The Zong: A Massacre, the Law and the End of Slavery* (New Haven, CT: Yale University Press, 2011).

33 Arthur Zilversmit, *The First Emancipation: The Abolition of Slavery in the North* (Chicago: University of Chicago Press, 1967).

34 Numerous studies provide chapter and verse for these generalizations, including Gary B. Nash, *Race and Revolution* (Madison, WI: Rowman & Littlefield Publishers, 1990) and Richard S. Newman, *The Transformation of American Abolitionism: Fighting Slavery in the Early Republic* (Chapel Hill, NC: University of North Carolina Press, 2002). Gradual

emancipation laws were passed in Pennsylvania in 1780, in New York in 1799, and in New Jersey in 1804.

35 Morgan, 'Proscription by Degrees', p. 9; Eva Sheppard Wolf, *Race and Liberty in the New Nation: Emancipation in Virginia from the Revolution to Nat Turner's Rebellion* (Baton Rouge, LA: Louisiana State University Press, 2006), pp. 14, 24–5, 28; Gary B. Nash and Jean Soderlund, *Freedom by Degrees: Emancipation in Pennsylvania and its Aftermath* (New York: Oxford University Press, 1991), p. 102.

36 David N. Gellman, *Emancipating New York: The Politics of Slavery and Freedom 1777–1827* (Baton Rouge, LA: Louisiana State University Press, 2006), pp. 52–3; Graham Russell Hodges, *Root and Branch: African Americans in New York and East Jersey, 1613–1863* (Chapel Hill, NC: University of North Carolina Press, 1999), p. 169; Patrick S. Brady, 'The Slave Trade and Sectionalism in South Carolina, 1787–1808', *Journal of Southern History*, 38/4 (1972), pp. 601–20; Ruth Scarborough, *The Opposition to Slavery in Georgia prior to 1860* (Nashville, TN: University of Tennessee Press, 1933), pp. 108–10.

37 Anstey, *The Atlantic Slave Trade and British Abolition*, pp. 269–70, 275, 330–1.

38 Bruce A. Ragsdale, *A Planters' Republic: The Search for Economic Independence in Revolutionary Virginia* (Madison, WI: University of Wisconsin Press, 1996), pp. 135, 251.

39 Rachel N. Klein, *Unification of a Slave State: The Rise of the Planter Class in the South Carolina Backcountry, 1760–1808* (Chapel Hill, NC: University of North Carolina Press, 1990), pp. 131–2.

40 James LoGerfo, 'Sir William Dolben and "The Cause of Humanity": The Passage of the Slave Trade Regulation Act of 1788', *Eighteenth-Century Studies*, 6/4 (1973), pp. 431–51.

41 Davis, *The Problem of Slavery in the Age of Revolution*, p. 24.

42 Morgan, 'Proscription by Degrees', pp. 7–8.

43 Paul Finkelman, 'Slavery and the Constitutional Convention: Making a Covenant with Death', in Richard R. Beeman, Edward C. Carter II and Stephen Botein (eds), *Beyond Confederation: Origins of the Constitution and American National Identity* (Chapel Hill, NC: University of North Carolina Press, 1987), pp. 195–217.

44 Kenneth Morgan, 'Slavery and the Debate over Ratification of the United States Constitution', *Slavery and Abolition*, 22/3 (2001), p. 45.

45 Davis, *The Problem of Slavery in the Age of Revolution*, pp. 123–5.

46 See, for example, Nash, *Race and Revolution*, pp. 27–9; Gary B. Nash, *The Forgotten Fifth: African Americans in the Age of Revolution* (Cambridge, MA: Harvard University Press, 2006), pp. 79–85.

47 Paul Finkelman, 'The Founders and Slavery: Little Ventured, Little Gained', *Yale Journal of Law & the Humanities*, 13/2 (2001), p. 422.

48 Donald L. Robinson, *Slavery in the Structure of American Politics, 1765–1820* (New York: W.W. Norton & Co., 1971), pp. 302–10; Howard A. Ohline, 'Slavery, Economics, and Congressional Politics, 1790', *Journal of Southern History*, 46/3 (1980), pp. 335–60.

49 Fehrenbacher, *The Slaveholding Republic*, p. 136.
50 Brady, 'The Slave Trade and Sectionalism', pp. 601–20.
51 Brown, *Moral Capital*.
52 Oldfield, *Popular Politics and British Anti-Slavery*, p. 114.
53 Ibid., pp. 155–66; Marcus Wood, *Blind Memory: Visual Representations of Slavery in England and America, 1780–1865* (Manchester: University of Manchester Press, 2000), pp. 16–21, 25–9; M. Guyatt, 'The Wedgwood Slave Medallion', *Journal of Design History*, 13/2 (2000), pp. 93–105.
54 David Geggus, *Slavery, War, and Revolution: The British Occupation of Saint Domingue, 1793–1798* (Oxford: Clarendon Press, 1982).
55 Jed Handelsman Shugerman, 'The Louisiana Purchase and South Carolina's Reopening of the Slave Trade in 1803', *Journal of the Early Republic*, 22/2 (2002), pp. 253–90.
56 Michael Duffy, 'The French Revolution and British Attitudes to the West Indian Colonies', in David Barry Gaspar and David Geggus (eds), *A Turbulent Time: The French Revolution and the Greater Caribbean* (Bloomington, IN: Indiana University Press, 1997), pp. 78–101.
57 Davis, *The Problem of Slavery in the Age of Revolution*, pp. 441–3.
58 See the data in www.slavevoyages.org (accessed 18 March 2015).
59 Anstey, *The Atlantic Slave Trade and British Abolition*, pp. 364–402.
60 Eric Williams, *Capitalism and Slavery* (Chapel Hill, NC: University of North Carolina Press, 1944); Drescher, *Econocide*. See also Ryden, *West Indian Slavery and British Abolition*, pp. 254–70; Selwyn H. H. Carrington, *The Sugar Industry and the Abolition of the British Slave Trade, 1775–1810* (Gainesville, FL: University Press of Florida, 2002); David Richardson, 'The Ending of the British Slave Trade in 1807: The Economic Context', in Stephen Farrell, Melanie Unwin and James Walvin (eds), *The British Slave Trade: Abolition, Parliament and People* (Edinburgh: Edinburgh University Press, 2007), pp. 127–40.
61 Lacy K. Ford, *Deliver Us from Evil: The Slavery Question in the Old South* (New York: Oxford University Press, 2009), pp. 96–102, 105.
62 Michael Tadman, *Speculators and Slaves: Masters, Traders, and Slaves in the Old South*, 2nd edn (Madison, WI: University of Wisconsin Press, 1996); Steven M. Deyle, *Carry Me Back: The Domestic Slave Trade in American Life* (New York: Oxford University Press, 2006).
63 Stephen J. Goldfarb, 'An Inquiry into the Politics of the Prohibition of the International Slave Trade', *Agricultural History*, 68/2 (1994), pp. 29–30.
64 Morgan, 'Proscription by Degrees', p. 1.
65 Blackburn, *The Overthrow of Colonial Slavery*, p. 286.
66 The legislative history of the two bills is covered in Du Bois, *Suppression of the African Slave Trade*, pp. 107–15.
67 Ford, *Deliver us from Evil*, p. 125.
68 Drescher, *Abolition*, pp. 135–6.
69 For a summary of the debates see Robinson, *Slavery in the Structure of American Politics*, pp. 324–7. See also Matthew Mason, 'Slavery Overshadowed: Congress Debates Prohibiting the Atlantic Slave Trade

to the United States, 1806–1807', *Journal of the Early Republic*, 20/1 (2000), pp. 59–81.

70   David Eltis, 'Was Abolition of the U.S. and British Slave Trade Significant in the Broader Atlantic Context?', *William and Mary Quarterly*, 3rd series, LXVI/4 (2009), pp. 722, 724.

71   Christopher Lloyd, *The Navy and the Slave Trade: The Suppression of the African Slave Trade in the Nineteenth Century* (London: Longmans, Green and Co., 1949).

72   Christopher L. Brown, 'Abolition of the Atlantic Slave Trade', in Gad Heuman and Trevor Burnard (eds), *The Routledge History of Slavery* (London: Routledge, 2011), pp. 287, 290–1; James F. King, 'The Latin American Republics and the Suppression of the Slave Trade', *Hispanic American Historical Review*, XXIV/3 (1944), p. 391.

73   Leslie Bethell, 'The Mixed Commissions for the Suppression of the Transatlantic Slave Trade in the Nineteenth Century', *Journal of African History*, 7/1 (1966), pp. 79–93; Farida Shaikh, 'Judicial Diplomacy: British Officials and the Mixed Commission Courts', in Keith Hamilton and Patrick Salmon (eds), *Slavery, Diplomacy and Empire: Britain and the Suppression of the Slave Trade, 1907–1975* (Eastbourne: Sussex Academic Press, 2009), pp. 42–64.

74   Robin Law, 'Abolition and Imperialism: International Law and the British Suppression of the Atlantic Slave Trade', in Derek R. Pearson (ed.), *Abolitionism and Imperialism in Britain, Africa, and the Atlantic* (Athens, OH: Ohio University Press, 2010), pp. 150–74.

75   David Eltis and David Richardson, *Atlas of the Transatlantic Slave Trade* (New Haven, CT: Yale University Press, 2010), p. 272.

76   Andrew Lambert, 'Slavery, Free Trade and Naval Strategy, 1840–1860', in Hamilton and Salmon (eds), *Slavery, Diplomacy and Empire*, pp. 65–80; Brown, 'Abolition of the Atlantic Slave Trade', p. 292.

77   Eltis, 'Was Abolition of the U.S. and British Slave Trades Significant in the Broader Atlantic Context?', p. 729.

78   Marika Sherwood, *Abolition: Britain and the Slave Trade Since 1807* (London: I.B.Tauris, 2007); Chris Evans, 'Brazilian Gold, Cuban Copper and the Final Frontier of British Anti-Slavery', *Slavery and Abolition*, 34/1 (2013), pp. 118–34.

79   Johannes Menne Postma, *The Dutch in the Atlantic Slave Trade, 1600–1815* (New York: Cambridge University Press, 1990), pp. 290–1.

80   Pieter C. Emmer, 'Abolition of the Abolished: The Illegal Dutch Slave Trade and the Mixed Courts', in Eltis and Walvin (eds), *The Abolition of the Atlantic Slave Trade*, pp. 177–92.

81   Lawrence C. Jennings, *French Anti-Slavery: The Movement for the Abolition of Slavery in France, 1802–1848* (Cambridge: Cambridge University Press, 2000), pp. 1–5.

82   Paul Michael Kielstra, *The Politics of Slave Trade Suppression in Britain and France, 1814–48* (Basingstoke: Palgrave Macmillan, 2000), p. 58.

83   Victor Bulmer-Thomas, *The Economic History of the Caribbean since the Napoleonic Wars* (Cambridge: Cambridge University Press, 2012), p. 52.

84 Jennings, *French Anti-Slavery*, pp. 32, 36; Serge Daget, 'The Abolition of the Slave Trade by France: The Decisive Years 1826–1831', in David Richardson (ed.), *Abolition and its Aftermath: The Historical Context, 1790–1916* (London: Cass, 1985), pp. 141–67.

85 João Pedro Marques, *The Sounds of Silence: Nineteenth-Century Portugal and the Abolition of the Slave Trade* (New York: Berghahn Books, 2006), pp. 35–98.

86 C. Duncan Rice, *The Rise and Fall of Black Slavery* (Baton Rouge, LA: Louisiana State University Press, 1975), p. 234.

87 Hugh Thomas, *The Slave Trade: The Story of the Atlantic Slave Trade: 1440–1870* (New York: Simon and Schuster, 1997), p. 739.

88 Leslie M. Bethell, *The Abolition of the Brazilian Slave Trade: Britain, Brazil, and the Slave Trade Question, 1807–1869* (Cambridge: Cambridge University Press, 1970), pp. 13, 15, 19.

89 David Eltis, *Economic Growth and the Ending of the Transatlantic Slave Trade* (New York: Oxford University Press, 1987), p. 93.

90 Bethell, *The Abolition of the Brazilian Slave Trade*, pp. 47, 60–1, 72, 85, 121, 150.

91 Jeffrey D. Needell, *The Party of Order: The Conservatives, the State, and Slavery in the Brazilian Monarchy, 1831–1871* (Stanford, CA: Stanford University Press, 2006), p. 152.

92 Marques, *The Sounds of Silence*, p. 165.

93 Dale T. Graden, *Disease, Resistance, and Lies: The Demise of the Transatlantic Slave Trade to Brazil and Cuba* (Baton Rouge, LA: Louisiana State University Press, 2014), pp. 62, 70, 78–9, 140.

94 Bethell, *The Abolition of the Brazilian Slave Trade*, pp. 214, 267, 284, 310, 321, 324, 330. See also Jeffrey D. Needell, 'The Abolition of the Brazilian Slave Trade in 1850: Historiography, Slave Agency and Statemanship', *Journal of Latin American Studies*, 33/4 (2001), pp. 681–711.

95 Eltis, *Economic Growth and the Ending of the Transatlantic Slave Trade*, p. 213.

96 Bethell, *The Abolition of the Brazilian Slave Trade*, pp. 327–63. See also John Macmillan, 'Myths and Lessons of Liberal Intervention: the British Campaign for the Abolition of the Atlantic Slave Trade to Brazil', *Global Responsibility to Protect*, 4/1 (2012), pp. 98–124.

97 Eltis, *Economic Growth and the Ending of the Transatlantic Slave Trade*, pp. 214–17; Drescher, *Abolition*, pp. 290–1.

98 David Murray, *Odious Commerce: Britain, Spain and the Abolition of the Cuban Slave Trade* (Cambridge: Cambridge University Press, 1980), pp. 67, 69, 71, 78, 90, 97, 100–1, 201.

99 Graden, *Disease, Resistance, and Lies*, pp. 12–25.

100 Murray, *Odious Commerce*, pp. 241, 248, 269; Lambert, 'Slavery, Free Trade and Naval Strategy', pp. 74–5.

101 Eltis, *Economic Growth and the Ending of the Transatlantic Slave Trade*, pp. 218–19; Murray, *Odious Commerce*, pp. 305–6, 308.

102 Ibid., p. 219; Drescher, *Abolition*, pp. 333–5; Murray, *Odious Commerce*, pp. 311, 315–16, 319, 322–3.

Chapter 6: Slave Emancipation

1   For examples of this procedure in the seventeenth-century Chesapeake, see T. H. Breen and Stephen Innes, *'Myne Owne Ground': Race and Freedom on Virginia's Eastern Shore, 1640–1676* (New York: Oxford University Press, 1980), pp. 72–7.

2   Hubert H. S. Ames, 'Coartación: A Spanish Institution for the Advancement of Slaves into Freedom', *Yale Review*, 17 (1909), pp. 412–31; Herbert S. Klein, *Slavery in the Americas: A Comparative Study of Cuba and Virginia* (Chicago: University of Chicago Press, 1967), pp. 196–200.

3   Laird W. Bergad, *The Comparative History of Slavery in Cuba, Brazil, and the United States* (New York: Oxford University Press, 2007), p. 196.

4   Sue Peabody and Keila Grinberg, *Slavery, Freedom, and the Law in the Atlantic World: A Brief History with Documents* (Boston: Bedford/ St. Martin's, 2007), p. 137.

5   Philip D. Morgan, 'The Black Experience in the British Empire, 1680–1810', in P. J. Marshall (ed.), *The Oxford History of the British Empire. Volume 2. The Eighteenth Century* (Oxford: Oxford University Press, 1998), p. 471.

6   Jerome S. Handler and John T. Pohlmann, 'Slave Manumissions and Freedmen in Seventeenth-Century Barbados', *William and Mary Quarterly*, 3rd series, XLI/3 (1984), pp. 390–408.

7   Stuart B. Schwartz, 'The Manumission of Slaves in Colonial Brazil: Bahia, 1684–1745', *Hispanic American Historical Review*, 54/4 (1974), pp. 603–35.

8   Lyman L. Johnson, 'Manumission in Colonial Buenos Aires, 1776–1810', *Hispanic American Historical Review*, 59/2 (1979), pp. 258–79.

9   This is illustrated in Kathleen J. Higgins, *'Licentious Liberty' in a Brazilian Gold-Mining Region: Slavery, Gender, and Social Control in Eighteenth-Century Sabará* (University Park, PA: Pennsylvania State University Press, 1999), pp. 145–74.

10   Carl N. Degler, *Neither Black nor White: Slavery and Race Relations in Brazil and the United States* (New York: Macmillan, 1971), pp. 38–47.

11   These themes are discussed in Andrew Fede, *Roadblocks to Freedom: Slavery and Manumission in the United States South* (New Orleans, LA: Quid Pro, 2011).

12   T. Stephen Whitman, *The Price of Freedom: Slavery and Manumission in Baltimore and Early National Maryland* (Lexington, KY: University Press of Kentucky, 1997), pp. 93–118.

13   Herbert S. Klein, 'The African American Experience in Comparative Perspective: The Current Question of the Debate', in Sherwin K. Bryant, Rachel Sarah O'Toole and Ben Vinson III (eds), *Africans to Spanish America: Expanding the Diaspora* (Urbana, Chicago and Springfield, IL: University of Illinois Press, 2012), p. 211.

14   Bernard Moitt, *Women and Slavery in the French Antilles, 1635–1848* (Bloomington, IN: Indiana University Press, 2001), p. 151.

15 David Brion Davis, *The Problem of Slavery in the Age of Emancipation* (New York: Oxford University Press, 2014), pp. 54–5.

16 Wayne Ackerson, *The African Institution (1807–1827) and the Antislavery Movement in Great Britain* (Lampeter: Edwin Mellen, 2005).

17 B. W. Higman, 'Slavery and the Development of Demographic Theory in the Age of the Industrial Revolution', in James Walvin (ed.), *Slavery and British Society, 1776–1846* (London: Macmillan, 1982), pp. 164–94.

18 David Brion Davis, *Slavery and Human Progress* (New York: Oxford University Press, 1984), pp. 179–82.

19 Quoted in Vincent Harlow and A. F. Madden (eds), *British Colonial Developments 1774–1834* (Oxford: Oxford University Press, 1953), p. 560.

20 Quoted ibid., p. 560.

21 Similarities between amelioration and gradual emancipation, even though different outcomes were expected, are analysed in Christa Dierksheide, *Amelioration and Empire: Progress and Slavery in the Plantation Americas* (Charlottesville, VA: University of Virginia Press, 2014).

22 Michael Craton, *Sinews of Empire: A Short History of British Slavery* (New York: Oxford University Press, 1974), pp. 273–4.

23 Kenneth Morgan, *Slavery and the British Empire: From Africa to America* (Oxford: Oxford University Press, 2007), p. 181.

24 Emilia Viotti da Costa, *Crowns of Glory, Tears of Blood: The Demerara Slave Rebellion of 1823* (New York: Oxford University Press, 1994), pp. 252–74, 290–1.

25 James Walvin, 'The Propaganda of Anti-Slavery', in Walvin (ed.), *Slavery and British Society*, pp. 60–3.

26 Clare Midgley, *Women against Slavery: The British Campaigns, 1780–1870* (New York: Routledge, 1992), pp. 1–118.

27 Seymour Drescher, 'Two Variants of Anti-Slavery: Religious Organization and Social Mobilization in Britain and France, 1780–1870', in Christine Bolt and Seymour Drescher (eds), *Anti-Slavery, Religion and Reform* (Folkestone: Archon Press, 1980), p. 48.

28 Mary Turner, *Slaves and Missionaries: The Disintegration of Jamaican Slave Society, 1787–1834* (Urbana, IL: University of Illinois Press, 1982), pp. 65–101.

29 David Brion Davis, 'The Emergence of Immediatism in British and American Antislavery Thought', *Mississippi Valley Historical Review*, 49/2 (1962), pp. 209–30; Morgan, *Slavery and the British Empire*, p. 187.

30 Craton, *Sinews of Empire*, pp. 277–8; Turner, *Slaves and Missionaries*, pp. 148–91.

31 Seymour Drescher, *The Mighty Experiment: Free Labor versus Slavery in British Emancipation* (New York: Oxford University Press, 2002), pp. 54–9.

32 William A. Green, *British Slave Emancipation: The Sugar Colonies and the Great Experiment 1830–1865* (Oxford: Oxford University Press, 1976), p. 118.

33 Ibid., pp. 120–2. Details of the compensation paid out are analysed in Nicholas Draper, *The Price of Emancipation: Slave-ownership, Compensation and British Society at the End of Slavery* (Cambridge: Cambridge University Press, 2010).

34 Craton, *Sinews of Empire*, p. 280.

35 Richard Huzzey, *Freedom Burning: Anti-Slavery and Empire in Victorian Britain* (Ithaca, NY: Cornell University Press, 2012).

36 Neville A. T. Hall, ed. B. W. Higman, *Slave Society in the Danish West Indies: St Thomas, St John, and St Croix* (Mona: University of the West Indies Press, 1992), p. 208.

37 Ibid., p. 209; Drescher, *Abolition: A History of Slavery and Antislavery* (New York: Cambridge University Press, 2009), p. 280.

38 Laurent Dubois, *Avengers of the New World: The Story of the Haitian Revolution* (Cambridge, MA: Harvard University Press, 2004).

39 Lawrence C. Jennings, *French Reaction to British Slave Emancipation* (Baton Rouge, LA: Louisiana State University Press, 1988).

40 Lawrence C. Jennings, *French Anti-Slavery: The Movement for the Abolition of Slavery in France, 1802–1848* (Cambridge: Cambridge University Press, 2000), pp. 8–12, 16–19, 166–8, 193–5, 263–4, 283–4.

41 Ibid., pp. 203–4, 239.

42 Seymour Drescher, 'Public Opinion and the Destruction of British Colonial Slavery', in Walvin (ed.), *Slavery and British Society*, p. 26.

43 Andre Midas, 'Victor Schoelcher and Emancipation in the French West Indies', *Caribbean Historical Review*, 1 (1950), pp. 110–30.

44 Jennings, *French Anti-Slavery* pp. 273–84; Lawrence C. Jennings, 'Cyril Bissette, Radical Black French Abolitionist', *French History*, 9/1 (1995), pp. 48–66.

45 John J. McCusker and Russell R. Menard, *The Economy of British America, 1607–1789*, 2nd edn (Chapel Hill, NC: University of North Carolina Press, 1989), pp. 118–25, 130, 132, 175–80.

46 Mary Ellison, *Support for Secession: Lancashire and the American Civil War* (Chicago: University of Chicago Press, 1972); Peter Kolchin, *American Slavery* (Harmondsworth: Penguin, 1993), p. 95.

47 Michael Tadman, *Speculators and Slaves: Masters, Traders, and Slaves in the Old South*, 2nd edn (Madison, WI: University of Wisconsin Press, 1996); Walter Johnson, *Soul by Soul: Life Inside the Antebellum Slave Market* (Cambridge, MA: Harvard University Press, 1999).

48 Joseph C. G. Kennedy, 'Population of the United States in 1860; Compiled from the Original Returns of the Eighth Census under the Direction of the Secretary of the Interior' (Washington DC: HardPress Publishing, 1864), p. vii.

49 The major issues are discussed in Robert W. Fogel and Stanley L. Engerman, *Time on the Cross: The Economics of American Negro Slavery* (Boston: Little Brown & Co., 1974); Herbert G. Gutman, *Slavery and the 'Numbers Game': A Critique of Time on the Cross* (Urbana, IL: University of Illinois Press, 1975); Mark M. Smith, *Debating American Slavery* (Cambridge: Cambridge University Press, 1998).

50 For Southern attitudes towards slavery, see James Oakes, *Slavery and Freedom: An Interpretation of the Old South* (New York: W.W. Norton & Co., 1998).

51 Larry E. Tise. *Proslavery: A History of the Defense of Slavery in America, 1701–1840* (Athens, GA : University of Georgia Press, 1987). Calhoun's comments on slavery as a 'positive good' were made in the US Senate on 6 February 1837: see Richard K. Cralle (ed.), *Works of John C. Calhoun* (New York: n.p., 1856), pp. 631–2.

52 Matthew E. Mason, 'Slavery Overshadowed: Congress debates Prohibiting the Atlantic Slave Trade to the United States', *Journal of the Early Republic*, 20/1 (2000), pp. 59–72.

53 Glover Moore, *The Missouri Controversy, 1819–1821* (Lexington, KY: University of Kentucky Press, 1953); Richard H. Brown, 'The Missouri Crisis, Slavery, and the Politics of Jacksonianism', *South Atlantic Quarterly*, 65 (1966), pp. 55–72; Robert Pierce Forbes, *The Missouri Compromise and its Aftermath: Slavery and the Meaning of America* (Chapel Hill, NC: University of North Carolina Press, 2007).

54 Peter J. Parish, *Slavery: History and Historians* (New York: Perseus, 1989), p. 26.

55 For an account which questions the existence of a conspiracy, see Michael P. Johnson, 'Denmark Vesey and his Co-Conspirators', *William and Mary Quarterly*, 3rd series, LVIII/4 (2001), pp. 915–76.

56 William W. Freehling, *Prelude to Civil War: The Nullification Crisis in South Carolina, 1816–1836* (New York: Oxford University Press, 1965).

57 Martin B. Duberman, 'The Northern Response to Slavery', in Duberman (ed.), *The Antislavery Vanguard: New Essays on the Abolitionists* (Princeton, NJ: Princeton University Press, 1965), pp. 395–413.

58 Leonard L. Richards, *'Gentlemen of Property and Standing': Anti-Abolition Mobs in Jacksonian America* (New York: Oxford University Press, 1971).

59 William W. Freehling, *The Road to Disunion: Secessionists at Bay, 1776–1854* (New York: Oxford University Press, 1990), pp. 213–86.

60 Davis, *The Problem of Slavery in the Age of Emancipation*, pp. 53–4, 61–3, 79, 172, 176, 179, 185.

61 David M. Potter, *The South and the Sectional Conflict* (Baton Rouge, LA: Louisiana State University Press, 1968).

62 Richard H. Sewell, *Ballots for Freedom: Antislavery Politics in the United States, 1837–1860* (New York: Oxford University Press, 1976), pp. 234–5; James Brewer Stewart, *Holy Warriors: The Abolitionists and American Slavery* (New York: Hill & Wang, 1976), pp. 160–2.

63 Thomas B. Alexander, *Sectional Stress and Party Strength: A Study of Roll-Call Voting Patterns in the United States House of Representatives, 1836–1860* (Nashville, TN: Vanderbilt University Press, 1967), p. 111.

64 Robert W. Fogel, *Without Consent or Contract: The Rise and Fall of American Slavery* (New York: W.W. Norton & Co., 1989), pp. 370–1, 379–80.

65 Don E. Fehrenbacher, *The Dred Scott Case: Its Significance in American Law and Politics* (New York: Oxford University Press, 1978).

66 Kenneth M. Stampp, *America in 1857: A Nation on the Brink* (New York: Oxford University Press, 1992), pp. 167–80.

67 Robert W. Johannsen, *Stephen A. Douglas* (Urbana, IL: University of Illinois Press, 1973), pp. 664–6, 668–77.

68 James Oakes, *The Scorpion's Sting: Antislavery and the Coming of the Civil War* (New York: W.W. Norton & Co., 2014), p. 85.

69 Quoted in William E. Gienapp, *Abraham Lincoln and Civil War America: A Biography* (New York: W.W. Norton & Co., 2002), p. 124.

70 Eric Foner, *The Fiery Trial: Abraham Lincoln and American Slavery* (New York: W.W. Norton & Co., 2010).

71 The best modern single-volume surveys of the war are Peter J. Parish, *The American Civil War* (New York: Holmes and Meier Publications, 1975) and James M. McPherson, *Battle Cry of Freedom: The Era of the Civil War* (New York: Oxford University Press, 1988).

72 For this interpretation, see Ira Berlin, 'Who Freed the Slaves? Emancipation and its Meaning', in David W. Blight and Brooks D. Simpson (eds), *Union and Emancipation: Essays on Politics and Race in the Civil War Era* (Kent, OH: Kent State University Press, 1997), pp. 105–21.

73 James Oakes, *Freedom National: The Destruction of Slavery in the United States, 1861–1865* (New York: W.W. Norton & Co., 2013), p. 379; Steven Hahn, *A Nation under our Feet: Black Political Struggles in the Rural South from Slavery to the Great Migration* (Cambridge, MA: Harvard University Press, 2003), pp. 91–2, 95–6, 99; James McPherson, *The War that Forged a Nation: Why the Civil War Still Matters* (New York: Oxford University Press, 2015) p. 101.

74 Oakes, *Freedom National*, p. 380; Paul D. Escott, *'What shall we do with the Negro?': Lincoln, White Racism, and Civil War America* (Charlottesville, VA: University of Virginia Press, 2009), p. 136. For a further argument that slave resistance contributed to the defeat of the Confederacy, see Armstead Robinson, *Bitter Fruits of Bondage: The Demise of Slavery and the Collapse of the Confederacy, 1861–1865* (Charlottesville, VA: University of Virginia Press, 2004).

75 Eric Foner, *Reconstruction: America's Unfinished Revolution, 1863–1877* (New York: HarperCollins 1988).

76 Escott, *'What shall we do with the Negro?'*, pp. 242–3.

77 Seymour Drescher, 'The Long Goodbye: Dutch Capitalism and Antislavery in Comparative Perspective', in Gert Oostindie (ed.), *Fifty Years Later: Antislavery, Capitalism and Modernity in the Dutch Orbit* (Leiden: Brill, 1995), pp. 35–6, 44.

78 Marten Kuitenbrouwer, 'The Dutch Case of Antislavery: Late and Elitist Abolitionism', in ibid., p. 72.

79 Ibid., pp. 78–9; Gert Ooostindie, 'Same Old Song? Perspectives on Slavery and Slaves in Suriname and Curaçao', ibid., pp. 143, 148; Pieter C. Emmer, 'The Ideology of Free Labor and Dutch Colonial Policy, 1830–1870', ibid., p. 207.

80 Pieter Emmer, 'Between Slavery and Freedom: The Period of Apprenticeship in Suriname (Dutch Guiana), 1863–1873', *Slavery and Abolition*, 14/1 (1993), pp. 87–113.

81 George Reid Andrews, *Afro-Latin America 1800–2000* (Oxford: Oxford University Press, 2004), pp. 64–5.

82 Camilla Townsend, 'In Search of Liberty: The Efforts of the Enslaved to attain Abolition in Ecuador, 1822–1852', in Darién J. Davis (ed.), *Beyond Slavery: The Multilayered Legacy of Africans in Latin America and the Caribbean* (Lanham, MD: Rowman and Littlefield Publishers, 2007), pp. 37–56.

83 Peabody and Keila Grinberg, *Slavery, Freedom, and the Law*, p. 122.

84 See two studies by Christopher Schmidt-Nowara: *Empire and Antislavery: Spain, Cuba, and Puerto Rico, 1833–1874* (Pittsburgh, PA: University of Pittsburgh Press, 1999), pp. 105, 115; 'Anti-slavery in Spain and its Colonies, 1808–86', in William Mulligan and Maurice Bric (eds), *A Global History of Anti-Slavery Politics in the Nineteenth Century* (Basingstoke: Palgrave Mamillan, 2013), pp. 137–8.

85 Rice, *The Rise and Fall of Black Slavery*, pp. 381–2, 384.

86 Ibid., pp. 383, 387–8.

87 Drescher, *Abolition*, p. 342; Rebecca J. Scott, *Slave Emancipation in Cuba: The Transition to Free Labor, 1860–1899* (Pittsburgh, PA: University of Pittsburgh Press, 1985), pp. 65–7.

88 Schmidt-Nowara, *Empire and Antislavery*, pp. 49–50, 119, 153–4.

89 Franklin W. Knight, *Slave Society in Cuba during the Nineteenth Century* (Madison, WI: University of Wisconsin Press, 1970), p. 168.

90 See two studies by Ada Ferrer: *Insurgent Cuba: Race, Nation, and Revolution, 1868–1898* (Chapel Hill, NC: University of North Carolina Press, 1999), pp. 8, 15, 29, 72, 74, 77; 'Armed Slaves and Anticolonial Insurgency in Late Nineteenth-Century Cuba', in Christopher Leslie Brown and Philip D. Morgan (eds), *Arming Slaves: From Classical Times to the Modern Age* (New Haven, CT: Yale University Press, 2006), pp. 304–29.

91 Laird Bergad, *Cuban Rural Society in the Nineteenth Century: The Social and Economic History of Monoculture in Matanzas* (Princeton, NJ: Princeton University Press, 1990), pp. 252–3.

92 Scott, *Slave Emancipation in Cuba*, p. 107.

93 Ibid., pp. 127–9; Drescher, *Abolition*, pp. 346–7.

94 César J. Ayala, *American Sugar Kingdom: The Plantation Economy of the Spanish Caribbean, 1898–1934* (Chapel Hill, NC: University of North Carolina Press, 1999), pp. 188–9, 191.

95 This internal slave trade is discussed in Robert Edgar Conrad, *The Destruction of Brazilian Slavery 1850–1888*, 2nd edn (Malabar, FL: Krieger Publishing, 1993), pp. 33–47.

96 James Walvin, *Crossings: Africa, the Americas and the Atlantic Slave Trade* (London: Reaktion Books, 2013), p. 212.

97 Drescher, *Abolition*, pp. 352, 354.

98 P. A. Martin, 'Slavery and Abolition in Brazil', *Hispanic American Historical Review*, XII/2 (1933), pp. 172–4.

99   Roderick J. Barman, *Citizen Emperor: Pedro II and the Making of Brazil, 1825–91* (Stanford, CA: Stanford University Press, 1999), p. 208.
100   Drescher, *Abolition*, p. 357; Rice, *The Rise and Fall of Black Slavery*, pp. 376–7.
101   Conrad, *The Destruction of Brazilian Slavery*, pp. 87–9; Dale Torston Graden, *From Slavery to Freedom in Brazil: Bahia, 1835–1900* (Albuquerque, NM: University of New Mexico Press, 2006), p. 158.
102   Drescher, *Abolition*, pp. 360, 363–7; Rice, *The Rise and Fall of Black Slavery*, pp. 378–9.
103   Drescher, *Abolition*, pp. 368–9; Rice, *The Rise and Fall of Black Slavery*, pp. 379–81.

The Legacy of Slavery

1   William A. Green, *British Slave Emancipation: The Sugar Colonies and the Great Experiment, 1830–1865* (Oxford: Clarendon Press, 1976), pp. 124–5.
2   Thomas C. Holt, *The Problem of Freedom: Race, Labor, and Politics in Jamaica and Britain, 1832–1938* (Baltimore, MD: John Hopkins University Press, 1992), pp. 55–112.
3   Douglas Hall, 'The Flight from the Estates Reconsidered: The British West Indies, 1838–1842', *Journal of Caribbean History*, 10/11 (1978), pp. 16–24.
4   Michael Craton, *Sinews of Empire: A Short History of British Slavery* (Garden City, NY: Anchor Press, 1974), p. 286.
5   Laurent Dubois, *Haiti: The Aftershocks of History* (New York: Oxford University Press, 2012), pp. 48–54; Jeremy D. Popkin, *You are All Free: The Haitian Revolution and the Abolition of Slavery* (Cambridge: Cambridge University Press, 2010), p. 137.
6   Dubois, *Haiti*, pp. 105–7; David Nicholls, *From Dessalines to Duvalier: Race, Colour, and National Independence in Haiti* (Cambridge: Cambridge University Press, 1979), p. 54.
7   B. W. Higman, *A Concise History of the Caribbean* (Cambridge: Cambridge University Press, 2011), pp. 166–7.
8   Eric Foner, *Reconstruction: America's Unfinished Revolution, 1863–1877* (New York: HarperCollins, 1988), pp. 253–61, 446–9.
9   V. L. Wharton, *The Negro in Mississippi, 1865–1890* (Chapel Hill, NC: University of North Carolina Press, 1947), pp. 157–80; J. Williamson, *After Slavery: The Negro in South Carolina during Reconstruction, 1861–1877* (Chapel Hill, NC: University of North Carolina Press, 1965), pp. 363–417.
10   Richard B. Drake, 'Freedmen's Aid Societies and Sectional Compromise', *Journal of Southern History*, 29/2 (1963), pp. 175–86.
11   C. Duncan Rice, *The Rise and Fall of Black Slavery* (Baton Rouge, LA: Louisiana State University Press, 1975), p. 359; Paul A. Cimbala and Hans L. Trefousse (eds), *The Freedmen's Bureau: Reconstructing the*

American South after the Civil War (Huntington, NY: Kreiger Publishing, 2005).

12 Roger L. Ransom and Richard Sutch, One Kind of Freedom: The Economic Consequences of Emancipation (New York: Cambridge University Press, 1977), pp. 87–103.

13 George Reid Andrews, Afro-Latin America 1800–2000 (New York: Oxford University Press, 2004), pp. 120, 126, 132, 134–6, 142–4.

14 Many issues concerning reparations are outlined in Hilary Beckles, Britain's Black Debt: Reparations for Caribbean Slavery and Native Genocide (Kingston: University of the West Indies Press, 2013).

15 Modern studies of the memorialization and representation of slavery include Gert Oostindie (ed.), Facing up to the Past: Perspectives on the Commemoration of Slavery from Africa, the Americas and Europe (Kingston: James Currey Ltd, 2001); Douglas Hamilton and Robert J. Blyth (eds), Representing Slavery: Art, Artefacts and Archives in the Collections of the National Maritime Museum (Farnham: Lund Humphries, 2007); J. R. Oldfield, Chords of Freedom: Commemoration, Ritual and British Transatlantic Slavery (Manchester: Manchester University Press, 2007).

16 See two books by Joel Quirk: Unfinished Business: A Comparative Survey of Historical and Contemporary Slavery (Paris: United Nations Educational, 2009); The Anti-Slavery Project: From the Slave Trade to Human Trafficking (Philadelphia, PA: University of Pennsylvania Press, 2011).

Index

Index